CAN IT
HAPPEN
HERE?

CAN IT HAPPEN HERE?

AUTHORITARIANISM IN AMERICA

EDITED BY

CASS R. SUNSTEIN

DEY ST.

An Imprint of WILLIAM MORROW

"Lessons from the American Founding" contains content adapted from Introduction, *The Federalist* (Cambridge: Harvard University Press, 2009).

HarperCollins books may be purchased for educational, business, or sales promotional use. For information, please email the Special Markets Department at SPsales@harpercollins.com.

FIRST EDITION

Designed by Renata De Oliveira

Library of Congress Cataloging-in-Publication Data has been applied for.

ISBN 978-0-06-269619-9

18 19 20 21 22   DIX/LSC   10 9 8 7 6 5 4 3 2 1

CONTENTS

INTRODUCTION
CASS R. SUNSTEIN

The United States is living under a military dictatorship. No one dares to call it that—but that's what it is. Here's what happened.

A year ago, a terrorist organization launched a successful attack in Chicago. Two thousand people were killed. President Donald Trump declared a national emergency and imposed martial law. With overwhelming popular support, he ramped up existing surveillance policies. The government is now monitoring all emails and telephone calls. Americans know that they are being monitored. Most of them don't mind.

In President Trump's words, "Privacy just isn't smart."

Harkening back to the late 1800s, the Trump administration made "sedition" a crime. Sedition includes "disloyalty to the United States," which includes "actions that demonstrate sympathy to our nation's enemies." Under the sedition laws, thousands of people have been arrested. No one knows exactly how many.

Muslim-Americans must register with the authorities, and

if they engage in "suspicious behavior," the authorities will pay them a visit. Preventive detention has become routine. No one knows how many people have been detained. There is a lot of private violence against people who are thought to be "disloyal." As a precautionary measure, tens of millions of people are displaying American flags on their automobiles and homes.

It's not easy to leave the country. If you do, beware: it's tough to get back in. If you aren't an American citizen, good luck.

Since the Chicago attack, Congress has capitulated to the president's demands and enacted the laws he favors. The federal judiciary has upheld his programs. So far, the press remains free, at least as a formal matter. But the most popular news outlets enthusiastically embrace President Trump's programs. They are careful not to criticize him.

The majority of Americans dismiss the president's critics as sources of "fake news." The Department of Justice is starting to investigate some sources of fake news for possible sedition. Whether or not the investigations result in prosecution, the dissenting news outlets are increasingly marginal. In terms of impact, they're failing, and their economic situation is increasingly dire.

In a recent speech to a joint session of Congress, President Trump declared that the war on Islamic terrorism "had no beginning and has no end."

Sure, I made all that up, and it's just a story; it's hardly likely. (Some of the chapters here will defend that view.) But if you find anything in the narrative even close to imaginable, we could try a few others. North Korea attacked Guam, and the president claimed "emergency powers." China did something frightening and horrific, and the president claimed, "We are now at war." The economy took a horrific downturn, and the president contended that he must "do whatever needs to be done to protect the country." Better yet: a catastrophe or a threat took a form that we cannot even imagine, producing something like the situation just described.

Fiction writers, like Sinclair Lewis, Philip K. Dick, and Philip Roth, have ventured alternative histories of the United States, in which some kind of authoritarianism ends up triumphant. Maybe Germany won World War II. Maybe the United States fell under the spell of an authoritarian ruler. If you like alternative history (and I confess that I love it), it's probably for one of two reasons. First, a tale of what-might-have-been can tell us something important and even profound about ourselves. It seizes on some feature of our national character—small or large, hidden or overt—or some inclination that some people have, and it shows what might have happened if that feature or tendency had somehow flowered. Roth's book *The Plot Against America* is a masterpiece in that vein.

What-might-have-beens warn us: inside every human heart, there's a fascist waiting to come out. George Orwell's *Nineteen Eighty-Four* remains the best analysis of that point, and it might well be true. After the attacks of 9/11, a lot of people discovered something like that, and their political party didn't matter.

Second, what-might-have-beens make an intriguing claim about a nation's history: with a little push or shove—

with an illness here, a death there, a single act of cowardice or courage, a coincidence around the corner—our world could have ended up a whole lot different. If Adolf Hitler had been smarter, maybe most of Europe would have ended up under the Nazis. Without Franklin Delano Roosevelt, the United States might have gone in all sorts of different directions in the 1930s and '40s. In 1936, Lawrence Dennis wrote a book titled *The Coming American Fascism*. It's not a warning. It's hopeful and optimistic.

With some twists and turns in the future, maybe Islamic terrorists will turn significant parts of the world in their preferred directions. *Submission*, by Michel Houellebecq, is all about that. It's not optimistic, but its arresting narrative arc makes the tale something other than totally implausible.

Houellebecq's focus is unusual. Since the 1930s, the question whether it can happen here typically asks about the rise of fascism. But that's a failure of imagination. Things can go wrong in a thousand different ways. Actually, they have. If the United States did not have the history it has had, speculative writers would spin tales that would defy belief, including the enslavement of millions of people in the American South; lynching countless people because of their skin color; decades of racial segregation; denial of the vote to women (until 1920, no less); the internment of more than 100,000 Japanese Americans on the West Coast—and also (less bad, but not good) the rise of McCarthyism in the 1950s and Nixon's grotesque abuses in the 1970s.

This is not a book about Donald Trump, not by any means, but there is no question that many people, including some of the authors here, think that Trump's words and deeds have put the can-it-happen-here question on the table. Several of the essays engage his election and his presidency. Some of the authors fear that an election of a left-wing extremist could create its own form of "it."

But the discussions here reach well beyond President Trump, left-wing extremists, and any other contemporary figure. They are focused on big and enduring questions. For example:

Is a powerful central government a threat to liberty—or a safeguard against it?

If a president wants to be a dictator, what steps would he take?

Can populism produce authoritarianism?

What's the Deep State, and should we worry about it?

How robust is freedom of speech?

Can we rely on our courts?

Does the American Constitution solve the problem?

What can we learn from history?

If some of the chapters are a bit academic, well, that should be taken as a tribute to the seriousness of the topic, and to the importance of confronting it with more than a quick glance at politics, law, and history.

So: Can it happen here? My own summary of this book: Absolutely. It has happened before. It will happen again. To many Americans, something like it is happening now.

That's mysterious, I know. Read on.

THE DICTATOR'S HANDBOOK, US EDITION

ERIC A. POSNER[1]

Tyrannophobia, the fear of the dictator, is as old as the American republic.[2] The founders worried about being governed by a Caesar or Cromwell, and ever since, as regular as the election cycle, Americans have accused the serving president of harboring dictatorial ambitions.

Although none of the forty-five men who have occupied the presidency so far have succeeded in their supposed dictatorial goals, the public's tyrannophobia has never been stronger. George W. Bush and Barack Obama, for example, were both routinely compared to Hitler based on their alleged dictatorial behavior and ambition.

With the presidency of Donald Trump, tyrannophobia has reached a fever pitch. Even before taking office, Trump was labeled a dictator. The accusations no longer come from the wings but have taken center stage. Journalists, politicians, academics, and other people with centrist, establishment credentials genuinely fear that Trump will inaugurate authoritarian rule in the United States. Their fears are based on Trump's statements and actions during the campaign:

> *Trump has flouted the norms of American elections and governance at every turn, including calling for the jailing of an opposing candidate, encouraging violence against protesters, endorsing the torture of prisoners, suggesting he might not respect the results of the election, falsely claiming that millions of illegal votes were cast, failing to resolve unprecedented conflicts of interest or to even disclose his tax returns, and attacking a federal judge based on his ethnicity (and that's of course a highly incomplete list).*[3]

While it's possible that this was all bombast, the stakes are high, and we should take seriously the claim that Trump seeks some level of authoritarian rule, whether or not "dictatorship" in its scariest sense is on the table. Is it possible that he can succeed? Can it happen here?

To answer this question, let's assume that Trump does seek to become a dictator in the fullest sense. The problem he faces is that powerful institutions stand between him and the scepter. He would need to subvert these institutions in order to seize the prize. It's worthwhile, if only as an exercise, to imagine how this subversion might work.

TACTICS

Attack the press. On the campaign trail, Trump threatened to "open up" libel laws, to make it easier for him to sue journalists who defame him. In office, he called the press "the enemy of the people." Authoritarian leaders have used libel laws to bully journalists in other countries—in Russia and Turkey, for example, where thousands of libel lawsuits have targeted journalists critical of the regime.[4] But Trump has his work cut out for him in the United States. Trump could try to persuade Congress to enact a new version of the Sedition Act of 1798, which criminalized defamation of the president of the United States, or he could invoke the Espionage Act of 1917, which criminalized various forms of disloyalty to the government. But the Supreme Court has made it extremely difficult for the government to prosecute journalists and for public figures like Trump to win civil actions against journalists and others who criticize them.

How could Trump evade this restriction? A frontal assault on the Court's First Amendment jurisprudence would fail for the time being. Justices on the left and right are committed to strong protections for political speech; Trump would need to replace at least five of them, securing the Senate's consent in each case, and it would be hard, perhaps impossible, for him to find even a single qualified, mainstream jurist who would supply the vote he needs.

But Trump could intimidate the press in other ways. He could order the Justice Department to prosecute journalists who are complicit in leaks of secret documents. While this approach would break with Justice Department precedent, it would be legal. And while it may be difficult to prevail in these prosecutions because of skepticism from judges and hostility from juries, cash-strapped media organizations may be deterred from aggressive investigations of executive-branch misconduct. Following the examples of Franklin Roosevelt and Richard Nixon, Trump could also threaten to slow down broadcast license approvals of media that displease him, or interfere with mergers that they seek for business reasons. Again, while courts would not go along, even the threat of dragging out the process might be consequential.

Trump might also be able to secure favorable but narrow legislation from Congress, and a degree of acquiescence from the courts, if a national emergency takes place and the legislation is tied to the threat in question. Suppose, for example, that a 9/11-style terrorist attack occurs, and Congress passes a law that prohibits anyone from celebrating radical Islam or promoting terrorism. Conceivably, courts could relax First Amendment protections for journalists who criticize Trump's counterterrorism program, though this is highly speculative.

In the meantime, Trump has attacked or circumvented the press in lawful, creative ways. He has used Twitter to send messages to the public without the intermediation of press reports, analysis, and editing. He has publicly chastised journalists who are, in his view, excessively critical of him, pursuing a divide-and-conquer strategy by blasting some journalists and media organizations who have criticized him or reported unflattering facts about him while praising others for their fairness. Using tweets, he has directed public attention to fly-by-night media organizations that support his line, giving them traffic from which they profit, and in this way stimulating the production of fake or biased news, and perhaps in the process creating an overall atmosphere of skepticism toward the press as a whole. Perhaps he can persuade a significant portion of the public that anything the press says is wrong. He has even said "the public doesn't believe" journalists anymore. "Now, maybe I had something to do with that." But whether this strategy succeeds or fails remains to be seen.

Trump, following in the footsteps of Obama and other presidents, can also attempt to control the press by restricting the dissemination of information from the government. The Freedom of Information Act and other statutes compel the government to disclose some information, and whistleblower statutes encourage government employees to disclose certain lawful secrets, but Trump can use his executive power to push back against these requirements—for example, by refusing to disclose in the absence of a court order.

Finally, Trump can adopt a tactic of authoritarian governments the world over, which enforce generally applicable laws (tax, regulatory, criminal, and so on) more vigorously against journalists, as well as political opponents of all kinds, than against supporters and other people. The executive has nearly unlimited discretion to inflict burdensome investigations on people of its choice, the prospect of which may deter criticism even if prosecutions or convictions do not follow.

Attack (or evade) Congress. Successful dictators who come to power in democracies need to push aside the legislature, which is the major institutional barrier to dictatorial rule. Some dictators shut down the legislature, but most maintain it as a fig leaf or as a subordinate body for airing public concerns but not for making policy. These dictators bribe or intimidate legislators, or simply disregard them, ruling by diktat through the military or security forces. And some dictators prevail over the legislature simply because they are immensely popular and can call on the public to punish legislative opponents in the polls. None of these approaches are open to Trump. But he has other means to enforce his will.

The US president possesses immense powers to act without congressional authorization.

He can order the military to conduct operations. He can order the FBI, CIA, and IRS to harass his opponents, as we saw with Nixon. He can also refuse to enforce certain laws—as a series of presidents, including President Obama, refused to enforce the immigration law. And he can order the regulatory agencies to follow priorities that reflect his political interests. All these things can already be done, lawfully, subject to weak and ambiguous limitations.

For example, Trump has, on his own, ordered immigration authorities to crack down on illegally present aliens, and directed the EPA to ease up on climate regulation. He can impose retaliatory tariffs against China. He can withdraw US forces from the Baltic states and send them to Taiwan.

But all these actions require the cooperation of the bureaucracy and the acquiescence of Congress. We will discuss the bureaucracy next; Congress could be roused to action if Trump's actions are too unpopular. Congress retains the power to withdraw delegations on which the president relies, or to pass new statutes that bar his actions. In passing legislation imposing new sanctions on Russia despite Trump's opposition, Congress has done just that. Congress can also use its spending power to block actions that Trump seeks to take, just as it did to prevent Obama from closing Guantánamo. In the end, these conflicts will be resolved either by the courts or by political power. Trump can narrowly interpret new statutes or claim that they violate his constitutional powers—as we saw on repeated occasions during the Bush administration when Congress tried to restrict its counterterrorism actions. Trump, taking a page from Richard Nixon (and Abraham Lincoln), might try to reallocate funds from programs that Congress favors to programs that he favors. Congress could also withdraw cooperation in other areas where Trump needs legal authority (for example, to raise the debt ceiling); this would create new confrontations.

Attack the bureaucracy. Presidents rule through the bureaucracy. If the bureaucracy fails to cooperate, then the president cannot be effective. Trump faces not one but multiple bureaucracies, and the different agencies may respond differently to him. The immigration authorities might enthusiastically participate in crackdowns, while the EPA could drag its feet when asked to deregulate. The most important bureaucracy for an aspiring dictator is the military, on which most dictators depend for their power.

To control the federal government's vast civil service, Trump needs to appoint loyalists to leadership positions. In most cases, the Senate must consent. Strikingly, Trump has had trouble filling positions. Trump is hampered by the small number of truly loyal supporters who also have significant government experience and hence the ability to control the agencies they are asked to head. Independent political appointees and members of the civil service will almost certainly disobey any orders from Trump requiring that they violate the law and be put in legal jeopardy. He will also have trouble motivating them to obey even lawful orders that are greatly at variance with precedents, their political preferences, and their agencies' historical missions.

What can Trump do? In the long term, Trump, if successful, may be able to replace disloyal appointees with loyal appointees, and may be able to attract loyalists to civil service positions. In the short term, he can threaten to undermine agencies that fail to do his bidding or in any other way pose a threat to his power.

Trump did just this, even before he entered office. He lashed out at the intelligence agencies, likening them to the Gestapo, because they reported to the press that Russian meddling helped Trump win the election. This was a high-stakes gambit. It is possible that the intelligence agencies, fearing that they will lose popular support, will think more carefully before crossing Trump. It is also possible that they will work to undermine him. Trump's attack on the intelligence agencies may also serve as a warning to other agencies that might otherwise be inclined to defy him.

Once in office, Trump followed this script. He fired FBI director James Comey for refusing to stop investigations of his aides. He fired acting attorney general Sally Yates because of her refusal to defend Trump's travel ban. He even publicly chastised his hand-picked attorney general, Jeff Sessions, because Sessions recused himself from the Russia investigation. But these actions backfired. A special counsel was appointed, and, thanks to Trump's egregious actions, the special counsel enjoys considerable political support in Congress, even from Republicans.

A full-blown dictator needs military support. US military leaders have shown exemplary refusal to meddle in politics or challenge civilian leadership—with the notable but short-lived exception of Douglas MacArthur during the Truman administration. This cuts both ways. Trump can expect loyalty from the military as long as he maintains his position in office and uses the military in lawful ways—even, one suspects, if he engages in unconstitutional behavior like harassing the press. But it is currently unimaginable that the military would cooperate if Trump called on it to shut down government institutions, as so many dictators in other countries have done.

Attack the courts. With a few exceptions, confined to early American history, the US president has given significant respect to the courts. Courts can thwart a dictator's ambitions in many ways. They can protect dissenters from prosecution, civil litigation, and harassment. They can strike down regulations and block executive orders. American judges are protected by life tenure; they benefit from a tradition of independence and are trusted by the public.

But there are significant limits on judicial power. The judiciary is largely reactive, and can rarely block the executive branch when the president acts swiftly. The courts have for the most part refrained from interfering with military orders and foreign policy. They give deference to the president's interpretation of treaties and have permitted the president to withdraw from them, while not interfering with "executive agreements" with foreign countries that evade the requirement of Senate consent under the Treaty Clause of the Constitution.

Moreover, if Trump obtains the cooperation of Congress, he can make significant inroads on judicial power. With legislation, he can strip courts of jurisdiction. He could also follow in the footsteps of Franklin Roosevelt and attempt to increase his support on the Supreme Court by packing it—increasing the number of justices and appointing a majority. But even though Roosevelt was immensely popular when he proposed to pack the Court, he failed to convince Congress. The episode seriously damaged his own political standing. Court packing is not a plausible tool for Trump.

Trump could order executive officials to disregard judicial orders, putting them at risk of contempt of court. He has not done that so far, but he has publicly criticized judges who have ruled against him, mocking one as a "so-called judge" and attacking another group of judges as biased. (He actually said: "I don't ever want to call a court biased, so I won't call it biased. But courts seem so political . . ." You know what he means.) While such personal attacks on the judiciary are almost unprecedented in the United States, it seems unlikely that Trump will intimidate the courts in the short term.

Attack the states and local governments. A dictator who sought total control over the country would need to punch through the walls created by the federal system. Consider, for example, the dictator's strategy of enforcing generally applicable laws more harshly against his political opponents than against ordinary people, who might be left alone completely. Most generally applicable laws are enforced by the states and local police, not by the federal government. Even enforcement of federal laws, which overlap with state laws in many ways, requires cooperation with local authorities. Already some cities have announced that they will not cooperate with Trump's plan to round up illegal immigrants; they could even actively shield illegal immigrants from federal authorities.

The federal government can impose its will on the states in many ways—by, for example, bestowing or withholding funds, or simply enacting new laws and enforcing them with federal agents. But limits on such control are formidable. The large number of states, their historical independence, the important role that state officials play in the party system, and numerous other factors suggest that they will present significant pockets of resistance to any president who seeks to be dictator. The only practical way for the federal government to seize states' police powers is through martial law, last accomplished on a wide scale during the Civil War. Barring a catastrophe, this can't happen here. Indeed, Trump's efforts along these lines so far—an attempt to ban funds to so-called sanctuary cities—are modest and have been received skeptically by the courts.

Attack the party system. The party system, though not recognized in the Constitution, has emerged as a significant constraint on presidential power. Parties are vast networks in which patronage and other benefits are transferred to the ranks in return for political support for the parties' leaders. Most presidents obtain power by working their way up a party hierarchy, in the process being vetted for talent and ideological reliability. Once in power, they continually repay the party by distributing offices and other resources to prominent party members and supporting the party's goals, and in return receive support from party members who occupy government offices and positions in the press and elsewhere in civil society. By the same token, a president's party can turn on him if he defies it. And the party that is out of power will marshal its own resources to undermine the president—by offering benefits to its own members who, by virtue of their positions in government or in civil society, can subvert the president and bring their own members to power.

Trump is unique in modern history as an outsider who came to power by overcoming his party's leadership. And while the Republican Party gave him its support once he won the primary, he must continue to maintain that support, and he is vulnerable if it withdraws that support. Trump also must contend with the Democratic Party, which seeks to undermine him. An ordinary president will rely as much as possible on his own party and occasionally govern with support of moderates of both parties. But such a president is constrained by the party system.

What is an aspiring dictator to do?

Some dictators and aspiring dictators create new parties outside the established system (Huey Long, for example, if he can be considered an aspiring dictator), or rely on other groups to support them, like an ethnic or regional population, the military, or the security services.

Trump has not moved in this direction. The only likely route to dictatorship involves subordinating the Republican Party establishment to his will. And Trump has not been shy about attacking Republicans who defy him. But it's unclear whether his attacks can bring the Republicans in line. One possible approach is to achieve such a high layer of popularity that party members are afraid to defy him. But Trump is unpopular, and even very popular presidents—like Franklin Roosevelt—have been unable to dominate their parties except for short periods of time. Another approach is to use patronage to keep the party in line. But Trump—like previous presidents—does not have access to sufficient patronage. There are only so many offices that can be distributed, and these offices are worth only so much. Imaginably, an extremely wealthy president could keep party members in line by using his personal funds—or the funds of wealthy supporters—to (legally) bribe them with campaign contributions. But even if Trump is as rich as he says he is, he does not have that kind of money, nor does he appear to be willing to spend his own money for this purpose.

Attack civil society. The vague term *civil society* encompasses groups outside government, including the press and parties, which have already been discussed, but other groups play a role as well. Trump already faces significant opposition from the legal profession and from academics. Lawyers will bring lawsuits against virtually any major executive action that smacks of executive overreaching—in many cases funded out of their own pocket, or by law firms, or by public interest groups. Government agencies constantly draw on the expertise of scientists and other researchers, who might boycott a Trump administration or (more likely) refuse to provide research and technical support to policies they disapprove of.

Public interest groups, religious groups, and other organizations will also organize marches and petitions, publicize executive overreaching, and take other actions to oppose Trump. Although one suspects that many such groups will support him as well, the overall effect is likely to turn the public against Trump if he overreaches, which in turn will embolden Congress, the courts, and the bureaucracy to constrain him.

Could a dictator attack civil society? In many countries, they have done just that—by harassing critics and offering rewards to those who give support to the regime. Recep

Tayyip Erdoğan has purged Turkish universities as well as the press and bureaucracy. But, in the United States, all such efforts would be nearly unprecedented. The closest analogy is the McCarthy era, but in that case the impetus came from Congress, not the president, and the era was short-lived and ended with Joseph McCarthy's disgrace.

Stir up the mob. The most tried-and-true method of becoming a dictator in the twentieth century has been to rely on extralegal methods, typically involving a mob of supporters who use violence to intimidate opponents, whether they are journalists, bureaucrats, judges, politicians, or ordinary citizens. This was the method of Hitler and Mussolini, which Sinclair Lewis translated into the American setting for his novel *It Can't Happen Here.* This method relies on a large group of disaffected people, usually young men, with little to lose, who are fired up by the promises and ideological aspirations of the would-be dictator. In principle, Trump could try to create his own Brownshirts by rewarding supporters for their loyalty with offices and other compensation, along with pardons if they are convicted of crimes. But while Trump has winked at violence on occasion, he has not tried to create a paramilitary to do his bidding.

American soil seems especially unpropitious for such a transplant, perhaps because the country has always been too rich, large, and diverse, or the political system has always been effective at addressing the interests of groups that are large enough to pose this kind of threat. Trump has, however, shown considerable imagination in stirring up divisions. His public comments on white nationalists who marched in Charlottesville, on NFL players who kneel during the national anthem to protest police brutality, and on many other topics have exacerbated the already-deep divisions in the country. It remains unclear whether Trump can take advantage of these divisions in order to consolidate his power, but the possibility cannot be dismissed.

CAN IT HAPPEN HERE?

An aspiring dictator would do best by pushing against all these margins rather than trying to crush the institutional barriers seriatim. Imagine that Trump simultaneously: (1) harasses only the toughest and most critical journalists while encouraging a squid cloud of disinformation that keeps the public in the dark about his mistakes and failures; (2) defies Congress only in carefully selected cases where his goals are popular and Congress is divided; (3) harasses agencies that pose a threat to his power (intelligence agencies?) while lavishing resources and attention on those that support him (immigration agencies?); (4) disobeys a particularly unpopular judicial order while scorning the integrity of the judge; (5) divides both parties through skillful distribution of patronage; and (6) manages to inspire some of his supporters to threaten violence against journalists and government employees who dissent from Trump's rule. Could steady pressure against all these institutions, all at once, cause them to crumble because they cannot rely on one another for support?

A point that emerges from the discussion is that the institutions that may block an aspiring dictator depend on one another for mutual support. Journalists can resist a dictator through courageous reporting, but not—or less so—if the dictator's supporters have infiltrated the judiciary, causing it to relax First Amendment protections that keep journalists out of jail or spare them from paying large fines. The judiciary can block illegal orders, but maybe not if judges fear that Congress will impeach them or strip them of jurisdiction. Congress can defy a dictator, but maybe not if it believes that voters love their leader and will vote against members of Congress who oppose him. Congress may fear even an unpopular dictator if they suspect that the dictator can influence electoral outcomes—by manipulating and pressuring the press, or controlling the agencies that conduct elections (which, unfortunately for the US president, are mostly state agencies), or (the point can't be ignored) inviting a foreign power to distribute propaganda. Thus, while a frontal assault by the would-be dictator on a single institution standing alone seems bound to fail, it is possible that a series of more modest actions on multiple fronts, executed patiently over a long period of time, could eventually produce dictatorial power.

But, at the time of this writing, this turn of events seems unlikely. Trump took office as one of the most unpopular presidents in history, widely distrusted and even loathed by elected officials, journalists, and the public, and (one suspects) judges and a good portion of the bureaucracy. He has only lost popularity and trust over his first year, thanks to his divisive fulminations and reckless actions. With a long record of lies and broken promises, he can hardly expect enthusiastic cooperation even from people who sympathize with his goals. With critics in civil society nipping at his heels and the public skeptical about his temperament and integrity, Trump is more dependent on the party establishment, the bureaucracy, and other institutions than any president in recent memory. And, as of this writing, he has predictably accomplished very little, with most of his campaign promises unfulfilled.

NOTES

1. University of Chicago Law School. The first part of the title is filched from Bruce Bueno de Mesquita and Alastair Smith, *The Dictator's Handbook: Why Bad Behavior Is Almost Always Good* (New York: Public Affairs, 2012), whose book also provided some general inspiration for this piece.
2. Eric A. Posner and Adrian Vermeule, *The Executive Unbound* (New York: Oxford University Press, 2010).
3. See Thomas B. Edsall, "What Does Vladimir Putin See in Donald Trump?" *New York Times*, January 19, 2017 (quoting political scientist Brendan Nyhan), https://www.nytimes.com/2017/01/19/opinion/what-does-vladimir-putin-see-in-donald-trump.html?action=click&pgtype=Homepage&clickSource=story-heading&module=opinion-c-col-right-region&region=opinion-c-col-right-region&WT.nav=opinion-c-col-right-region.
4. See Ozan O. Varol, "Stealth Authoritarianism," *Iowa Law Review* 100, 1673 (2015).

CONSTITUTIONAL ROT
JACK M. BALKIN

When you think about politics these days, it's hard to avoid focusing on Donald Trump's remarkable rise to power and his even more remarkable presidency. It's even harder to avoid thinking about the scandals swirling around him day to day. While these are important, they are not the subject of this essay. Instead, I want to look at the big picture. In this picture, Trump is merely a symptom. He is a symptom of a serious problem with our political and constitutional system.

Trump outrages and flusters his opponents; so much so that as we lurch from controversy to controversy, many people wonder whether we are currently in some sort of constitutional crisis. We are not. Rather, we are in a period of constitutional rot.

By "constitutional rot," I mean decay in the features of our system that maintain it as a healthy republic. Constitutional rot has been going on for some time in the United

States, and it has produced our current dysfunctional politics.

Constitutional dysfunction isn't the same thing as gridlock—after all, the three branches of government are currently controlled by the same party. Rather, it is a problem of *representation*. Over time, our political system has become less democratic and less republican. It has become increasingly oligarchical.

By "democratic," I mean responsive to popular will and popular opinion. By "republican," I mean that representatives are devoted to the public good, and responsive to the interests of the public as a whole—as opposed to a small group of powerful individuals and groups. When representatives are responsive not to the interests of the public in general but to a relatively small group of individuals and groups, we have oligarchy.

REPUBLICS ARE ESPECIALLY SUSCEPTIBLE TO CONSTITUTIONAL ROT

Republics are governments premised on the pursuit of the common good. Representatives are given power for the sole purpose of achieving the public good. The framers of our Constitution understood that republics are fragile things. They are easily corrupted, and over time, they are likely to turn into oligarchies or autocracies.

Everybody knows the famous story that when Benjamin Franklin was asked what kind of government the Philadelphia Convention had produced, he replied, "A republic . . . if you can keep it." [1] He wasn't joking. The framers knew

20

that every previous republic in history had eventually fallen apart. At the very end of the convention, Franklin predicted that the new American government "is likely to be well administered for a course of years, and can only end in Despotism, as other forms have done before it, when the people shall become so corrupted as to need despotic Government, being incapable of any other."[2]

When a government becomes oligarchical, leaders spend less and less time working for the public good. Instead, they spend more and more time enriching a small group of important backers that keep them in power. Because the general public feels abandoned by politicians, it gradually loses faith in the political system. This leads to the rise of demagogues, who flatter people with promises that they will make everything right again.

In the United States, oligarchy has resulted from the gradual breakdown of the party system that selects candidates and keeps political parties responsive to the public. It has also resulted from changes in how political campaigns are financed; and from long-term changes in the structure of mass media, which have encouraged political distrust, exacerbated polarization, and merged politics with entertainment.

Both parties have been affected by these developments, but the problems are especially pronounced in the Republican Party, which styles itself as a populist party but is anything but. A small class of wealthy donors has disproportionate control over the Republican policy agenda. The influence of the donor class over that agenda is the best explanation of developments in Congress.

What are the deeper causes of constitutional rot? There are four interlocking features, which we might call the Four Horsemen of Constitutional Rot: (1) political polarization; (2) loss of trust in government; (3) increasing economic inequality; and (4) policy disasters, a term coined by Stephen Griffin to describe important failures in decision-making by our representatives, like the Vietnam War, the Iraq War, and the 2008 financial crisis.[3]

Today, one of the most important, overarching policy failures is America's inadequate response to globalization. The 2008 financial crisis is a special case of this larger policy failure.

A democracy requires a broad-based, stable, and economically secure middle class to create the right incentives for government officials to pursue the public good.[4] If economic inequality gets too pronounced, the wealthiest tend to grab disproportionate political power, and they will use it to further entrench and enrich themselves. A globalized economy threatens a broad-based, stable, and economically secure middle class because it puts serious pressure on social insurance programs and on the economic stability and self-sufficiency of Americans.

Political and economic elites have not navigated globalization's changes well. They have taken pretty good care of themselves, but they have not taken care of the whole country. This inadequate response to globalization has hastened constitutional rot.

These four horsemen—polarization, loss of trust, economic inequality, and policy disaster—mutually reinforce each other. Political scientists have pointed out that rising economic inequality exacerbates polarization, which in turn helps produce policies that exacerbate inequality.[5] Rising inequality and polarization also encourage loss of trust. Polarization and oligarchy create overconfidence and insulate decision makers from necessary criticism, which makes policy disasters more likely; policy disasters, in turn, further undermine trust in government, and so on.

In an oligarchical system, regardless of its formal legal characteristics, a relatively small number of backers effectively decide who stays in power. In such a system, politicians will have strong incentives to divert resources to the relatively small group of backers who keep them in power. Not surprisingly, the power of government and resources for government are often wasted or diverted from important public goods. Our constitutional system is still formally democratic, but it has become more oligarchical in practice over time. As a result, the United States has wasted a great deal of money on policy disasters, it has shaped the tax code so that most of the benefits of economic growth have gone to the wealthiest Americans, and through unwise tax and fiscal policy, it has diverted a lot of money that could have been used for public services and public goods to the wealthy.

CONSTITUTIONAL DEFENSES AGAINST CONSTITUTIONAL ROT

Our Constitution is designed to ward off both oligarchy and demagogues and preserve a republic. For the most part, it has been quite successful in the face of a wide variety of changes and challenges. Some of these features of our constitutional system, however, don't work very well anymore in preventing oligarchical tendencies. Separation of powers between Congress and the president is a good example. Richard Pildes and Daryl Levinson have pointed out that our system is better described as separation of parties rather than separation of powers.[6] When the president and Congress are from the same party, there will be little oversight of the president. The Republican Congress's almost complete disinterest in checking Donald Trump is a particularly worrisome example.

Even so, the United States still has many other republican defenses. We still have an independent judiciary, regular elections, and a free press. Many other countries that have eventually succumbed to autocracy are not so fortunate. Moreover, in the United States, from the founding onward, lawyers have played a crucial role in defending the republic: in staffing an independent judiciary; in promoting rule-of-law values in the bureaucracy; and in bringing cases to protect constitutional rights and check executive overreach. Once again, many other countries that have become autocratic are not as fortunate as the United States.

PROPAGANDA AND CONSTITUTIONAL ROT

One should not underestimate the value of our free press, even as it comes under assault from the Trump administration. Reporters have not been cowed into silence as they have been in other countries. If anything, Trump's shenanigans and his successful manipulation of the press in 2016 have caused the press to think more deeply about its democratic responsibilities.

Even so, the power of the press to protect republican government has been weakened. Part of this is due to economics, and part of it is due to other factors. The American system of freedom of the press was seriously undermined in 2016. It was undermined not by state censorship but by Trump's very effective hacking of the media; he has proved to be both a master manipulator and a very effective demagogue in the digital era.

The system of free press was also undermined by the production of effective propaganda, both from within the United States and from outside it. These two forms of propaganda come from different sources, but they reinforced each other in a perfect storm in 2016.

We now have domestic propaganda machines that have thrown their support behind Trump and now engage in shameless forms of propaganda that would have done Soviet-era apparatchiks proud. The only difference is that instead of propping up communism, they prop up Trump. In addition, Russia and allied groups in Eastern Europe engaged in successful propaganda campaigns during the 2016 election season, designed to enhance Trump's chances and sow discord and confusion in the United States.

Propaganda's effects corrode republican institutions and encourage constitutional rot. Propaganda enhances polarization; it increases distrust of political opponents, as well as those elements of government held by one's political opponents.

Propaganda tries to foster controversies that divide the country and enhance mutual distrust and hatred among fellow citizens. It seeks to convert politics into a particularly brutal opposition between virtuous friends and evil enemies who must be stopped at all costs and by any means necessary.

Propaganda also undermines the crucial role of deliberation and the search for truth in a democracy. It attempts to put everything in dispute, so that nothing can be established as true and everything becomes a matter of personal opinion or partisan belief. Because everything is a matter of opinion, one can assume that anything a political opponent says can be disregarded, and that factual claims contrary to one's own beliefs can also be disregarded. Thus, successful propaganda builds on motivated reasoning and encourages even more motivated reasoning. It undermines shared criteria of reasoning, good-faith attempts at deliberation, and mutual accommodation between political opponents in democracies.

Moreover, if people stop believing in the truth of what they read, they don't have to think hard about political questions. Instead, they can simply make political decisions based on identity or affiliation with their political allies. Propaganda, in other words, undermines truth to destroy the concept of the public good and to encourage tribalism.

As a political system becomes increasingly oligarchical, it also becomes less equal and more polarized, and generates greater distrust, both of government in general and of political opponents. People not only lose trust in government but also in other people who disagree with them. Political opponents appear less as fellow citizens devoted to the common good and more like internal threats to the nation.

Another way of putting it is that in a well-functioning republic, there are friends and potential friends. Potential friends are people you currently disagree with but might ally with in the future because both of you are devoted to the public good. In a system of constitutional rot, the country falls into something like Carl Schmitt's view that all politics is divided between friends and enemies.[7] From the perspective of a well-functioning republic, Schmitt's friend/enemy distinction is a corruption of politics, rather than its essential nature.

TRUMP AS A SYMPTOM OF CONSTITUTIONAL ROT

Loss of trust in the government and in political opponents eventually produces demagogues who attempt to take advantage of the situation. Demagogues don't spring up unawares. People see them coming from miles away. But by this point people have lost so much faith in government that they are willing to gamble on a demagogue. They hope that the demagogue can make things right again and restore past glories.

Trump is a demagogue. We might even say that he is straight out of central casting for demagogues: unruly, uncouth, mendacious, dishonest, and cunning. His rise is a symptom of constitutional rot and constitutional dysfunction. Constitutional rot not only allowed Trump to rise to power; it also has given him incentives to increase and exacerbate constitutional rot to stay in power. Many of his actions as president—and his media strategy—make sense from this perspective.

Polarization helps keep Trump in power because it binds his supporters to him. He exacerbates polarization by fomenting outrage and internal division. He also confuses and distracts people, keeping them off balance and in a state of emotional upheaval. Emotional upheaval in turn increases fear, and fear increases mutual distrust.

Trump doesn't care if his opponents hate him, as long as his base hates and fears his political opponents more. Because his supporters hate and fear his enemies, they are more likely to cling to him, because they are quite certain that his enemies are even worse.

Polarization also helps keep most professional politicians in his party from abandoning him. Many Republican politicians do not trust Trump, and many regard him as unqualified. But if Republican politicians turn on Trump, they will be unable to achieve anything during one of the infrequent periods in which they control both Congress and the White House. This will infuriate the base and anger the wealthy group of donors who help keep Republicans in power. Republican politicians who oppose Trump may face primary challenges. Finally, Republican politicians can't be sure that enough of their fellow politicians will follow them if they stick their necks out. In fact, they may provoke a civil war within the Republican Party, in which Trump's supporters accuse them of stabbing Trump (and the party) in the back.

Many people think that the sense of upheaval that Trump has created in American politics means that he cannot keep going this way for long, and that his presidency is about to crack apart at any moment. This is a mistake. Polarization and upheaval are good for him. Crisis is his brand.

WHY TRUMP HAS BEEN A POPULIST TURNCOAT

If you understand the relationship between polarization and oligarchy, you will understand a remarkable feature of American politics. Although Trump ran as a populist who promised to protect the working class from the depredations of globalization, as soon as he entered the White House, he reversed course. His cabinet is full of wealthy individuals, and many of his top advisors are from the very financial class that he excoriated in his campaign. Moreover, he has quickly allied himself with the most conservative elements of the Republican Party, and he has supported a health care bill that is likely to harm many working-class Americans.

The Republican Party in Congress depends on its donor class to stay in power. The central goal of the Republican agenda, therefore, is to deliver benefits to the donor class, either through tax cuts, government expenditures, or deregulation.

Congress's repeated attempts to repeal Obamacare are a case in point. The House bill, passed in March 2017, was actually a tax cut disguised as a health care measure. It offered a $600 billion tax cut to the wealthiest Americans, which it paid for by removing some of Obamacare's insurance protections and gradually eliminating its Medicaid expansion.[8] Moreover, by locking in tax cuts in a health care bill, Republicans hoped to make it easier to achieve still other tax reforms that would please their donors. The Senate attempted to pass multiple versions of an Obamacare repeal without success; the basic strategy in these bills was either cutting the taxes supporting Obamacare or cutting its entitlements, particularly Medicaid. Cutting entitlements, in turn, reduces budgetary obligations, thus making it easier to—you guessed it—cut taxes for wealthy donors.

From the standpoint of populism, the Republicans' proposed health care bills have been an utter travesty; they withdraw important benefits and protections from working-class Americans to benefit the very wealthiest. Commentators repeatedly pointed out that the bills made no sense if the goal was actually to improve health care. But the bills made perfect sense from the standpoint of oligarchy. Even so-called moderate Republicans depend heavily on the donor class, and therefore they have faced enormous pressures to cave and support the leadership's proposals. In the House, establishment and more moderate Republicans capitulated through a face-saving (but ineffectual) compromise. They did so not because the Freedom Caucus is so powerful, but because the powerful donors who shape the party's policy agenda wanted their tax cuts. Because Senators knew that their version was likely to be deeply unpopular with the general public, they drafted it in secret, rushing it through to avoid public scrutiny until shortly before votes were taken. After all, as one Senate aide explained, the Republicans aren't stupid.[9] They knew that their bill was toxic. But it pleased their donors, and so they were determined to sacrifice any pretense of procedural regularity to achieve their goals.

The health care bill is a prime example of constitutional rot. Our nominally republican system of government has become so infected by oligarchy that the party in power has no scruples about acting in an entirely shameless manner, as long as the interests of its masters are well served.

Which brings us back to Trump's about-face. Trump ran as a populist but he now governs as a sellout. This is not an unusual phenomenon among populist revolutionaries. Once they take power, they often quickly discard the people who put them in power; they substitute new backers who are easier to deal with and/or pay off to stay in power.

Trump is a huckster, with few actual ideological commitments. So he has few qualms about changing course. It is much easier for Trump to ally himself with congressional Republicans than to attempt a seriously populist legislative agenda, which would be very costly and would be opposed by members of his own party. Working across the aisle with Democrats is complicated because of the very polarization Trump has helped foster. Democrats do not trust him, and working with them might lead his Republican allies in Congress to abandon him. And he needs loyalty among Republicans to fend off the scandals swirling around him.

Thus, ironically, Trump's very strategies for gaining power—dividing the country and fomenting mutual hatred—mean that he should align his policies with members of his own party against the Democrats. That means that he will not govern as an economic populist, although his rhetoric will remain rabidly populist. But there will be little substance behind it. It is far easier to align with congressional Republicans, who will protect him from Democrats who despise him and want to topple him with scandals.

Having cast his lot with congressional Republicans, that means that he, too, will serve the same donor class. Trump may have run a populist campaign, but now that he is in power, he has pretty much embraced oligarchy. His populism is mostly sloganeering—it is a Potemkin village. We might say that it takes a Potemkin village to make a Trump presidency.

THE FUTURE

That's the bad news. Here is the good news.

First, Trump represents the end of a cycle of politics rather than the future of politics. American politics is divided into regimes in which one party's agenda tends to dominate. Eventually that party runs out of steam, its coalition fragments, its political agenda becomes irrelevant and inadequate to solve current problems, and the evolution of the political system undermines it.

Trump is the last president in the Reagan regime. During this period, the dominant party was the Republican Party; the regime's policy agenda was tax cuts and deregulation above all; its coalition was white voters plus professionals and wealthy business elites; and it fostered and exacerbated the polarization of political parties that began with the 1968 election.

The Reagan regime's electoral coalition is falling apart: from 1992 to 2016, the Republican Party won the presidential popular vote only once; twice the party has had to depend on an electoral college victory. This is a sign of weakness, not strength.

The regime is crumbling; Trump is the last Reaganite. In the next few election cycles, a new regime will begin, offering the possibility of a new beginning in American politics.

Second, despite the influx of propaganda and the decline of separation of powers in restraining the president, many features of the constitutional system remain robust. We still have an independent judiciary, a free press, and regular elections.

Third, we should not confuse what's been happening in the past several months with constitutional crisis. Constitutional crisis means that the Constitution is no longer able to keep disagreement within politics; as a result, people go outside the law and/or turn to violence or insurrection.[10] However unpleasant our politics may be, all of our current struggles are still within politics.

Fourth, we are headed for a big showdown in electoral politics over the next several election cycles. One of the two parties will have to find a way to restore trust in government and renounce oligarchical politics. The next decade will tell the tale. I remain hopeful.

Even if Trump left office tomorrow and was replaced with Mike Pence, there would still have to be a reckoning over these issues. Indeed, even if Hillary Clinton had won the election, there would still have to be a reckoning—perhaps even more urgently if Clinton won, because she ran a campaign that paid so little attention to populist concerns. The United States has failed to reconcile globalization with democracy. It has not accommodated the demands of republican government to global economic change. This is a serious policy failure, and it has contributed to constitutional rot. The bill for this neglect is coming due. We will have to pay it.

The central question is how to preserve republican government in the face of a changing global economy. Trump is merely a symptom of the larger problem. So my advice is: keep your eye on the larger issue, and not on the president's latest tweets.

This is not the first time that the American experiment in democracy has been threatened by oligarchy, although the problem arises each time in a different form. The Jacksonians fought the financial aristocracy of their day; the early Republican Party fought the Slave Power, and the populists and progressives fought the "malefactors of great wealth" that dominated the country during its First Gilded Age.[11] Now, in our Second Gilded Age, there is no guarantee that the pattern of success will continue. Even so, Americans should organize themselves on the assumption that they have the ability to defend republican government from oligarchy as they have done many times before.

I believe we will get through this, together. But we have to pay attention to the real sources of constitutional dysfunction, halt the rot that threatens our constitutional system, and preserve our republic. The history of the American Constitution is a series of struggles for greater democracy, equality, and inclusiveness in the face of well-entrenched opposition. Trump's presidency signals the beginning of yet another contest.

NOTES

1. Walter Isaacson, *Benjamin Franklin: An American Life* (New York: Simon & Schuster, 2003), 459.
2. Max Farrand, ed., *The Records of the Federal Convention of 1787* (New Haven, CT: Yale University Press, 1911, revised edition 1966), 641.
3. Stephen M. Griffin, *Broken Trust: Dysfunctional Government and Constitutional Reform* (Lawrence: University Press of Kansas, 2015).
4. For the most recent version of this argument, which was well known to the framers, see Ganesh Sitaraman, *The Crisis of the Middle Class Constitution* (New York: Albert A. Knopf, 2017).
5. See, e.g., John Voorheis, Nolan McCarty, and Boris Shor, "Unequal Incomes, Ideology and Gridlock: How Rising Inequality Increases Political Polarization" (2015), at https://www.princeton.edu/csdp/events/McCarty10012015/McCarty-10012015.pdf.
6. Daryl J. Levinson and Richard H. Pildes, "Separation of Parties, Not Powers," *Harvard Law Review* 2311 (2006): 119.
7. See Carl Schmitt, *The Concept of the Political*, trans. George Schwab (Chicago: University of Chicago Press, 1996).
8. See Dylan Matthews, "The GOP Health Bill Is a $600 Billion Tax Cut—Almost Entirely for the Wealthy," *Vox*, March 7, 2017, at https://www.vox.com/policy-and-politics/2017/3/7/14844362/ahca-ryancare-trumpcare-tax-cut-rich.
9. Caitlin Owens, "Senate GOP Won't Release Draft Health Care Bill," *Axios*, June 12, 2017, at https://www.axios.com/senate-gop-wrapping-up-health-care-bill-but-wont-release-it-2440345281.html.
10. Sanford Levinson and Jack M. Balkin, "Constitutional Crises," *University of Pennsylvania Law Review* 707 (2009): 157.
11. Theodore Roosevelt, "Address of President Roosevelt on the Occasion of the Laying of the Corner Stone of the Pilgrim Memorial Monument, Provincetown, MA," August 20, 1907 (Washington, DC: Government Printing Office, 1907), 47.

COULD FASCISM COME TO AMERICA?

TYLER COWEN

Could it ever happen here? Fascism, that is. That question is a standard refrain from American history, dating back at least to the 1930s and also related to the classic Sinclair Lewis novel *It Can't Happen Here*. It was asked with increasing frequency after the ascent and election of Donald Trump, both on the left and by "Never Trump" commentators on the right.

Most of us are familiar with the dictum "Prediction is difficult, especially when it concerns the future." Still, I would like to hazard the prediction that no, it cannot happen here. I won't claim it could never happen over the centuries, rather that it can't happen in anything recognizably like the America of today.

My argument is pretty simple: American fascism cannot happen anymore because the American government is so large and unwieldy. It is simply too hard for the fascists, or for that matter other radical groups, to seize control of. No matter who is elected, the fascists cannot control the bureaucracy, they cannot control all the branches of American government, they cannot control the judiciary, they cannot control semi-independent institutions such as the Federal Reserve, and they cannot control what is sometimes called "the deep state." The net result is they simply can't control enough of the modern state to steer it in a fascist direction.

This point also will help us see a new defense of big government: *big government is useful precisely for (among other reasons) helping to keep government relatively small.* That sounds counterintuitive, but a big, sprawling government is harder to take over, and harder to "turn bad," than is many a smaller government. Surely it ought to give us pause that the major instances of Western fascism came right after a time when government was relatively small, and not too long after the heyday of classical liberalism in Europe, namely the late nineteenth century. No, I am not *blaming* classical liberalism for Nazism, but still it is easier to take over a smaller and simpler state than it is to commandeer one of today's sprawling bureaucracies.

I commonly hear arguments from classical liberals suggesting that a "night watchman state," or some slightly expanded version thereof, provides government with greater efficacy and focus. If government is concentrating on its essential functions, and what it can do well, maybe it does a better job. Imagine for instance a government that doesn't try so hard to regulate broccoli stems, but delivers on limiting crime and providing speedy and fair trials to the accused.

Yet the greater focus of the night watchman state, for all its virtues, is part of the reason why it is easy to take over. There is a clearly defined center of power, a clearly defined set of lines of authority, and furthermore the main activity of the state is to enforce property rights through violence or the threat of violence. That means such a state will predominantly comprise policemen, soldiers, possibly border authorities, Coast Guard employees, and others in related support services. The culture and ethos of such a state is likely to be relatively masculine and also relatively martial and tolerant of a certain amount of risk, and indeed violence. The state will be full of people who are used to the idea of applying force to achieve social ends, even if, under night watchman assumptions, those deployments of force are for the most part justified.

A would-be fascist basically has to court those groups and promise them a new social order in which violence is raised in social status, and in which violence is deployed for something other than just the protection of property rights. I'm not suggesting that is an easy sell, and indeed most societies do not fall prey to fascist temptations, nor do their soldiers lean in that direction. I'm merely suggesting that as intellectual leaps go, that is an imaginable one. I believe that even in today's American state there is more support among policemen, border guards, and soldiers for some semi-fascistic ideas than there is, say, in the regular bureaucracy. The conversion exercise becomes all the easier if there is a communist threat on the horizon, and fascism can be sold to the populace and to the members of the state as

superior to the nationalization of property and the dictatorship of the proletariat. Fascism, at least in some of its forms,
sounds closer to the status quo and thus less scary to many
conservatives, moderates, and members of the middle class,
as indeed was the case for part of the 1930s in many locales,
not just in Nazi Germany.

Compare that struggle to trying to persuade a complex
social welfare bureaucracy to adopt fascism. The social welfare bureaucracy will be more scattered, have a larger number of people, probably a greater diversity of types, and it is
likely to employ a much higher percentage of women and
also relatively old people—men and women at ages who
likely would be out of the armed forces and possibly out of
police forces as well. The bulk of that bureaucracy will have
had no experience with violence, either directly or indirectly, and it probably dreads the notion of a country where
violence is more prevalent. They are not used to thinking of
criminals or foreign forces as an enemy in any kind of active, daily way, again unlike the police forces and soldiers.
In short, as an audience they are far less likely to embrace or
even tolerate ideals of fascism.

You already may know that about 4.3 percent of the
population of Washington, DC, voted for Donald Trump. I
do not myself consider Trump to be an appropriate stand-in
for the concept of fascism, but the point is that a lot of these
people did make that association, to varying degrees, and
they voted accordingly.

And since being elected, Trump has found that the traditional bureaucracy has been trying to thwart his will. The

courts have ruled against his executive orders; a Republican Congress has not been a rubber stamp for his ideas on trade, immigration, and health care reform; and agencies have been slow-walking the Trumpian ideas they do not like. The Pentagon and even the State Department have reexerted their traditional control over foreign policy. The Trump administration has found it does not have the ability to staff the federal government with Trump sympathizers, and so there is a mix of radical understaffing and staffing with traditional Republican types. None of those developments is conducive to radical change in government, whether or not you think the Trump agenda ever was a fascistic one. The problem with Trumpian rule has been one of chaos much more than totalitarianism.

Furthermore, the Trump associates who sometimes are considered the "most fascistic" (it is beyond the scope of this essay to evaluate such charges, so here I am simply referring to the perception) largely have been forced out or lost influence, including Michael Flynn and Steve Bannon. Actual fascists these days don't have extensive experience in government at high levels, and they are unlikely to find such environments conducive to their goals and temperaments. That makes it very hard for a potential fascistic revolution to get off the ground. And the larger, more diverse, and more decentralized the federal government is, the more of a "fascist shock force" would be required to bring about fundamental change. Fascistic ideas just don't seem to be in the running to produce such kinds of change. You might think that someday American fascism will acquire a better-developed infrastructure in terms of ideas and personnel, but still a larger and more complex government raises the bar significantly on how much ideological infrastructure would be needed to effect real fascistic change.

COMPARISON WITH SOME OTHER VIEWS

A relevant perspective can be found in Eric Frank Russell's science fiction novel *The Great Explosion*. In Russell's treatment, external conquerors find it virtually impossible to take over the anarchistic society of the Gands, who practice passive resistance. The would-be conquerors arrive and demand obedience, but literally no one has the authority, or for that matter the will, to surrender. The demands are ignored, and the assailants are not sure what to do next. They could attempt violent reprisals, but there is no one exactly with the responsibility of responding to such attempted deterrence. Imagine for instance trying to do a corporate takeover of "the blogosphere," or some other distributed and decentralized entity. Who exactly is supposed to sign over the keys to the castle? One is reminded of the various English attempts to take over semi-anarchistic Ireland in medieval times. Various chieftains could be subdued or bought out, but colonizing the whole island took centuries, in part because there was no single king to depose and thus no simple way to commandeer the whole country.

I am suggesting that there is something to Russell's portrait of why it is hard to take over an anarchistic society. But if we consider that actual anarchy is unlikely as an alternative (and probably also undesirable), what might be the next best thing? I am suggesting that rather than the night watchman state, a diverse, decentralized, and complex bureaucracy might be much harder to take over, precisely because it is more anarchistic in some key respects.

It is also interesting to compare my perspective to the views of the Austrian economists Ludwig von Mises and Friedrich A. Hayek, and also the American economist Milton Friedman. There are some differences between those writers, but overall they all stress how losses of economic freedom and political freedom come together. Mises wrote a famous essay called "Middle-of-the-Road Policy Leads to Socialism," first published in 1950, and also covered this topic in later writings. Although Mises in this piece focuses on socialism, more broadly he considers socialism and fascism to be two branches of the more fundamental disease of extreme statism. Hayek's best-selling *The Road to Serfdom* stressed how economic regulation and nationalization tend to lead to totalitarianism, and if you are skeptical, keep in mind that he wrote the book in the 1940-to-1943 period, when successful democracies were few and far between and the world scene looked remarkably bleak. Milton Friedman, in his 1980 book *Free to Choose*, made related arguments about how economic freedom underpins political freedom, so I'm going to consider these views as a kind of composite, while again noting that some differences remain among these authors.

In the composite model, one economic intervention creates some problems from its unintended secondary consequences, and that in turn leads to another intervention, which in turn creates the perceived need for yet further interventions. For instance, you can imagine a price control leading to a decline in product quality, which in turn motivates further government regulations on business and product quality, which in turn renders many businesses unprofitable, and which eventually leads to yet further control or even nationalization. Eventually government controls so much of the economy that political liberties are lost too. For instance, if a government owns the media and printing presses, and plays a major role in regulating occupations and land use, liberty will dwindle, and eventually democracy will disappear as well. Too many decisions will be concentrated in the hands of the centralized state.

It is easy to see the intuitive appeal of this model, especially in the middle parts of the twentieth century. But I am suggesting it is mostly wrong, at least circa 2017, and indeed we have seen governments take on ever-larger roles in taxing and regulating economies, and in providing public goods, without there being a general move toward totalitarian outcomes. Democracy is alive and well, if not everywhere, at the very least in the social democracies with government running at 40 to 55 percent of GDP. Part of this has been because a larger government is harder to take over, but another part is that militaries and police functions have declined in relative importance compared to the other parts of government.

So what does the composite Mises-Hayek-Friedman model miss? For one thing, for better or worse, voters desire a lot of these expansions of government activity, and so they tend to cement citizens' belief in liberal democratic capitalism, albeit with a lot of government involvement. But more fundamentally, these successive state interventions in some ways actually dilute the power of the state. Even though the state does more, it has less coherence and more decentralization and diversity. The state may end up overextended or overregulating in a manner that is hard to correct or pull back. Still, such a state will not be very vulnerable to a hostile takeover by a fascist or otherwise totalitarian party. Bureaucracy actually isn't up to pushing through a fascist takeover, and only rarely will it have that desire in the first place. And indeed the history of the Western (and some non-Western) democracies since World War II suggests this alternative perspective is closer to the truth than are the claims of Mises, Hayek, and Friedman.

HOW LARGE WERE THE GERMAN AND ITALIAN STATES ON THE EVE OF FASCISM?

Upon its election, the Nazi state moved the German government away from transparency, including fiscal transparency, and there are reasons to doubt the strict veracity of German governmental economics statistics dating back at least as far as the 1920s. Still, everything we know about that time period, including comparisons with other, economically similar nations, suggests that the overall size of government on the eve of the Nazi revolution was not massively large.

For instance, if we look at available data on German government spending as a percentage of GDP, it measures at about 36.6 percent as of 1932, at least according to Suphan

Andic and Jindřich Veverka. That is considerably smaller than what the German government would grow to after the denazification following World War II, when government rose to 44 percent of GDP by 1958 and to much more later. Vito Tanzi and Ludger Schuknecht offer an alternate estimate of 34.1 percent of GDP for the Nazi government in 1937, and 31.1 percent of GDP for government expenditure in Mussolini's Italy, again for 1937. We also should adjust our interpretation of these numbers by the reality that government regulation in those days was extremely underdeveloped, making the states of that time, relative to contemporary states, smaller yet.[1]

The history of fascism more generally has been characterized by conflict between party and state, and extreme fascist victories typically have required the ascendancy of party and thus a relatively weak state. Hitler, for instance, used a variety of persuasion, force, and terror to make the state do his bidding. In these situations, party militants typically wanted to try to take over the state altogether, as Lenin (more or less) managed to do in Russia, but the more successful fascist leaders, including Hitler, resisted this tendency and accommodated their programs to the demands of the bureaucracy to a considerable extent, so as to not alienate those bureaucracies.[2]

Robert O. Paxton summed it up nicely: "In Nazi Germany, the party came to dominate the state and civil society, especially after war began." In other words, the key parts of the German state had to be small enough, and easy enough to manage, to be taken over by a political party. In

Italy the situation was different, as, in the words of Paxton, ". . . the traditional state wound up with supremacy over the party," and thus Italian fascism was more moderate and less destructive than in Germany. This difference in outcome did not spring from a larger Italian state, but arose in large part because Mussolini did not trust his own most militant forces and thus preferred for the traditional Italian state to remain largely in place.[3]

After the Nazis took control of Germany, they trimmed welfare spending somewhat, in part because the country had been in a recession. But they kept most of the basic welfare state apparatus in place, with the biggest change being forms of racial and ethnic exclusion from benefits. And contrary to what most people have been led to believe, the German economic recovery of the 1930s was not driven by Nazi fiscal policy. In reality, real consumption fell over that decade, and most of the spending boosts were for the military, which inflated measured GDP but did not create real wealth for the citizenry. So the Nazis didn't move to big government, in terms of overall economic and regulatory issues, as much as many people might think.[4]

The Nazi history on privatization also is consistent with my hypotheses. After the Nazis took power, they sold off public ownership in a variety of previously state-owned industries, including steel, mining, banking, local public utilities, shipyards, ship lines, and railways. In part they did this for the revenue, and in part they may have done it to cultivate business loyalty. Still, the Nazis did not see any contradiction between fascism and partial privatization, in contrast to the theories of Mises, Hayek, and Friedman discussed above. At however intuitive a level, the Nazi regime may have sensed that they needed a government they could control, rather than a government that was as large and interventionist as possible. Privatization fit into that vision, or at least did not contradict it. I am not suggesting that all or even most fascist regimes have been privatizers (though Augusto Pinochet's Chile is another example), only that we need a theory where privatization and fascism do not necessarily clash.[5]

The history of Latin American fascistic dictatorships is more broadly consistent with this general approach. They typically have sprung from weak and insecure states, often rife with corruption but not massively interventionist, as might fit the predictions of Mises, Hayek, and Friedman. Arguably the strongest and best developed fascistic state was Pinochet's Chile, which also had an extensive (albeit imperfect) social welfare apparatus, which in fact Pinochet supported and increased over time. That is perhaps one reason why Pinochet's Chile made a relatively smooth transition out of autocracy into a stable democracy once Pinochet lost the referendum and stepped down.

It is interesting to consider contemporary China in light of this analysis, and fortunately most of the implications are positive ones. In 1993, for instance, the Chinese central government's share of direct revenue absorbed only 3 percent of the country's economy, which of course is a very low figure, reflecting the fiscal immaturity of the Chinese state. The widespread prevalence of state-owned enterprises meant the actual Chinese government was much bigger and more influential than that single number would suggest, but still the Chinese central government proper was not so sprawling and complex. At that time, arguably there was a higher risk of an outside takeover of the Chinese government, perhaps by a dissident "fundamentalist" communist faction rather than by explicit fascists, but a takeover nonetheless. It wasn't so hard to seize control of the centralized state, and the relevant constraints probably came from the provinces and other local authorities, raising the traditional specter of a Chinese civil war.[6]

These days, the Chinese central government is more bureaucratized, there is a value-added tax, and the government has been evolving toward the bureaucratic structures found in the developed world, albeit with the nondemocratic backdrop of the Communist Party. Most of all, the Chinese central government is more complex, and it represents a more diverse series of interests. It is probably harder for extremists to take over such a government and plunge China back into either total tyranny or chaos. China has become more normalized, and although the associated bureaucratization of society brings some very real costs, overall that is a favorable development.

In contrast to contemporary China, consider the Khmer Rouge movement in Cambodia in the 1970s. Whatever label you wish to attach to their ideas, the Khmer Rouge took over the government of Cambodia at the time and ended up massacring well over a million Cambodians and brutalizing many more. There do not seem to be systematic numbers on the size of the Cambodian state right before the Khmer Rouge takeover, but it is widely recognized that governmental institutions mostly were primitive in terms of their size and scope, modern bureaucracy was hard to come by, and the army was a central part of the apparatus of Cambodian rule. Those are exactly the conditions that raise the probability of a takeover followed by the brutal oppression of the domestic population, namely few parts to take over and a predominance of coercive power in the active parts of the government that do exist. And indeed the Khmers did take over the Cambodian government and redirect the coercive institutions of that state toward their own brutal, preferred ends.

Those are exactly the conditions China has moved away from, and thus China's own historical experiences with massacres, brutal rule, and oppression seem to be growing less rather than more likely.

IS BIGGER GOVERNMENT ALWAYS BETTER?

No, of course not. A government that is too big involves high costs in terms of efficiency and arguably justice as well. The former Soviet Union would be one example of such a disastrous system, and the state controlled so many different aspects of individual, economic, and political life. Still, the path toward fascism, or for that matter greater communist tyranny, may not have been through a simple extension and expansion of the power of the Soviet state. The Soviet government became weakened and bureaucratized over time, compared to its earlier years, and it also became less oppressive (for the most part). Khrushchev and Brezhnev were less brutal and totalitarian than was Stalin, for instance. And at the time when Lenin seized power, the Russian state very much fit the model of being weak, institutionally immature, and not having a well-developed social welfare bureaucracy by modern standards.

In the model I have in mind, excess government may cause slow growth, and if government is far too large it may cause a more general breakdown of social order and thus also a collapse of rule. And that actually is the most plausible path from very large government to fascism, namely through an intermediate state of political chaos, including, for a while, what is likely to be a much smaller government. If you consider the collapse of the Soviet Union, for instance, the Soviet economic model failed, the Soviet government lost its support, the Soviet empire fell apart, revenue dried up, and there was a power vacuum throughout parts of the 1990s. The eventual result of that vacuum was Vladimir Putin and the construction of a new fascism. The point here is not whether Putin is better or worse than the old Soviet Union (I would say better, at least so far). Rather, even a highly statist system required an intermediate period of collapse and smaller government, and a partial falling away of the preexisting bureaucracy, before making a phase transition to a new fascism.

Choosing a complex governmental structure to minimize the risk of a fascist takeover also involves forgoing some potential upside from major reforms. If a harmful governmental takeover is more difficult, a beneficial set of major, radical reforms may be more difficult to implement as well. The society will be more prone to ossification and stagnation, as the permanent bureaucracy will overregulate the economy and be very difficult to pare back. And indeed this does reflect one side of the recent Western experience, namely that it is very difficult to get rid of excess bureaucracy and regulation, to the detriment of dynamism and economic growth. Just as we are insulated from a fascist takeover, so are we probably stuck with some of the less efficient features of modern social democracies. This is all part of a more general process of pacification, feminization, and bureaucratization of just about everything, a process I have outlined in my recent book *The Complacent Class: The Self-Defeating Quest for the American Dream.*

For all the bipartisan agreement that regulatory reform in some manner is needed, very few Western societies have succeeded with it. The biggest example of a deregulatory success in the United States has been airline deregulation, which was done directly by an act of Congress and which abolished the regulating agency, the Civil Aeronautics Board (CAB), outright. This did not have to be done by cutting through a jungle of regulations with the proverbial machete, and the sheer act of outright agency abolition cannot be applied to, say, the Environmental Protection Agency or the Food and Drug Administration, as those institutions perform far too many valuable functions, unlike the CAB. Internationally, the biggest deregulatory success may have been the waves of reform in New Zealand in the 1980s and '90s, and that instance is notable for the almost complete absence of checks and balances in the cabinet-led New Zealand system of government. But even in that case, New Zealand has kept a modern bureaucracy and modern social welfare state, albeit with a fair amount of regulatory repeal, improvements in the quality of regulation, and consolidations of regulatory authority. In terms of functions, the New Zealand government just doesn't look that different from those of other Western states.

It can be said that the ongoing evolution and cementing in of big government, in the social welfare and bureaucratic senses of that term, is an extended exercise in risk aversion. Since Western governments became more bureaucratic and complex, we just haven't had much in the way of fascist takeovers, or even serious attempts in those directions. We also haven't had that much in the way of sweeping reforms in the deregulatory direction. What I am suggesting is that these are two sides of the same coin, and they represent a deliberate decision to opt for, or at least to allow, a relatively stable course with a minimum of risk of excess deviation toward any particular extreme political direction.

CONCLUDING REMARKS

No, it can't happen here. Not anytime soon. That is both our blessing and, when you think through all of its implications, our curse as well.

REFERENCES
Andric, Suphan, and Jindřich Veverka. "The Growth of Government Expenditure in Germany Since the Unification." *Public Finance Analysis*, 1963/64, 23, 2, 169–278.

Bel, Germa. "Against the Mainstream: Nazi Privatization in 1930s Germany." *The Economic History Review*, February 2010, 63, 1, 34–55.

Cowen, Tyler. *The Complacent Class: The Self-Defeating Quest for the American Dream.* New York: St. Martin's Press, 2017.

Friedman, Milton, and Rose Friedman. *Free to Choose: A Personal Statement.* New York: Harcourt, Brace, Jovanovich, 1980.

Hayek, Friedrich A. *The Road to Serfdom.* Chicago: University of Chicago Press, 1944.

Mises, Ludwig. "Middle-of-the-Road Policy Leads to Socialism." Online, Mises Institute, https://mises.org/library/middle-road-policy-leads-socialism. First published 1950.

Paxton, Robert O. *The Anatomy of Fascism.* New York: Vintage Books, 2005.

Payne, Stanley G. *A History of Fascism 1914–1945.* Madison: University of Wisconsin Press, 1995.

Ritschl, Albert. "Deficit Spending in the Nazi Recovery, 1933–1938: A Critical Reassessment." *Journal of the Japanese and International Economies*, December 2002, 16, 4, 559–82.

Russell, Eric Frank. *The Great Explosion.* New York: Dodd, Mead, and Company, 1962.

Tanzi, Vito, and Ludger Schuknecht. *Public Expenditure in the 20th Century: A Global Perspective.* Cambridge, UK: Cambridge University Press, 2000.

Tooze, Adam. *The Wages of Destruction: The Making and Breaking of the Nazi Economy.* New York: Penguin Books, 2006.

Wong, Christine P. W., and Richard M. Bird. "China's Fiscal System: A Work in Progress." In Loren Brandt and Thomas Rawski, editors, *China's Great Economic Transformation.* Cambridge, UK: Cambridge University Press, 2008, 429–66.

NOTES

1. See Andic and Veverka (1963/64, p. 183). See also Tanzi and Schuknecht (2000, pp. 6–7), and for background information, Tooze (2006).
2. Paxton (2005, p. 133).

3. Paxton (2005, p. 147).
4. On Nazis and the welfare state, see Paxton (2005, p. 146). On fiscal policy, see Ritschl (2002).
5. On Nazi privatization and its motives, see Bel (2010).
6. On the 1993 figure, see Wong and Bird (2008, p. 440).

LESSONS FROM
THE AMERICAN FOUNDING
CASS R. SUNSTEIN

Is the United States of America truly exceptional? Is that why it can't happen here? (In my view, it really can't.)

To answer those questions, let's start at the beginning—not with the firing of shots at Lexington and Concord but with the founding document, and with what remains its best explanation and defense, which was, astonishingly, offered in real time.

To many modern readers, *The Federalist Papers* seem formal, musty, old, and a bit tired—a little like a national holiday, celebrating events long past but lacking a sense of struggle and excitement, or even a clear message. But under remarkable time pressure, Alexander Hamilton, James Madison, and John Jay, writing under the name of "Publius," produced the best historical record, by far, of the ideas that gave birth to American exceptionalism. If authoritarianism can't happen here (and it probably can't), Publius helps explain why.

It is important and true that the explanation was a product of a concrete historical drama, involving the fate of an emerging nation that was having an exceedingly difficult time governing itself. But Publius's claims, and the structure he defended, bear not only on American debates of the eighteenth century but also those of the nineteenth, twentieth, and twenty-first. They offer lessons for making war and making peace, and for domestic challenges of many different kinds. Indeed, they provide guidance for constitutional democracies all over the globe, not least when peace, prosperity, and self-government itself are endangered.

In a nutshell, Publius contends that republican governments do best, and are most stable and most protective of liberty, not in a small, homogenous area but in a large, diverse one, complete with a system of checks and balances. According to *The Federalist Papers*, small republics and tightly knit groups often end up destroying liberty, and themselves, simply because of the power of well-organized factions.

But in a large republic, heterogeneity can be a creative force, promoting circumspection and introducing safeguards against bias, error, confusion, and oppression. In Madison's boldest words, the constitutional design, offering checks and balances in a large republic, provides "a Republican remedy for the diseases most incident to Republican government. And according to the degree of pleasure and pride we feel in being Republicans, ought to be our zeal in cherishing the spirit and supporting the character of Federalists." Those words are bold, because Republicanism and Federalism were widely thought to be opposed. (We'll see why.)

Publius argues on behalf of a distinctive and novel kind of democracy—a deliberative one. He insists that in a well-functioning deliberative democracy, a wide range of perspectives and diversity of views are a virtue rather than a vice, at least if the constitutional framework has the correct structure. In this way, Publius explicitly repudiates classical republicanism and Montesquieu, the great theorist of republican thought and an important authority for post-revolutionary America.

The repudiation yielded something altogether new and different. That novel conception of republicanism—one that cherishes the spirit of federalists—provides a clue to the longevity of the United States Constitution. It also helps to explain why it has served, for so many, as a model of self-government under law. It helps explain, finally, why it has operated as a robust set of safeguards against (full-scale) authoritarianism in many forms.

HISTORICAL BACKGROUND

To appreciate *The Federalist Papers*, it is indispensable to have some understanding of the Articles of Confederation, which the Constitution replaced. The Articles were adopted shortly after the Revolution in order to ensure a degree of unification of the states for the solution of common foreign and domestic problems, but the overriding understanding was that the states would remain sovereign. The first substantive provision of the Articles announced that "each state retains its sovereignty, freedom, and independence, and every Power, Jurisdiction, and right, which is not by this confederation expressly delegated to the United States, in Congress assembled."

A number of powers were, however, conferred on "the United States in Congress assembled." These powers included "the sole and exclusive right and power of determining on peace and war"; the authority to resolve disputes between the states; the power to regulate "the alloy and value of coin struck by their own authority, or by that of the respective states"; and the authority to control dealings with Indian tribes, to establish or regulate post offices, and to appoint naval and other offices in federal service.

By contemporary standards, the Articles of Confederation had conspicuous gaps. Two of the most important powers of the modern national government were missing altogether—the power to tax and the power to regulate commerce. Moreover, two of the three branches of the national government were altogether absent. There was no executive authority. There was no general national judicial authority; the only relevant provision authorized Congress to establish a national appellate tribunal to decide maritime cases. Of course, there was no bill of rights.

By the middle years of the 1780s, many prominent leaders agreed that amendments to the Articles were required. James Madison, along with numerous others, identified a series of concrete problems: encroachments by the states on federal authority, trespasses by some states on others, unjust state laws, and a disastrous absence of mechanisms for coordinated action in domains such as naturalization, commerce, and literary property. Seeking to address those problems, reformers agreed that a prime imperative was to prevent any form of authoritarianism, especially as it had been experienced under British rule, and thus to carry forward the goals for which the Revolution had been fought.

In 1786, state representatives met in Annapolis to discuss the problems that had arisen under the Articles; they adopted a resolution to hold a convention in Philadelphia to remedy those problems. The resulting Constitution developed an altogether novel framework, one that went beyond the Articles of Confederation in a number of ways.

Among the most important changes were the creation of a powerful executive branch; the grant to Congress of the powers to tax and to regulate commerce; and the creation of a federal judiciary, including the Supreme Court and, if Congress chose, lower federal courts. The tenth amendment, added two years later, was a pale echo of the first provision of the Articles of Confederation, deleting the word *expressly*, and it was countered by the clause granting Congress the authority to make "all laws necessary and proper" to effectuate its enumerated powers. To its defenders and to its critics, the most noteworthy feature of the new Constitution was its dramatic expansion of the authority of the national government, giving it a range of fresh powers and authorizing both the executive and the judiciary to exercise considerable authority over the citizenry.

The Constitution was sent to the states for ratification in September 1787. At the time, it proved extremely controversial, and powerful objections were offered against it. There was no assurance that it would be ratified. Opposition was especially intense in New York. Seeking to persuade voters in that state, Alexander Hamilton was the major impetus behind *The Federalist Papers*; he recruited John Jay and James Madison for the effort. Because Jay was injured in a street riot at an early stage, he turned out to be only a modest contributor. The name "Publius" was chosen by Hamilton.

THE ANTIFEDERALIST CASE

In many periods in American history, there has been enthusiasm for the arguments of the antifederalists—committed opponents of the proposed Constitution who claimed that the document amounted to a betrayal of the principles underlying the Revolution. We cannot understand Publius's originality without exploring the relationship between his arguments and those of the antifederalists, whom Publius attempted to rebut.

Many of the antifederalists emphasized the importance, for republican government, of civic virtue. Governmental outcomes were, in their view, to be determined by citizens devoted to a public good separate from the struggle of private interests; and one of government's key tasks was to ensure the flourishing of the necessary public-spiritedness. In part for this reason, the antifederalists insisted on the importance of decentralization. Only in small communities would it be possible to check a potentially oppressive government, and to find and develop the unselfishness and devotion to the public good on which genuine freedom depends.

In emphasizing the value of small communities, the antifederalists echoed traditional republican theory. Consider the words of Montesquieu, a crucial authority for antifederalists and federalists alike: "In a large republic, the public good is sacrificed to a thousand views; it is subordinate to exceptions, and depends on accidents. In a small one, the interest of the public is easier perceived, better understood, and more within the reach of every citizen; abuses are of less extent, and of course are less protected." [1]

Emphasizing this point, the antifederalists were deeply hostile to the idea of a dramatic expansion of the powers of the national government. Only a decentralized society would allow the homogeneity and dedication to the public good that would prevent the government from threatening liberty and degenerating into a war among private interests. A powerful national government would create heterogeneity and distance from the sphere of power—and thereby threaten liberty and undermine the public's willingness to participate in politics as citizens.

The antifederalist Brutus, a close follower of Montesquieu, was most explicit on the point of the importance of homogeneity: "In a republic, the manners, sentiments, and interests of the people should be similar. If this be not the case, there will be a constant clashing of opinions; and the representatives of one part will be continually striving against those of the other. This will retard the operations of government, and prevent such conclusions as will promote the public good." [2]

Many of the antifederalists also sought to avoid extreme

disparities in wealth, education, or power. Such disparities would poison the spirit of civic virtue and prevent achievement of the homogeneity of a virtuous people. Thus the antifederalists complained of "the factitious appearances of grandeur and wealth." [3]

From this perspective, the grounds on which the antifederalists based their opposition to the proposed Constitution should be clear. They believed that the Constitution would destroy the system of decentralization on which true liberty depended. Citizens would lose effective control over their representatives. Rule by remote national leaders would attenuate the scheme of representation, rupturing the alliance of interests between the rulers and the ruled. The antifederalists feared that the proposed Constitution would effectively exclude the people from the realm of public affairs and provide weakly accountable national leaders with enormous discretion to make policy and law.

Some of the antifederalists were also skeptical of the emerging interest in commercial development that had played such a prominent role in the decision to abandon the Articles of Confederation in favor of the new Constitution. In the antifederalists' view, commerce was a threat to the principles underlying the Revolution because it gave rise to ambition, avarice, and the dissolution of communal bonds.

PUBLIUS'S RESPONSE

The antifederalist objections to the proposed Constitution provoked Publius to offer a theoretical response that amounted to a new conception of self-government. This conception reformulated long-standing principles of republicanism, in the process rejecting some of its apparently deepest commitments.

The authors of *The Federalist Papers* were fully aware of the originality of the American project. No. 1, written by Hamilton, begins in this way: "It has been frequently remarked that it seems to have been reserved to the people of this country, by their conduct and example, to decide the important question, whether societies of men are really capable or not of establishing good government from reflection and choice, or whether they are forever destined to depend for their political constitutions on accident and force."

What is especially noteworthy here is the distinction between "reflection and choice" on the one hand and "accident and force" on the other, with the suggestion that many constitutions were a product either of random events or of simple power. In suggesting that cherished and time-honored traditions might actually be a product of "accident and force," Publius is hoping for a fresh path.

But how might the apparently powerful objections of the antifederalists be shown to be unconvincing?

It is best to start with Madison's No. 10, probably the very greatest of the papers. For Madison, the primary problem for self-government is the control of faction, understood in his famous formulation as "a number of citizens, whether amounting to a majority or minority of the whole, who are united and actuated by some common impulse of passion, or of interest, adverse to the rights of other citizens, or to the permanent and aggregate interests of the community." Madison urges that for a well-constructed union, no advantage "deserves to be more accurately developed than its tendency to break and control the violence of faction."

Note Madison's emphasis on both passion and interest—and his suggestion that either one can be harmful to "the rights of other citizens" and to "the permanent and aggregate interests of the community." We can see Nazi Germany and the Soviet Union as animated mostly by passion rather than interest; the same is true of many nations that have stifled liberty. But interest also plays a role, as when nations confiscate property, or when majorities harm minorities whom they see as competitors. The disgraceful internment of Japanese-Americans during World War II was a product of passion, but it was unquestionably based on perceived interest.

In standard republican fashion, the antifederalists rooted the problem of faction in that of corruption; their solution was to control the factional spirit and limit the power of elected representatives. In their view, those close to the people, chosen locally, would not stray from the people's interests. The civic virtue of the citizenry and of its representatives would work as a safeguard against tyranny. In emphasizing the importance of small republics, the need for civic virtue, the risk of corruption, and the importance of homogeneity, the antifederalists directly followed Montesquieu.

Madison saw things very differently. He transformed the question of corruption into that of faction. He saw the "corruption" that created factions as a natural, though undesirable, product of liberty and inequality in human faculties. This redefinition meant that the basic problems of governance could not be solved by the traditional republican means of education and inculcation of virtue.

Crucially, the problem of faction was likely to be most, not least, severe in a small republic. In a small republic, a self-interested private group could easily seize political power and distribute wealth or opportunities in its favor. Indeed, in the view of the federalists, this was precisely what had happened in the years since the Revolution. During that period, factions had usurped the processes of state government, putting both liberty and property at risk.

Madison viewed the recent history as sufficient evidence that sound governance could not rely on traditional conceptions of civic virtue and public education to guard against factional tyranny. Such devices would be unable to overcome the natural self-interest of men and women, even in their capacity as political actors. "The latent causes of faction are thus sown in the nature of man. . . ." Self-interest, in Madison's view, would inevitably result from differences in natural talents and property ownership. To this point, Madison added the familiar idea that attempting to overcome self-interest would carry a risk of tyranny of its own.

MADISON'S SOLUTION

All this justified rejection of the antifederalist belief that the problem of faction could be overcome, but it supplied no positive solution to the problem. In developing a solution Madison was particularly original. He began with the notion that the problem posed by factions is especially acute in a small area, for a "common passion or interest will, in almost every case, be felt by a majority of the whole"—and there will be no protection for the minority. Liberty and self-government would be at risk. But a large republic would provide crucial safeguards. There, the diversity of interests would ensure against the possibility that sufficient numbers of people would feel a common desire to oppress minorities.

A large republic thus contained a built-in check against the likelihood of factional tyranny. "The smaller the society, the fewer probably will be the distinct parties and interests composing it." But "[e]xtend the sphere, and you take in a greater variety of parties and interests; you make it less probable that a majority of the whole will have a common motive to invade the rights of other citizens." An extended republic, with diverse interests, creates a built-in protection against oppression.

This was not the only virtue of size. In a large republic, the principle of representation might substantially solve the problem of faction. In a critical passage, Madison wrote that representation would "refine and enlarge the public views by passing them through the medium of a chosen body of citizens, whose wisdom may best discern the true interest of their country and whose patriotism and love of justice will be least likely to sacrifice it to temporary or partial considerations." A large republic would simultaneously reduce the danger that representatives would acquire undue attachment to local interests. Emphasizing that risk, Madison favored large rather than small election districts and long rather than short periods of service.

This conception of representation appears throughout *The Federalist Papers*. No. 57 urges that: "The aim of every political constitution is, or ought to be, first to obtain for rulers who possess most wisdom to discern, and most virtue to pursue the common good of the society; and in the next place, to take the most effectual precautions for keeping them virtuous whilst they continue to hold their public trust."

In multiple places, Publius suggests that wisdom and virtue would characterize national representatives. Whereas the antifederalists accepted representation as a necessary evil, Publius regarded it as an opportunity for achieving governance by diverse officials devoted to a public good distinct from the struggle of private interests. Representatives would have the time and temperament to engage in a process of reflection. The hope was for a genuinely national politics. The representatives of the people would be free to engage in the process of discussion and debate from which the common good would emerge.

All this was sufficient to suggest that the standard view, rooted in Montesquieu and underlined by Brutus, was altogether wrong: small republics were far less promising than large ones. But what about the risk of "clashing opinions," which would seem to be greatly increased in a large republic? It is here that Publius offers one of his most important arguments. The central claim is that what Brutus sees as a vice is actually a virtue.

In No. 70, Hamilton writes, "the differences of opinion, and the jarrings of parties in [the legislative] department of the government, though they may sometimes obstruct salutary plans, yet promote deliberation and circumspection, and serve to check excesses in the majority." Publius views the system of bicameralism as a way of ensuring increased "deliberation and circumspection," in large part because it enlists diversity both as a safeguard and as a way of enlarging the range of arguments.

We might note here that in the very same number, Hamilton is actually defending the "unitary executive"—the decision to create a single president, who would be in charge of the executive branch and thus in a position to ensure "promptitude of decision" as well as energy. The unitary executive, in key ways subordinate to the legislature, was a crucial part of the system of deliberative democracy. As Hamilton explains in No. 79, an independent judiciary was also a crucial element: "The complete independence of the courts of justice is peculiarly essential in a limited constitution." A central function of the independent judiciary would be to interpret the Constitution, and thus to ensure that the other institutions would be kept within their lawful bounds as established by We the People.

In important respects, the departure from traditional republicanism could not have been greater. On Publius's account, the Constitution willingly abandoned the classical republican understanding that citizens generally should participate directly in the processes of government. Far from being a threat to freedom, a large republic could help to guarantee it. And in No. 55, Publius rejects explicitly the notion that political actions are inevitably vicious or self-interested: "As there is a degree of depravity in mankind which requires a certain degree of circumspection and distrust, so there are other qualities in human nature which justify a certain portion of esteem and confidence."

STRUCTURES AS SAFEGUARDS

Of course, representation in an extended sphere was hardly the entire story. The structural provisions of the Constitution attempted to increase the likelihood of public-spirited representation, to provide safeguards in its absence, and to ensure an important measure of popular control.

Bicameralism thus attempted not only to promote "jarring" but also to ensure that some representatives would be relatively isolated while others would be relatively close to the people. Indirect election of representatives played a far more important role at the time of ratification than it does today; the fact that state legislatures chose senators ensured that one house of the national legislature would have additional insulation from political pressure. The electoral college, puzzling to many modern observers, is another important example of the general effort to promote deliberation among those with different perspectives (see No. 68).

Perhaps most important, the separation-of-powers scheme was designed with the recognition that even national representatives may be prone to the influence of "interests" that are inconsistent with the public welfare. In No. 10, Madison notes that "enlightened statesmen will not always be at the helm." No. 51 elaborates this point and has a distinctive emphasis, relying on the celebrated "policy of supplying, by opposite and rival interests, the defect of better motives." Whereas conventional republicans emphasized virtue, Madison offered a different prescription: "Ambition," in the classic formulation, "must be made to counteract ambition."

The system of checks and balances within the federal structure was intended to operate as a check against both self-interested representation and factional tyranny. If a private group were able to achieve dominance over a certain part of the national government, or if a segment of rulers obtained interests that diverged from those of the people, other national officials would have both the incentive and the means to resist.

The federal system would also act as an important safeguard. The "different governments will control each other" and ensure stalemate rather than action at the behest of particular private interests. The jealousy of state governments and the attachment of the citizenry to local interests would provide additional protection against the aggrandizement of power in national institutions.

The result is a complex system of checks: national representation, bicameralism, indirect election, distribution of powers, and the federal-state relationship would operate in concert to counteract the effects of faction despite the inevitability of the factional spirit. And the Constitution itself, enforced by independent judges and adopted in a moment in which the factional spirit had been perhaps temporarily extinguished, would prevent both majorities and minorities from usurping government power to distribute wealth or opportunities in their favor.

A DELIBERATIVE DEMOCRACY

The picture that emerges is one of deliberative democracy. Publius rejects the view of his antifederalist adversaries on the ground that they missed the lessons of both theory and experience. They undervalued the likelihood that local government would be dominated by private interests instead of profiting from civic virtue. Publius doubts that the private interests of the citizenry could be subordinated by instilling principles of civic virtue. Finally, Publius thinks that commercial development is crucial to the new nation and could not be achieved without a considerable degree of centralization.

The notion that politics might be conducted solely as a process of bargaining and trade-offs was far from Publius's understanding. His suspicion of civic virtue, at least as a complete solution, and his relatively skeptical attitude toward the possibility that citizens could escape their self-interest led Publius to reject the traditional republican structure without rejecting important features of its understanding of politics. Hence Madison's stunning suggestion that the "pleasure and pride we feel in being Republicans" does not lead to the doubts and fears of the antifederalists; on the contrary, that very pleasure and pride lead directly to the hope and optimism of the Federalists.

Crucially, the system of checks and balances, in a large

republic, would help to improve deliberation. In this system, judicial review was hardly a means of frustrating the public will; on the contrary, it would help to ensure that We the People would remain superior to our rulers.

Perhaps the most significant element in federalist thought was the expectation that the constitutional system would serve republican goals better than the traditional republican solution of small republics, civic education, and close ties between representatives and their publics. The federalists insisted that the new system of deliberative democracy would preserve the underlying republican model of politics without running the risk of tyranny or relying on naive understandings about the human capacity to escape self-interest.

WAS PUBLIUS RIGHT?

Reasonable people have wondered whether Publius was right. The United States has been a beacon for people all over the globe, the clearest symbol of a system, and a culture, that stands opposed to authoritarianism in all its forms. But the national record is hardly spotless. For many decades, slavery was an accepted feature of the American system. In times of war, civil liberties and civil rights have been badly compromised. Protection of freedom of speech is a product of the second half of the twentieth century; before that time, speech could be punished if it was regarded as dangerous. The system of checks and balances did not prevent racial segregation, mandated by law.

This is not the place for a catalogue of abuses by the US

government or by the various states. But the very fact that it would be easy to produce one raises a cautionary note about any effort to argue that Publius was entirely right. Indeed, that same fact shows that the very question "Can it happen here?" contains some serious ambiguities. Above all, what is "it"? The question is typically understood to refer to a victory for authoritarianism—something close to Hitler's Germany or Stalin's Soviet Union. But nations that fall far short of full-scale authoritarianism can and certainly do engage in practices that violate the principles of free and self-governing societies, and that would make authoritarian nations proud.

Antifederalist themes can be found in long-standing American skepticism about a centralized and occasionally remote national government—and in corresponding enthusiasm for the authority of state and local officials. Over the last decades, those themes have come mostly from the political right, complaining of what many people have seen as excessively aggressive acts by Democratic leaders such as Lyndon Johnson, Bill Clinton, and Barack Obama. We may doubt whether those acts suggest anything like a failure of Publius's project, but it is noteworthy that the antifederalist objections have played a continuing role in American political debate.

At important times in American history, an independent judiciary has been seen not as a bulwark of liberty but as a threat to self-government, very much in line with the fears of the antifederalists. In the early part of the twentieth century, federal courts struck down progressive legislation, such as maximum hour and minimum wage laws. Decades later, they struck down legislation more likely to be favored by the right, such as prohibitions on abortion, sex discrimination, and departures from the idea of one person, one vote. No one can plausibly argue that an occasionally aggressive federal judiciary has meant that authoritarianism came to the United States. But Publius certainly did not anticipate it.

In a large republic, interest groups, or factions, have wielded considerable power, requiring serious qualifications of Madison's arguments in No. 10. Here, too, it would be difficult to argue that his arguments are fundamentally wrong, but the United States is, in important respects, far smaller than it once was, because it is so easy to communicate and organize across geographical barriers that were once formidable. In some areas, factions can and do take over the government's apparatus, at least for a time.

THE UNEXPECTEDLY POWERFUL PRESIDENCY

But it is the rise of an immensely powerful presidency, and the growth of the national security and administrative apparatus, that have raised the most serious questions about many of Publius's claims. At the time of the founding, and notwithstanding the fear of monarchies, the legislature was widely seen as the most dangerous branch. Today, it is often paralyzed, and when it is not, it tends to follow the president's lead.

Although Publius was greatly concerned to constrain the authority of the executive, he did not anticipate a situation of this kind. As he put it:

*In a government where numerous and extensive
prerogatives are placed in the hands of an hereditary
monarch, the executive department is very justly
regarded as the source of danger, and watched with all
the jealousy which a zeal for liberty ought to inspire.
In a democracy, where a multitude of people exercise
in person the legislative functions, and are continually
exposed, by their incapacity for regular deliberation
and concerted measures, to the ambitious intrigues
of their executive magistrates, tyranny may well be
apprehended, on some favorable emergency, to start up
in the same quarter. But in a representative republic,
where the executive magistracy is carefully limited;
both in the extent and the duration of its power; and
where the legislative power is exercised by an assembly,
which is inspired, by a supposed influence over the
people, with an intrepid confidence in its own strength;
which is sufficiently numerous to feel all the passions
which actuate a multitude, yet not so numerous as
to be incapable of pursuing the objects of its passions,
by means which reason prescribes; it is against the
enterprising ambition of this department that the
people ought to indulge all their jealousy and exhaust
all their precautions.*

It is a subtle argument, but its modern force is doubtful.
One reason is that in the twenty-first-century "representative republic" that is the United States, the power of the
executive magistracy is not so carefully limited in the extent

and the duration of its power. After the New Deal in particular, massive, awe-inspiring, occasionally fear-producing policymaking power has been wielded by presidents and those who work for them. It is a nice question whether Publius's particular claims about republican government remain convincing in light of the rise of an immensely powerful presidency. What, we might ask, can constrain it, if it is really determined to move in authoritarian directions?

Even centuries later, some of the central answers do come from Publius.

First: The system of checks and balances ensures, now as ever, that the president almost always needs legislative authorization in order to act. At least in the domestic domain, he cannot act unilaterally; Congress must give him the power to do what he wants. In theory, of course, a president could simply ignore that restriction of his authority. But no president is likely to do that. Publius might have been more focused on the dangers associated with Congress, but the design of the national government did serve to limit the president's room to maneuver, even under radically changed conditions.

Second: The federal judiciary is generally available to insist that the executive must obey the law. Most of the time, it acts as a deterrent to unlawful action and also as a corrective to such action when it occurs. When President Harry Truman seized the nation's steel mills in the midst of the Korean War, the Supreme Court struck down his action. When President Richard Nixon tried to prevent the publication of the Pentagon Papers, the Supreme Court stopped him. When President Donald Trump imposed what was widely seen as a "Muslim ban," the federal courts stood in his way, at least at the start. To be sure, the president appoints the nation's judges, and we can imagine a federal judiciary that is supine in the face of presidential aggression. But imagination is one thing; reality is another.

Third: The Bill of Rights has assumed far more importance than the founding generation expected. It is now a defining feature of American law and (equally important) culture. Arguably authoritarian measures are likely to run into serious objections under one or another provision of the Bill of Rights—the due process clause, the free exercise provision, the free speech provision, the right to a jury trial.

Fourth: In the American republic, the court of public opinion often reigns supreme, and that particular court imposes severe constraints on what national officials do. Publius was well aware of this point. And because respect for rights and for the central ingredients of self-government are culturally engrained, public opinion is a serious check on the executive—on both what it wants to do and what it can do, whatever it wants.

There is a cautionary note. Institutional safeguards can alter probabilities, but they do not offer guarantees. The system of checks and balances is far less robust than Publius expected, because legislatures generally support presidents of their political party—which means that ambition is less likely to counteract ambition. Some of the time, ambition reinforces ambition, as legislators bow to the will of the chief executive. We have also seen that when national security is threatened, legislatures tend to give the president the authority that he wants. If the American project is to be seriously jeopardized, it will almost certainly be because of a very serious security threat.

But let's not engage in speculative thought experiments. The sheer longevity of the constitutional framework that Publius defended, and the place it has maintained for both democracy and deliberation, continue to attest to the power of Publius's arguments. Taken as a whole, the American experience suggests that Publius did not go far wrong. Mostly, he has been proved right.

NOTES

1. Montesquieu, *The Spirit of the Laws* (Cambridge, UK: Cambridge University Press, 1989).
2. Herbert Storing, ed., *The Complete Anti-Federalist* (Chicago: University of Chicago Press, 2007).
3. See vol. 6 of *The Complete Anti-Federalist*, 201.

BEYOND ELECTIONS:
FOREIGN INTERFERENCE WITH
AMERICAN DEMOCRACY

SAMANTHA POWER

When President George Washington gave his Farewell Address in 1796, he urged the American people "to be constantly awake" to the risk of "foreign influence," which he called "one of the most baneful foes of republican government."

In the wake of Russia's meddling in the US election in 2016, President Washington's warning has a new, chilling resonance. In the immediate aftermath, the debate in the United States seemed concentrated on two dimensions of foreign interference—precisely who did what to influence the election, and how the United States and other democracies must fortify cybersecurity for our emails, critical infrastructure, and voting platforms. While pursuing these objectives is extremely important, we need to pay equal attention to an additional dimension of our vulnerability: our adversaries' ability to subvert our democratic processes by aiming falsehoods at a ripe subset of our population—and not only during our election cycles.

While a majority of Americans reported to Pew after the 2016 election that fake news had caused "a great deal" of confusion about current events, 84 percent described themselves as at least somewhat confident in their own ability to discern real from fake.[1] This confidence may well be misplaced, as a dramatically altered media environment in the United States gives propaganda and falsehoods far greater scope for influence than at any time in our history.

One possible source of our relative complacency now is that Russia's attempts to meddle in our democracy proved largely unsuccessful during the Cold War. Back then, the short- and long-term aims of Soviet influence and disinformation operations—so-called active measures—were simple: discrediting, and weakening, countries with opposing political agendas. In 1982, just months before succeeding Leonid Brezhnev as leader of the Soviet Union, KGB chairman Yuri Andropov told Soviet foreign intelligence officers abroad to more directly incorporate these "active measures" into their standard work. As the officially designated "Main Adversary," the United States was the top target, and the KGB followed up Andropov's order by designating an ambitious priority for the stepped-up operations: preventing the 1984 reelection of Ronald Reagan.

Soviet agents were instructed to infiltrate American party and campaign staffs in search of embarrassing information to leak to the press, while Soviet propagandists pushed a set of story lines to the Western media to try to reduce public support for the popular president. They sought to portray Reagan as a militarist who aided repressive regimes and fueled a dangerous arms race.[2] Soviet agents successfully seeded scores of negative news stories around the world while disseminating forged government communications to American allies and the press. Fake KGB documents spread word of a (nonexistent) CIA plot to give nuclear weapons to apartheid South Africa, for example, while Russia was also the source of a forged US embassy memorandum that led to erroneous press reports about a US plot to assassinate a Nigerian presidential candidate. A review of Soviet operations for 1982 and 1983 conducted by the KGB's chief foreign operations arm noted that "the range of questions dealt with by means of active measures has been continually widening."[3] These types of activities were, of course, not unique to Moscow; the CIA's own media interventions and manipulations during the Cold War have been well documented.[4]

Ultimately, the Soviets' "active measures" did not penetrate American public consciousness in a material way in the 1984 election. Ronald Reagan handily defeated Walter Mondale, taking forty-nine states and 525 of the 538 electoral college votes. Analogous efforts aimed at Margaret Thatcher during the UK's 1983 general election had also come up short, as she, too, won reelection in a landslide.

Reagan's victory was obviously overdetermined, but, even had the US presidential election been close, the Soviet Union faced huge obstacles during the Cold War in influencing the American electorate—or voters in other democracies—with its propaganda and disinformation. Indeed, as historian Christopher Andrew and former KGB archivist Vasili Mitrokhin observed in their definitive account of KGB activities in the West, Reagan's landslide "was striking evidence of the limitations of Soviet active measures within the United States."[5]

While it is not easy to quantify the impact of active measures, there is no question that foreign powers like Russia and China, or non-state actors like ISIS, today have a much greater ability to use "fake news" or "alternative facts" to influence a democratic electorate than they did during the Cold War. What exactly has changed in the three decades since the Soviet Union tried to thwart Reagan's reelection, making foreign propaganda far more likely to penetrate in the United States and other democracies?

First, during the Cold War, the vast majority of Americans received their news and information via mediated platforms. This meant that what appeared in print, on television, or via radio generally had to get by professional gatekeepers. Opinion still crept into news coverage, and cries of media bias were still sounded. But a foreign adversary who sought to reach Americans did not have great options for bypassing the umpires, who decided what was true and what was newsworthy. When reporters were found to have gotten a story wrong, it harmed the brand of the publication—and jeopardized the career of the implicated journalist.

In 1982, as the KGB was on the verge of initiating its campaign against Reagan's reelection, the House Intelligence

Committee undertook an investigation of the overall threat to US interests posed by Soviet active measures. Although investigators uncovered and publicized numerous Russian attempts to subvert American initiatives and policy abroad, their conclusion about the domestic threat was reassuring. Speaking on behalf of the FBI, Assistant Director Edward O'Malley confirmed that "the Soviet leadership continues to use and fund such operations on a large scale," but despite the Soviets' best efforts, O'Malley said, "We do not see Soviet active measures as having a significant impact on US decision makers." As he pointed out, "the American media is sophisticated and generally recognizes Soviet influence attempts."[6]

Nonetheless, even then, Russian *dezinformatsia* would occasionally make its way into major American publications. In profiling Andropov, for example, *Newsweek* and *Time* repeated descriptions of the longtime KGB leader as "a closet liberal" who "relaxed with American novels" and even "sought friendly discussions with dissident protestors"—all KGB-originated fictions designed to soften Andropov's image for Western audiences.[7]

Today, the American media environment bears only a passing resemblance to that of 1984. Television is the key constant: it was the "main source" of news about current events for 53 percent of Americans polled by Gallup in 1984, and for 51 percent in 2016. Yet today's television news-viewing audience tends to self-select according to their preexisting political preferences.[8] And while 27 percent of Americans turned to a daily newspaper in 1984, today only

8 percent do. The replacement is no surprise—26 percent of Americans now go online for their main source of news, with 20 percent depending on websites and other web-based platforms and 6 percent pointing to the wild, wild west of social media. Indeed, Pew has found that two-thirds of Americans are getting some of their news on social media.[9]

Russia has keenly exploited our growing reliance on new media—and the absence of real umpires. According to the declassified US intelligence assessment of Russian activities during the 2016 election that was made public in January 2017,[10] the Russian government supplemented the reach of RT and Sputnik—Russia's state-funded propaganda organs that are now available in various languages in Europe and the United States via YouTube, social media, cable, and the web—by employing a network of trolls and robot computer programs (known as "bots") that amplified damaging stories on Hillary Clinton, spread information obtained through Russia's parallel hacking campaign, and then sought to get the resulting "controversy" over the information picked up in mainstream reporting. Although initially effectively laundered to mask its fingerprints, the Russian role in manipulating the social media conversation is now more widely known and has been publicly acknowledged by Facebook and Twitter. After initially resisting the conclusion that their platforms had been compromised, these companies have now deactivated hundreds of accounts linked to Russian influence operations and Facebook has identified thousands of Russian-bought political advertisements aimed at American audiences that ran on its site. Many of the now-defunct

Facebook and Twitter accounts remained active until they were identified and deleted in mid-2017.[11]

Publicly available information about the content disseminated by these accounts and ads reveals a multifaceted strategy to support Trump's election (by both energizing and depressing turnout among key constituencies) and sow political discord among Americans. Posing as American citizens, organizations, or common interest pages with names like "Blacktivists," "Being Patriotic," and "Secured Borders," the Russia-controlled Facebook pages and accounts posted anti-Clinton messages, helped organize political rallies, and promoted links to inflammatory stories and websites. The ads, in turn, prompted users to "like" the Russian-controlled pages on Facebook and disseminated polarizing messages on topics like immigration, gun control, and race relations. A typical post on the "Being Patriotic" page, for example, claimed, "At least 50,000 homeless veterans are starving, dying in the streets, but liberals want to invite 620,000 refugees and settle them among us." Among the Russian-bought ads is an image of an African-American woman firing a gun at the viewer.[12] Russia followed a similar playbook on Twitter, helped in particular by bots that saturated users' feeds with divisive memes and fake news—a tactic that appears to have been especially pronounced in swing states.[13]

These revelations demonstrate how Russia, using a combination of covert human agents and bots, helped bring attention to a ridiculous claim originating on alt-right websites that Secretary Clinton had been involved in an underage sex ring. Many Americans—Democrats and Republicans alike—dismissed this absurd "Pizzagate" story as a sideshow until an armed man turned up at the pizzeria in question, seeking answers. Yet the ability of such a far-fetched story to gain traction illustrates the way in which political bots can be deployed to manufacture interest in a nonstory and create the illusion of widespread anger (or support) that then burrows into the consciousness of some in the broader public.[14] According to Jonathan Albright, the research director of the Tow Center for Digital Journalism at Columbia University and a leading researcher in mapping how fake news spreads, the #pizzagate hashtag was tweeted thousands of times daily, with a disproportionate number of accounts (many of them bots) tweeting from the Czech Republic, Cyprus, and Vietnam. As Albright told the *Washington Post*, "What bots are doing is really getting this thing trending on Twitter. These bots are providing the online crowds that are providing legitimacy."[15]

It is significant that, according to the declassified US intelligence assessment, the Russians had prepared a social media campaign, in anticipation of Secretary Clinton's victory, to amplify doubts about the validity of the results and "cripple her presidency from its start." With polling in late October 2016 showing that over half of Republicans believed Clinton could win only due to illegal voting or vote rigging, the Russian campaign would likely have resonated with a significant number of voters had Clinton won.[16]

The evolution of stories like Pizzagate from alt-right stalking horse to trending Twitter discussion and even front-page news underscores one of the great dangers of a media environment manipulated by targeted social media interventions. As demonstrated by decades of behavioral science research on agenda-setting, "elements emphasized by the mass media come to be regarded as important by the public."[17] More recently, social scientists have begun to produce empirical evidence that media coverage not only directs public attention but also influences how people think about a given issue or person. Thus, for example, countries that receive extensive media coverage are more likely to be considered by Americans as "vitally important" to US interests.[18] With regard to political candidates the attributes most emphasized by the media come to be associated with individuals.[19] These findings suggest potentially high rewards for flooding people's online feeds with misleading narratives for months at a time. As credible gatekeepers disappear and news is increasingly mediated through open platforms like Facebook and Twitter, we become more susceptible to measures that deploy volume and repetition to attract our attention and influence our perspectives.

Research conducted over the course of the election found that "political bot activity reached an all-time high for the 2016 campaign,"[20] with one study concluding that during the critical final weeks of the race, bots accounted for 3.8 million tweets—essentially one-fifth of the entire Twitter conversation about the election.[21] Meanwhile, the sheer quantity of misleading stories shared on Facebook is staggering. Using a database of 156 election-related news stories that fact-checking websites deemed "false," economists from NYU and Stanford determined that these false stories had been shared by American social media users 38 million times in the final three months of the 2016 presidential election alone.[22]

European countries have been on the receiving end of similar Russian measures, characterized by National Security Advisor H. R. McMaster as a "very sophisticated campaign of subversion and disinformation and propaganda . . . to break apart Europe and . . . sow dissention and conspiracy theories."[23] The May 2017 hack of Emmanuel Macron's campaign and dissemination of internal emails on election eve, when Macron was legally prohibited from responding, was well publicized. Less well known among Americans is Russian interference in elections and policymaking in Bulgaria (where Russia attempted to harm the chances of the pro-EU party in recent elections)[24] or Sweden (where a leading think tank documented how Russia had forged documents and fabricated stories over the course of years to rally public opinion against joining NATO).[25] In Germany, European intelligence officials believe that Russian hackers stole a huge trove of emails from German members of Parliament in anticipation of the September 2017 elections. However, importantly, the major political parties reportedly made a pact not to use any leaked information for political gain—so determined were they not to abet Russian meddling. The emails were not released, although they presumably remain in Russia's pocket for future use.[26]

Overall, America's European allies have responded more aggressively to Russian media manipulation after watching its scope in—and impact on—the US presidential election.

The EU has increased resources for its East StratCom office, a task force initiated in 2015 expressly to counter Russian active measures on social media. For example, as *The Guardian* reported, East StratCom spent weeks "correcting a widely shared and entirely false story that claimed that a 1,000-strong mob chanting 'Allahu Akbar' burned down Germany's oldest church." [27]

Non-state actors are becoming adept at exploiting this media landscape too. As ISIS explained in an official handbook circulated to its social media amplifiers, strategically used "media weapons [can] actually be more potent than atomic bombs" and are "no less important than the material fight." [28] At the height of its military successes, ISIS was each day releasing thirty-eight unique pieces of news and propaganda through its social media channels. [29] A study conducted by the Combating Terrorism Center at West Point determined that more than 50 percent of some 8,500 ISIS media posts covered nonmilitary aspects of the group's activities (such as religious ideology, daily life, and governance of its territories). Less than 10 percent featured the graphic violence often highlighted in Western media coverage of the group's propaganda. The study concluded that "this diverse array of themes portrayed by the group provides a likely explanation for the Islamic State's ability to attract such a diverse group of fighters and supporters from around the world . . . The group is going to great lengths to paint a picture of a caliphate that is not just a military and religious entity, but one that engages in the diverse range of activities a citizen might expect from a state." [30] This attempt to lure foreign recruits by depicting the utopian nature of life in ISIS territory was a particularly misleading—and, according to subsequent ISIS defectors, a particularly effective—form of "fake news."[31]

Beyond the explosion of new media platforms, a second major difference between the Cold War and today is that while the larger existential struggle against communism created a mainstream consensus about what America was against, and a great suspicion of anything that would have originated in the Soviet Union, our society today is defined by a virulent "partyism"—where divisions between Democrats and Republicans are more numerous, more strenuously held, and more accompanied by personal animus than we have ever seen before. These divisions mean that, in the recent election, falsehoods that aimed to discredit Secretary Clinton—without evident inquiry into their origins—were repeated and amplified on Fox News. The insularity of political and social media communities means that the average Facebook user has five politically like-minded friends for every one friend from the other party.[32] The information that comes to us has increasingly been tailored to appeal to our prior prejudices, *and* it is unlikely to be challenged by the like-minded with whom we interact day-to-day.

Indeed, the echo chamber's walls are so soundproof that, even after President Putin's well-documented interference in our election, his aggression against his neighbor Ukraine, and his atrocities in Syria, his favorability among Republicans rose substantially between 2015 and President Trump's inauguration, from 12 percent to 32 percent, while almost doubling among Independents, from 12 percent to 23 percent.[33]

Most worrisome, suspicion over differing interpretations has grown in the absence of inclusive, reasoned debate about the issues of the day. Many Americans are questioning not only whether they are obtaining objective facts—60 percent believe news stories today are "often inaccurate," according to Gallup, a major increase from 34 percent in 1985—but also whether objective facts exist at all. It is no secret that large numbers of Americans now view as opinion what were once seen as verifiable facts (e.g., the science of a warming planet; the number of noncitizen voters in the presidential election; or the utility of vaccines in inoculating children). In this environment, where our most important elected official feels no allegiance to well-established truths, the sense of an epistemological free-for-all provides an opening to all comers—especially those who are sophisticated about where to find their audience.

The third ground for alarm, in 2017, is that any well-financed actor—including not only Super PACs but foreign governments—can harvest data on its target audience, personalize its message to suit the taste of the citizens it aims to reach, and employ this customized propaganda to try to skew a contemporary political debate. The Kremlin-linked Facebook ads reached millions of Americans, and some were geographically directed.[34] Many of the Russian ads also appear to have been designed and targeted to influence specific audiences, such as those that stoked fears about Black Lives Matter or highlighted Muslim support for Clinton's candidacy.[35]

Senior US intelligence officials have even cited evidence of Russia using algorithms to target the social media accounts of particular reporters and slanting the message in line with what they assess to be the reporters' political stances.[36] An electorate that in the Cold War would have been hard to differentiate today comprises individuals whose particular likes and dislikes are intimately understood by big business, technology companies, and political campaigns—and, seemingly, well-resourced foreign entities with an interest in impacting public opinion.

Both the Justice Department and Senate Intelligence Committee probes into the 2016 election are examining whether the Russian government had access to information that allowed its operatives to tailor their messages to specific voters—the "million-dollar question," as the top Democrat on the intelligence committee put it.[37] Looking ahead, Russia and China surely have the means to purchase or steal such data, enabling them to customize their propaganda in future attempts to influence Americans. Russia's success in identifying fault lines within the electorate—and then shaping and targeting outreach that would be either appealing or inflammatory—will surely be a blueprint for other actors.[38] Indeed, as the University of Oxford's Computational Propaganda Research Project recently highlighted, it is already commonplace for governments to manipulate public opinion over social media by contracting directly with strategic communication firms.[39] The quantity of data on Americans' habits and political preferences now allows outsiders to "virtually walk the precinct," with customized outreach deployed instead of the house-to-house canvassing of earlier eras.[40] Regardless of whether one believes that Russia's brazen interference changed the outcome of the 2016 election, the extent to which these tools can be used to manipulate our democratic system is alarming. Amid all the cries of "fake news," high-ranking Trump campaign staff (including his campaign manager and digital director) shared content during the campaign from a Twitter account later revealed to be run by the Russians. Much more disturbing is evidence that Russians personally targeted and contacted hundreds of unwitting Americans, successfully encouraging some to organize political protests.[41]

Many Americans have already come to terms with the new realities of a society that has evolved rapidly due to advances in technology and connectivity: 214 million Americans now share details of their lives on Facebook; the most reliable way to know what the president is thinking is to follow his Twitter feed; and a host of apps and websites allow those with no formal ties to terrorist groups to be indoctrinated and trained to harm others.

But there is a danger that we view foreign-placed falsehoods as a risk that will arise again only in our next election cycle. Unfortunately, because sowing divisions is seen by our adversaries to be in their interest regardless of whether there is an election occurring, we must be on our guard at all times. The Alliance for Securing Democracy, a critically important, bipartisan initiative established to track and expose these efforts, offers a disturbing, real-time look into what Russia is doing right now, out of cycle. On the afternoon of August 2, 2017, a busy day on which President Trump signed a bill imposing significant sanctions on Russia and the Dow closed above 22,000 for the first time, the top two stories being promoted by Twitter accounts linked to Russian influence operations were about Hillary Clinton's links to foreign arms sales and Trump's "hero's welcome" during a visit to Ohio.[42] The Alliance has also shown how Russia-linked accounts promoted alt-right conspiracies about the violence in Charlottesville, Virginia, as well as stories that slammed those—like Senator John McCain—who had criticized the president's equivocal response. In many ways, ASD's dashboard is the 2017 version of a series of "special reports" the State Department put out in the early 1980s that sought to undermine Soviet fake news by publishing lists of false stories.

It is a testament to our divided times that it now seems unthinkable that the State Department—much less the president—would publicly call out the misinformation being spread about the actions of our own government and citizens. But now that there is a genuine risk of foreign powers who, in Washington's words, "practice the arts of seduction, to mislead public opinion," it is incumbent on the rest of us to enhance our vigilance.

NOTES

1. "Many Americans Believe Fake News Is Sowing Confusion," Pew, December 2016, http://www.journalism.org/2016/12/15/many -americans-believe-fake-news-is-sowing-confusion/.
2. Christopher Andrew and Vasili Mitrokhin, *The Mitrokhin Archive: The KGB in Europe and the West* (New York: Penguin Press, 1999),

315–17; *Comrade Kryuchkov's Instructions: Top Secret Files on KGB Foreign Operations, 1975–1985*, eds. Christopher Andrew and Oleg Gordievsky (Palo Alto, CA: Stanford University Press, 1993), 97; and Christopher Andrew and Oleg Gordievsky, *KGB* (New York: HarperCollins, 1990), 589–91.

3. *Comrade Kryuchkov's Instructions*, 100.

4. For an overview, see Kevin O'Brien, "Interfering with Civil Society: CIA and KGB Covert Political Action During the Cold War," in *Strategic Intelligence: Windows Into a Secret World*, eds. Loch K. Johnson and James J. Wirtz (Los Angeles: Roxbury Publishing Company, 2004), 265–68.

5. Andrew and Mitrokhin, *The Mitrokhin Archive*, 317.

6. "Soviet Active Measures: Hearing Before the Permanent Select Committee on Intelligence, July 13–14, 1982," US Government Printing Office, 1982, 206.

7. Andrew and Gordievsky, *KGB*, 489.

8. For example, 40 percent of Trump voters and only 3 percent of Clinton voters made Fox News their primary news source for the 2016 election. There was also a significant difference among Trump and Clinton voters with regard to reliance on online outlets like the Drudge Report and Breitbart. See "Trump, Clinton Voters Divided in Their Main Source for Election News," Pew Research Center, January 18, 2017, http://www.journalism.org/2017/01/18/trump-clinton-voters-divided-in-their-main-source-for-election-news/. See also "Political Polarization & Media Habits," Pew Research Center, October 21, 2014, http://www.journalism.org/2014/10/21/political-polarization-media-habits/.

9. "Americans Increasingly Turn to Specific Sources for News," Gallup, July 8, 2016, http://news.gallup.com/poll/193553/americans-increasingly-turn-specific-sources-news.aspx; and "News Use Across Social Media Platforms 2017," Pew Research Center, September 7, 2017, http://www.journalism.org/2017/09/07/news-use-across-social-media-platforms-2017/.

10. "Assessing Russian Activities and Intentions in Recent US Elections," Office of the Director of National Intelligence, January 6, 2017, https://www.dni.gov/files/documents/ICA_2017_01.pdf.

11. Scott Shane, "The Fake Americans Russia Created to Influence

the Election," *New York Times*, September 7, 2017, https://www
.nytimes.com/2017/09/07/us/politics/russia-facebook-twitter
-election.html; Carol Leonnig, Tom Hamburger, and Rosalind
Helderman, "Russian Firm Tied to Pro-Kremlin Propaganda
Advertised on Facebook During Election," *Washington Post*,
September 6, 2017, https://www.washingtonpost.com/politics
/facebook-says-it-sold-political-ads-to-russian-company-during
-2016-election/2017/09/06/32f01fd2–931e-11e7–89fa-bb822
a46da5b_story.html; Dustin Volz and Joseph Menn, "Twitter
Suspends Russia-Linked Accounts, but U.S. Senator Says Response
Inadequate," Reuters, September 28, 2017, https://www.reuters
.com/article/us-usa-trump-russia-twitter/twitter-suspends-russia
-linked-accounts-but-u-s-senator-says-response-inadequate-idUSK
CN1C331G; Kevin Collier, "Twitter Was Warned Repeatedly
About This Fake Account Run by a Russian Troll Farm and
Refused to Take It Down," *Buzzfeed News*, October 18, 2017,
https://www.buzzfeed.com/kevincollier/twitter-was-warned
-repeatedly-about-this-fake-account-run.

12. Shane, "The Fake Americans Russia Created to Influence the
Election"; Ben Collins, Kevin Poulsen, and Spencer Ackerman,
"Russians Impersonated Real American Muslims to Stir Chaos
on Facebook and Instagram," *Daily Beast*, September 27, 2017,
http://www.thedailybeast.com/exclusive-russians-impersonated
-real-american-muslims-to-stir-chaos-on-facebook-and-instagram;
Ben Collins, Gideon Resnick, Kevin Poulsen, and Spencer
Ackerman, "Russians Appear to Use Facebook to Push Trump
Rallies in 17 U.S. Cities," *Daily Beast*, September 20, 2017;
Adam Entous, Craig Timberg and Elizabeth Dwoskin, "Russian
Operatives Used Facebook Ads to Exploit America's Racial and
Religious Divisions," *Washington Post*, September 25, 2017,
https://www.washingtonpost.com/business/technology
/russian-operatives-used-facebook-ads-to-exploit-divisions-over
-black-political-activism-and-muslims/2017/09/25/4a011242
-a21b-11e7-ade1-76d061d56efa_story.html; Adam Entous,
Craig Timberg and Elizabeth Dwoskin, "Russian Facebook Ads
Showed a Black Woman Firing a Rifle, Amid Efforts to Stoke
Racial Strife," *Washington Post*, October 2, 2017, https://www
.washingtonpost.com/business/technology/russian-facebook-ads

-showed-a-black-woman-firing-a-rifle-amid-efforts-to-stoke-racial
-strife/2017/10/02/e4e78312-a785-11e7-b3aa-c0e2e1d41e38_
story.html; and Craig Timberg, "Russian Propaganda May
Have Been Shared Hundreds of Millions of Times, New
Research Says," *Washington Post*, October 5, 2017, https://www
.washingtonpost.com/news/the-switch/wp/2017/10/05/russian
-propaganda-may-have-been-shared-hundreds-of-millions-of
-times-new-research-says/.

13. Elizabeth Dwoskin, Adam Entous and Karoun Demirjian,
"Twitter Finds Hundreds of Accounts Tied to Russian Operatives,"
Washington Post, September 28, 2017, https://www.washington
post.com/business/economy/twitter-finds-hundreds-of-accounts
-tied-to-russian-operatives/2017/09/28/6cf26f7e-a484–11e7
-ade1–76d061d56efa_story.html; Dylan Byers, Manu Raju, and
Jeremy Herb, "Twitter Tells Congress It Took Action on 200
Russia-Linked Accounts," CNN, September 28, 2017, http://
money.cnn.com/2017/09/28/media/twitter-russia-capitol-hill
/index.html; and Greg Gordon and Peter Stone, "'Fake news'
Tweets Targeted to Swing States in Election, Researchers Find,"
McClatchy, September 28, 2017, http://www.mcclatchydc.com
/news/politics-government/election/article175759241.html.

14. This cycle is explored in the context of the 2016 election in Samuel
Woolley and Douglas Guilbeault, "Computational Propaganda in
the United States of America: Manufacturing Consensus Online,"
Computational Propaganda Research Project Working Paper,
University of Oxford, May 2017, http://comprop.oii.ox.ac.uk/wp
-content/uploads/sites/89/2017/06/Comprop-USA.pdf.

15. Marc Fisher, John Woodrow Cox, and Peter Hermann, "Pizzagate:
From Rumor, to Hashtag, to Gunfire in D.C.," *Washington Post*,
December 6, 2016, https://www.washingtonpost.com/local
/pizzagate-from-rumor-to-hashtag-to-gunfire-in-dc/2016/12
/06/4c7def50-bbd4-11e6-94ac-3d324840106c_story.html.
Time has reported that the Senate investigation into Russia's
election intervention includes an examination of whether Russia
targeted Pizzagate and other anti-Clinton stories at specific
audiences, noting that Democratic operatives have produced
evidence showing that Google searches for Pizzagate "were
disproportionately higher in swing districts and not in districts

likely to vote for Trump." See Massimo Calabresi, "Inside Russia's Social Media War on America," *Time*, May 18, 2017, http://time .com/4783932/inside-russia-social-media-war-america/.

16. Maurice Tamman, "Half of Republicans Would Reject 'Rigged' Election Result if Hillary Clinton Wins," Reuters, October 21, 2016, http://www.reuters.com/article/us-usa-election-poll-rigging -idUSKCN12L2O2; Gabrielle Levy, "Voters Think Election Could Be 'Stolen,' " *US News and World Report*, October 17, 2016, https://www.usnews.com/news/politics/articles/2016–10–17/poll -shows-trumps-claims-of-a-rigged-election-are-working-with -voters.

17. Max McCombs, "Agenda-Setting," *International Encyclopedia of the Social and Behavioral Sciences*, eds. Neil Smelser and Paul Baltes (Amsterdam: Elsevier, 2001), 285.

18. Wayne Wanta, Guy Golan, and Cheolhan Lee, "Agenda Setting and International News: Media Influence on Public Perceptions of Foreign Nations," *Journalism & Mass Communication Quarterly* 81, no. 2 (Summer 2004): 364–77.

19. See, for example, Spiro Kiousis and Max McCombs, "Agenda-Setting Effects and Attitude Strength: Political Figures during the 1996 Presidential Election," *Communication Research* 31, no. 1 (February 2004): 36–57; Jakob-Moritz Eberl, Markus Wagner, and Hajo G. Boomgaarden, "Are Perceptions of Candidate Traits Shaped by the Media? The Effects of Three Types of Media Bias," *The International Journal of Press/Politics* 22, no. 1, (2017): 111–32; and Spiro Kiousis, "Compelling Arguments and Attitude Strength: Exploring the Impact of Second-Level Agenda Setting on Public Opinion of Presidential Candidate Images," *The International Journal of Press/Politics* 10, no. 2 (2005): 3–27. Such impacts continue to be documented in today's fragmented media environment. See Ki Deuk Hyun and Soo Jung Moon, "Agenda Setting in the Partisan TV News Context: Attribute Agenda Setting and Polarized Evaluation of Presidential Candidates Among Viewers of NBC, CNN, and Fox News," *Journalism & Mass Communication Quarterly* 93, no. 3 (2016): 509–29.

20. Bence Kollanyi, Philip Howard, and Samuel Woolley, "Bots and Automation over Twitter during the U.S. Election," Computational Propaganda Research Project Working Paper,

University of Oxford, November 2016, 4, http://comprop.oii
.ox.ac.uk/wp-content/uploads/sites/89/2016/11/Data-Memo-US
-Election.pdf.

21. Specifically, the study looked at election-related tweets from
September 16 to October 21, 2016. See Alessandro Bessi and
Emilio Ferrara, "Social Bots Distort the 2016 U.S. Presidential
Election," *First Monday*, November 2016, http://journals.uic.edu
/ojs/index.php/fm/article/view/7090/5653.

22. Hunt Allcott and Matthew Gentzkow, "Social Media and Fake
News in the 2016 Election," NBER Working Paper No. 23089,
National Bureau of Economic Research, June 2017, http://www
.nber.org/papers/w23089.

23. "National Security Advisor General H. R. McMaster on MSNBC
with Hugh Hewitt," August 5, 2017, http://www.hughhewitt.com
/national-security-advisor-general-h-r-mcmaster-msnbc-hugh/.

24. Joe Parkinson and Georgi Kantchev, "Document: Russia Uses
Rigged Polls, Fake News to Sway Foreign Elections," *Wall Street
Journal*, March 3, 2017, https://www.wsj.com/articles/how-does
-russia-meddle-in-elections-look-at-bulgaria-1490282352.

25. Jon Henley, "Russia Waging Information War against Sweden,
Study Finds," *The Guardian*, January 11, 2017, https://www
.theguardian.com/world/2017/jan/11/russia-waging-information
-war-in-sweden-study-finds.

26. Stefan Wagstyl, "Berlin Braced for Russian Meddling Before
September Election," *Financial Times*, July 4, 2017, https://www
.ft.com/content/6494853c-60a1–11e7–91a7–502f7ee26895;
Michael Schwirtz, "German Election Mystery: Why No Russian
Meddling?" *New York Times*, September 21, 2017, https://www
.nytimes.com/2017/09/21/world/europe/german-election-russia
.html.

27. Daniel Boffey and Jennifer Rankin, "EU Escalates Its Campaign
Against Russian Propaganda," *The Guardian*, January 23, 2017,
https://www.theguardian.com/world/2017/jan/23/eu-escalates
-campaign-russian-propaganda.

28. Charlie Winter, "Media Jihad: The Islamic State's Doctrine for
Information Warfare," International Center for the Study of
Radicalization and Political Violence, February 2017, 18.

29. Brendan Koerner, "Why ISIS Is Winning the Social Media

War," *Wired*, March 2016, https://www.wired.com/2016/03/isis
-winning-social-media-war-heres-beat/.

30. Daniel Milton, "Communication Breakdown: Unraveling the
Islamic State's Media Efforts," *Combatting Terrorism Center*,
October 2016, 30–31.

31. In Anne Speckhard and Ahmet S. Yayla's *ISIS Defectors: Inside
Stories of the Terrorist Caliphate* (2016), the expectation among
non-Syrians and Iraqis who travel to join ISIS that they will
be building and living in a utopian caliphate is particularly
pronounced. Peter Neumann's report "Victims, Perpetrators,
Assets: The Narratives of Islamic State Defectors" (2015)
documents that "ISIS is corrupt and un-Islamic" and "life under
ISIS is harsh and disappointing," two common narratives among
defectors. See also Kimiko de Freytas-Tamura, "ISIS Defectors
Reveal Disillusionment," *New York Times*, September 20, 2015,
https://www.nytimes.com/2015/09/21/world/europe/isis
-defectors-reveal-disillusionment.html.

32. Joshua Bleiberg and Darrell M. West, "Political Polarization on
Facebook," *Brookings*, May 13, 2015, https://www.brookings.edu
/blog/techtank/2015/05/13/political-polarization-on-facebook/.

33. "Putin's Image Rises in US, Mostly Among Republicans," Gallup,
February 21, 2017, http://www.gallup.com/poll/204191/putin
-image-rises-mostly-among-republicans.aspx.

34. Ben Collins, Kevin Poulsen, and Spencer Ackerman, "Russia's
Facebook Fake News Could Have Reached 70 Million Americans,"
Daily Beast, September 8, 2017, http://www.thedailybeast.com
/russias-facebook-fake-news-could-have-reached-70-million
-americans.

35. Entous, Timberg, and Dwoskin, "Russian Operatives Used
Facebook Ads to Exploit America's Racial and Religious Divisions."

36. "Inside Russia's Social Media War on America," *Time*, May 18,
2017, http://time.com/magazine/us/4783906/may-29th-2017-vol
-189-no-20-u-s/.

37. See "Trump-Russia Investigators Probe Jared Kushner-Run Digital
Operation," *McClatchy*, July 12, 2017, http://www.mcclatchydc
.com/news/nation-world/national/article160803619.html; Senate
Intelligence Committee Vice Chairman Mark Warner's comments
on *Pod Save the World*, available at https://www.justsecurity

.org/41199/connecting-dots-political-microtargeting-russia
-investigation-cambridge-analytica/; and Manu Raju and Jeremy
Herb, "Warner: 'Million-Dollar Question' How Russians Knew
Who to Target on Facebook," CNN, September 26, 2017, http://
www.cnn.com/2017/09/26/politics/senate-intelligence-committee
-russia-facebook-ads/index.html.

38. How this would likely occur is detailed in "Russia Could Easily
Spread Fake News Without Team Trump's Help," *Wired*, July 13,
2017, https://www.wired.com/story/russia-trump-targeting-fake
-news/.

39. Samantha Bradshaw and Philip Howard, "Troops, Trolls and
Troublemakers: A Global Inventory of Organized Social Media
Manipulation," Computational Propaganda Research Project
Working Paper, University of Oxford, July 2017, http://comprop
.oii.ox.ac.uk/2017/07/17/troops-trolls-and-trouble-makers-a
-global-inventory-of-organized-social-media-manipulation/.

40. Phillip Howard, "Digitizing the Social Contract: Producing
American Political Culture in the Age of New Media," *The
Communication Review* 6, no. 3 (2003): 233.

41. Betsy Woodruff, Ben Collins, Kevin Poulsen, and Spencer
Ackerman, "Trump Campaign Staffers Pushed Russian Propaganda
Days Before the Election," *The Daily Beast*, October 18, 2017,
https://www.thedailybeast.com/trump-campaign-staffers-pushed
-russian-propaganda-days-before-the-election; Shaun Walker,
"Russian Troll Factory Paid US Activists to Help Fund Protests
During Election," *The Guardian*, October 17, 2017, https://
www.theguardian.com/world/2017/oct/17/russian-troll-factory
-activists-protests-us-election; Rosalind Adams and Hayes Brown,
"These Americans Were Tricked Into Working for Russia. They Say
They Had No Idea," *Buzzfeed News*, October 17, 2017, https://
www.buzzfeed.com/rosalindadams/these-americans-were-tricked
-into-working-for-russia-they.

42. See the "Hamilton 68 Dashboard," Alliance for Securing
Democracy—German Marshall Fund, http://dashboard
.securingdemocracy.org/. The dashboard displays activity "from
600 monitored Twitter accounts linked to Russian influence
operations."

PARADOXES OF THE DEEP STATE

JACK GOLDSMITH

In April 1955, at the height of the Red Scare, University of Chicago political scientist Hans Morgenthau wrote an essay about the State Department's implementation of a 1953 order by President Dwight Eisenhower on security requirements for government employment.[1] That document, Executive Order 10450, fulfilled Eisenhower's campaign pledge to enhance security and loyalty in the department, an issue that had been the main focus of Senator Joseph McCarthy's anticommunist diatribes.[2] It required that "all persons privileged to be employed in the departments and agencies of the Government, shall be reliable, trustworthy, of good conduct and character," and should demonstrate an "unswerving loyalty to the United States." The Bureau of Security and Consular Affairs, run by McCarthy protégé Scott McLeod, enforced EO 10450 in the State Department. It purged several hundred State Department employees for suspected Communist sympathies, and hundreds more on suspicion of homosexuality.

Morgenthau decried the "persistent rumors" that the Bureau of Security deployed "tapped telephones, hidden microphones, steamed-open letters, special rooms and devices" against those suspected of disloyalty or bad character. Though Morgenthau did not know if the rumors were true (they largely were), he noted that their plausibility testified to "a spirit vastly different from that which is supposed to prevail in an agency of democratic government." Morgenthau argued that the Bureau's secret intelligence collection, combined with its power to condemn on the basis of that intelligence, enhanced its control over the operations and policies of the Department of State at the expense of the secretary of state and other senior political appointees. He described this phenomenon as "the dual state." The characteristic of the dual state, he maintained, is that "as a matter of law, the power of making decisions remains with the authorities charged by law with making them," while "as a matter of fact," the "agents of the secret police" can "at the very least exert an effective veto over the decisions."[3]

Morgenthau's "dual state" was a forerunner to an American "Deep State" consisting of national security bureaucrats who use secretly collected information to shape or check the actions of elected officials. Some see these American bureaucrats as a vital check on the law-breaking or authoritarian or otherwise illegitimate tendencies of democratically elected officials. Others decry it as a self-serving authoritarian cabal that illegally and illegitimately undermines democratically elected officials and the policies they were elected to implement. The truth is that the Deep State, which is a real phenomenon, has long been both a threat to democratic politics and a savior of it. The problem is that it is hard to maintain its savior role without also accepting its threatening role. The two go hand in hand, and are difficult to untangle. This essay seeks to explain these propositions through a study of Deep State leaks.

"DEEP STATE" IS A TERM USED MOST PROMINENTLY TO DESCRIBE cross-institutional clandestine forces in authoritarian states, including current and retired military and intelligence officials, that act to preserve certain national values when they are threatened by elected leaders. In Turkey, notoriously, the *derin devlet* has long used coups, assassinations, riots, and other forms of violence to preserve secular and anticommunist values.[4] Similar forces exist in Egypt and Pakistan.[5]

What I will call the "Deep State" in the United States is not nearly as sinister as in authoritarian countries. We don't have coups or tanks in the street or the like. But a Deep State exists here, and has for at least a century posed dangers to US constitutional democracy. The term is used in many different ways, often with negative connotations. To minimize confusion and focus the analysis, I will define *Deep State* narrowly and neutrally as the *US intelligence and related national security bureaucracies endowed with extraordinary powers of secret intelligence collection (or access to the fruits of that intelligence).*[6] (For present purposes, I have in mind primarily the Federal Bureau of Investigation, the National Security Agency, and the National Security Council.)

The Deep State so defined isn't an organized conspiracy or a formal entity that hands out membership cards. It is, rather, a metaphor for a national security bureaucracy that is "deep" in at least three senses. First, it collects intelligence and more generally operates in secret, protected by rules of classified information enforced through criminal and other sanctions. Second, it is entrenched by civil-service protection. Third, it has a general outlook and interests that persist across presidential administrations and that sometimes clash with an administration's outlook and interests.

The Deep State traces its origins to the establishment of the FBI in the 1930s, and it grew significantly with the National Security Act of 1947 (which created the CIA) and the formal creation by President Truman of the NSA in 1952.[7] From the beginning these agencies were controversial because they were hard to square with the ideals of democratic government. In a democracy, governmental action is presumptively open, subject to public criticism, analysis, and review in the press and by elected representatives and civil society and by courts, and ultimately subject to electoral check. Many worried that secret intelligence agencies, acting out of public sight, would abuse their intelligence collection and especially their electronic surveillance powers. In the 1950s, 1960s, and 1970s, this is exactly what happened.

The abuses during this period fell into two baskets. The first, which I'll call *political abuse*, involved the Deep State carrying out (or at least acting consistent with) the wishes of its political superiors to spy on and engage in operations against disfavored Americans or for political ends. FBI Director J. Edgar Hoover—at the direction of, or at least with the acquiescence of, presidents and attorneys general—used legally dubious wiretaps, bugs, break-ins, letter-openings, and the like to collect information about suspected communists, political dissidents, antiwar protesters, left-wing student groups, and others who engaged in "subversive" activities.[8] The NSA assisted these efforts by secretly collecting many millions of international communications of Americans on "watch lists" for suspected subversion. The FBI used the fruits of secret intelligence to covertly disrupt and discredit the activities of disfavored groups, including by surreptitiously destroying (or threatening to destroy) marriages, friendships, and job prospects. Martin Luther King Jr. is the most prominent example but far from the only one. In addition, every presidential administration from FDR through Nixon used the Deep State to collect political intelligence on potential rivals.[9]

The second type of abuse, which I'll call *sabotage*, occurred when the Deep State used secret intelligence opportunistically to further its institutional interests at the expense of or contrary to elected officials, sometimes to influence policy.[10] The key move here was to leak or threaten to leak secretly collected information to achieve a political end.[11] Hoover is the great (but not the only) example. He secretly collected and maintained compromising information about executive officials, members of Congress, and their friends and family, which he would share in ways that enhanced his power and influence over the elected official. "The moment [Hoover] would get something on a senator, he'd send one of the errand boys up and advise the senator that 'we're in the course of an investigation, and we by chance happened to come up with this data on your daughter," says William Sullivan, who led the FBI's domestic intelligence division under Hoover. "From that time on, the senator's right in his pocket." [12] For decades, politicians feared Hoover would collect and leak such information, and tended to give him what he wanted and not to cross him. [13] The FBI also covertly leaked its political intelligence to the news media in order "to influence social policy and political action" in accord with its preferences, the Church Committee, a Senate intelligence committee formed in 1975 to study intelligence abuses, found. [14] Sometimes it conveyed "distorted and exaggerated facts" to the media to support its political goals. [15] Deep State sabotage is close to the type of Deep State activities that some on the right decry today.

There were many institutional reasons why Deep State abuses occurred in that era, but two stand out. First, the Deep State lacked legal regulation. Practically no statutory laws governed Deep State activities inside the United States, and intelligence agencies "simply ignored" the Constitution, concluded the Church Committee. William Sullivan told the committee that in a decade on the U.S. Intelligence Board he never once heard or asked the question, "Is this course of action which we have agreed upon lawful, is it legal?"[16] Second was the absence of transparency within the government behind walls of secrecy. Congress exercised no oversight, and senior members of Congress frequently told intelligence officials not to inform them about intelligence activities.[17] There was not much more oversight within the executive branch of FBI and NSA activities, especially in the FBI, where presidents gave Hoover significant leeway to run his own ship. With no one with adverse interests watching carefully and internal responsibility blurred, abuse flourished.

The Deep State abuses of the 1950s through 1970s came to an end with their revelation in the early 1970s and with the 1976 Church Committee Report, which documented them publicly. The resulting reforms can be described as a "grand bargain."[18] The president and his intelligence bureaucracies were allowed to maintain robust surveillance and espionage capacities, including in the domestic arena. But in exchange, Congress imposed significant legal restrictions on how they collected, analyzed, and disseminated intelligence information; a bevy of lawyers (and, later, inspectors general) monitored and enforced those restrictions; domestic surveillance required a court order, including an order from a new court, the Foreign Intelligence Surveillance Court, for foreign intelligence collection; and two new committees, the Senate and House Intelligence committees, were to be kept "fully and currently informed" of all significant intelligence activities and were granted robust oversight authorities. The hope was that public oversight mechanisms could be replicated in secret by imposing legal restrictions, enhancing internal transparency, and creating multiple channels of accountability.

THE GRAND BARGAIN WAS SUCCESSFUL IN STAMPING OUT THE POLITI-cal abuses it aimed to address. In the four decades after the Church Committee, there has been no evidence that presidents and senior executive officials have used the Deep State to attack political enemies or subversive forces in the United States. Ironically, Edward Snowden's leak in 2013 of information about US signals intelligence practices confirmed the success of the grand bargain. Snowden revealed the massive scope of US signals intelligence collection at home and abroad. He also revealed a new and serious post–Church Committee problem: the rise of secret legal interpretation by executive lawyers and secret courts that can distort the meaning of public laws in ways that allow for intelligence collection against Americans that departs from public expectation.[19] But Snowden also showed that the political abuses of the pre-1975 era were gone. In many thousands of pages of highly classified material about numerous domestic collection programs and practices, not one pointed to anything like the political operations of the 1970s and before.

The grand bargain's imposition of legalism, process, and internal transparency also had a significant though more ambiguous impact on Deep State sabotage of democratic official action. None of the many intelligence revelations in the last few decades reveal anything like a concerted bureaucratic effort to exercise control over politicians or democratic policies akin to what Hoover's FBI did. One often reads that a president who betrays or fails to support intelligence agencies faces a threat of retaliation. But to the extent this has been true, it appears to be a species of typical bureaucratic resistance to presidential initiatives that cut against the bureaucracy's interests. Also, in recent years, intelligence agencies have sometimes been accused of skewing the information they feed a president, an accusation that is hard for the public to assess. The point for now is that we have never returned to the days in which an intelligence bureaucracy deployed its tools to in effect blackmail or threaten to destroy democratically elected officials, and thereby control them.

But there is a large caveat to this conclusion. A form of political sabotage that the grand bargain did not stop, and indeed a practice that has grown in the years since the Church Report, is leaks (or threats of leaks) of secret government information to achieve various ends. In the sabotage scenario sketched thus far, a national security bureaucrat discloses (or threatens to disclose) secretly collected information to harm the political principal for ends deemed *abusive*. Hoover's shenanigans are an example. But a member of the Deep State can also leak secret information or threaten to do so to sabotage the political principal in ways we deem *virtuous*. A classic pre–Church Committee example is Mark Felt, the associate director of the FBI who was Bob Woodward's infamous "Deep Throat" source for the Watergate revelations. Felt worked in the FBI for over thirty years and was heavily involved in its secret illegal actions, for which he eventually was convicted. But he was also "deeply offended that the President and his top aides ran what constituted a criminal operation out of the White House, and he risked everything to guide Woodward."[20]

It is sometimes hard to say precisely when and why opportunistic use of secret information to sabotage democratic leaders is deemed virtuous (Felt against the Nixon White House) as opposed to abusive (Hoover against scores of politicians). Felt was acting individually and taking personal risk, while Hoover was acting with the support of and on behalf of the FBI, and taking less personal risk. The bureaucracy as saboteur might pose a greater threat to democratic action than an individual acting alone. (It also might, in the right circumstance, be a more effective savior.) Felt might also be seen as a whistleblower who was exposing corrupt and illegal action by the government, while Hoover was an opportunist who was undermining democratic processes.

Felt's case is relatively easy to defend, because he disclosed no classified information and because he was ratting on one of the most corrupt presidencies in American history. A fuller assessment of virtuous sabotage must consider two complications. First, what if a Deep State agent leaks to expose corrupt or illegal action in the face of a criminal prohibition on the disclosure of that information? In that case, the intelligence official is acting illegally and contrary to the considered views of the political branches about the importance of maintaining secrecy. Can two wrongs make a right? And second, can we trust the Deep State leaker to leak the right kind of information? How can we be sure that the interests and judgments of Deep State leakers will, as in Felt's case, serve the national interest?

On the first question, it is pretty clear that, despite prohibition on leaks of classified information, the optimal rate of leaking such information to sabotage elected officials or their policies is not zero.[21] The president has complete control over the secrecy stamp, and he and his subordinates sometimes deploy it opportunistically to keep illegal or otherwise wrongful action out of the public realm. When the executive branch acts in the secret world it defines for itself, it may make more mistakes than usual, and any mistakes it does make are harder to correct, because the grand bargain is only a second-best solution to public transparency and accountability. Moreover, fear of leaks causes national security officials to think twice about what they do, and deters them from doing things that they should not do.

Finally, the proof is in the pudding. Leaks in the early 1970s revealed atrocious Deep State practices that led to the major reforms in the grand bargain. Numerous leaks of classified information in the last fifteen years—on matters ranging from black sites to interrogation to surveillance to drones—have disclosed practices deemed illegal or illegitimate by Congress, courts, or executive insiders, which proceeded to impose reform. In all these cases, sabotage via Deep State leaks performed a vital corrective. This is the sense in which the Deep State's manipulation can be a savior of democratic politics: it can preserve democratic values through the revelation and correction of antidemocratic action in secret.

The objection that the government, through democratic

processes, has considered the matter and spoken through criminal laws that prohibit leaks of classified information turns on an inaccurate picture of US law.[22] The general legal prohibitions on leaking classified information found in the century-old Espionage Act are old and full of loopholes that make many, and perhaps most, damaging leaks impossible to prosecute. Congress has considered but not closed these loopholes. Despite the recent press panic over leak investigations, the government prosecutes only a tiny fraction of leakers, and many it stays away from because they would be politically controversial.

The government is even more hands-off with the press, even though journalists publish much more classified information today than in the past, and with a lowered threshold of when such information is in the public interest.[23] It has never prosecuted a member of the media for publishing secret government information. It sometimes, though rarely, subpoenas journalists to assist in leak investigations, but under political pressure for restraint, the Justice Department has twice in recent years raised the hurdles to such subpoenas. A journalist in this situation can be jailed for refusing to reveal sources, but recently the Justice Department declined in a high-profile leak prosecution to force a journalist to testify against his source.[24] One reason the government constrains itself in punishing leakers and their publishers is that leaks of secret government information are not always an absolute bad, and indeed can serve a vital function in checking a too-secretive Deep State.[25]

To say that Deep State leaks of classified information

are sometimes justified is not to answer the second question about whether we can trust leakers to know which leaks are appropriate. Some leaks are intelligence operations by foreign adversaries. Those are viewed to be uncontroversially bad.[26] But even when leaks come from ostensible whistleblowers, they can be enormously costly in terms of national security harm, lost intelligence, blown sources, and significant financial investments ruined (especially when electronic surveillance techniques are disclosed).

Unfortunately, we don't have great conceptual tools for measuring these costs and benefits or for determining optimal trade-offs. The public lacks adequate information to really understand these harms, and intuitions about how to measure and trade them off vary widely. There are nonetheless plenty of reasons to think that leakers across the run of cases will lack adequate information, or proper incentives, or the right values, to get the trade-off right. Even those who see themselves as whistleblowers have many complex motivations and aren't reliable judges of when the benefits of leaks outweigh their costs. Sometimes they are right, but often they are wrong.

Some leakers, for example, misperceive the legality or legitimacy of government action. This happened with the leaks published by the *New York Times* in 2006 about how the government worked with a global banking consortium to collect financial information related to possible terrorist-related transfers. The author of the story, perhaps reflecting his source's motivation, defended it on the ground that it rested on a "largely untested legal theory" and was "arguably extralegal."[27] This judgment was simply wrong. The program violated no American privacy laws; it operated by administrative subpoenas pursuant to powers that Congress delegated to the president in the International Emergency Economic Powers Act.[28] Other times, leakers will misperceive the public-interest value of the leak compared to its national-security harm. We know this is so because American newspaper editors, who carry a heavy presumption in favor of publication, sometimes refuse to publish leaked classified information after weighing the value of publication against possible harms disclosed by the government.[29]

And then there is the complicated case of Edward Snowden. Snowden worked at the margins of the Deep State. He was technically a contractor, not a bureaucrat, although private-sector growth in the intelligence area has been significant enough to approach Deep State status in terms of what the intelligence contractors do and their distinctive and persistent interests and attitudes. Like Felt but unlike Hoover, Snowden acted alone rather than on behalf of the bureaucracy. And in contrast to Felt, Snowden aimed to hold accountable not just a president but the entire intelligence community.

Snowden's leaks can roughly be divided into two types of classified information: (1) surveillances practices inside the United States or involving American citizens, and (2) surveillance practices outside the United States involving non-US citizens. The leaks of practices in category 1 were the easier to justify because the practices were controversial under US statutory and constitutional law, were contrary to public expectations, and sparked reforms (and broader conversations about reforms). One could even argue that Snowden's category 1 disclosures *helped* US intelligence agencies by forcing them to be more transparent, by demonstrating that despite the legal controversy they were acting with the full knowledge and support of all three branches of government, and by sparking reform that strengthened the legality and legitimacy of their domestic collection practices while barely narrowing them.[30]

By contrast, the leaks of surveillance practices conducted abroad, against non-Americans, revealed operations that were lawful and consistent with general expectations (inside the United States) about US intelligence agencies' activities abroad.[31] Tellingly, these Snowden disclosures have not yet sparked significant changes to US law.[32] But they had a huge impact. They blew many sources and methods, caused enormous financial losses, severely strained relations with allies, and revealed to key adversaries (including China and Russia) how we monitor their activities. Snowden has justified his actions primarily on the basis of the oath he took to "support and defend the Constitution."[33] If so, he made a big mistake, since the practices he revealed did not violate the Constitution. Snowden might have been serving his oath when he leaked the Section 215 domestic metadata program, and also, perhaps, the aspects of the 702 programs (PRISM and upstream collection) that concerned US citizens. But it is hard to see how Snowden's oath to the US Constitution justified the theft and disclosure of the vast number of documents (probably more than 99 percent of the total) in category 2 about overseas activities that did not even arguably violate the laws or Constitution of the United States.

Snowden's actions in category 2 also reveal how the leaker may have whistleblowing motivations that cannot be credited within the US political system. Although Snowden has defended his actions mostly based on his oath, he has also suggested that he was motivated by cosmopolitan values to protect the privacy rights of foreigners and a free Internet.[34] But this motivation is antithetical to the very idea of a national intelligence service, whose job is to collect foreign intelligence, including by electronic means. There are any number of principals that it may be proper for national security bureaucrats to serve—the president, the Constitution and laws, the American people, the bureaucracy itself. But foreign citizens and governments cannot be a legitimate principal. No country can maintain an intelligence service and credit leaking for cosmopolitan ends.

In sum to this point: First-generation Deep State threats of political abuse and of bureaucratic (as opposed to individual) sabotage of government policies for illegitimate ends seem to have dissipated after the grand bargain. But leaks by individual officials have continued and indeed proliferated with the growth in the secrecy system that the Deep State manages. Although we don't have great metrics for assessing these leaks in every case, there are examples when the leaks serve valuable ends on balance and other examples when they don't. Leakers cannot be trusted to get this calculus right. But nor can the government be trusted to sort out and regulate Deep State leakers in ways that clamp down on the bad while maintaining the good—even assuming the government had the power to stop the leaks, which it doesn't, except at the margins. And so the US government muddles through with a massive secret intelligence bureaucracy that collects unfathomable amounts of information in the domestic realm but is unable to control its leakers, who for better or for worse possess enormous discretion to use the secretly collected information to sabotage persons, policies, and initiatives they do not like.

THE DEEP STATE HAS BEEN BLAMED FOR MANY THINGS SINCE DONALD Trump became president, including by the president himself (though he has not yet used the term *Deep State*).[35] Trump defenders have used the term *Deep State* promiscuously to include not just intelligence bureaucrats but a broader array of connected players in other administrative bureaucracies, in private industry, and in the media. I will continue to focus narrowly on the intelligence bureaucracies that conduct and use information collected secretly in the homeland. There is significant evidence that the Deep State so understood—either as part of a concerted movement or via individuals acting more or less independently—has used secretly collected information opportunistically and illegally to sabotage the president and his senior officials. The hard questions are whether this sabotage is virtuous or abusive, whether we can tell, and what the consequences of these actions are.

Since Trump was elected, unusually sensitive leaks of

intelligence information designed to discredit him and his senior leadership have poured forth from current and former intelligence officials in the Deep State. The first major one, in February 2017, concerned a court-approved NSA wiretap of a phone conversation between Russia's ambassador to the United States, Sergey Kislyak, and incoming National Security Advisor Michael Flynn that concerned, among other things, the possible removal of Russia sanctions imposed by President Obama.[36] Flynn had denied that the men discussed sanctions, and the leak revealing his lie led to his resignation.[37] Another major leak concerned communications intercepts during the campaign of Russian government officials discussing potentially "derogatory" information about Trump and top campaign aides.[38] Other leaks in this vein included intercepts of Russian officials claiming they could influence Trump through Flynn;[39] of Kislyak supposedly informing Moscow that he discussed campaign-related issues with then-Senator Jeff Sessions;[40] and of Kislyak discussing in a communication to Moscow that Trump's son-in-law, Jared Kushner, wanted to communicate via a secure channel.[41]

These leaks probably mark the first time ever that the content of foreign intelligence intercepts aimed at foreign agents that swept up US-person information was leaked.[42] They clearly aimed to damage US persons—ones who happen to also be senior US government officials.[43] They were unlawful and, beyond that, violated two until-now strict taboos about leaks—first on revealing the content of foreign intelligence information collected through electronic surveillance, and second on revealing the content of incidentally collected information about American citizens. The leaks were at least in some respects more damaging than Snowden's leaks, which involved information about *programs* but not discrete conversations that violated the privacy of the communicants involved and did not contain means and methods of intelligence collection at the level of granularity of the Trump-era leaks.[44]

Many people, including many who are not in the Trump camp, have interpreted these leaks to violate a third taboo by marking a return to the Hoover-era FBI's use of secretly collected information to sabotage elected officials with adverse political interests.[45] The comparison is plausible in light of the extensive efforts soon after the election to encourage the bureaucracy, including the intelligence bureaucracy, to resist the Trump administration, and the evidence that there was in some agencies such resistance.[46] We don't know if the leaks have come from uncoordinated Deep State individuals or via coordinated action akin to the type Hoover engaged in from the top of the FBI. (It might be something in between.) Moreover, while Hoover did many awful things in quiet, neither during his reign nor at any other time in American history have we seen such a profusion of sensitive leaks from the Deep State with such an overtly political aim to bring down senior leadership. Mark Felt's leaks may perhaps be the equivalent, but as noted above, they were not unlawful, and did not involve the most sensitive and guarded classified information that the government possessed.

The Felt example raises the possibility that the anti-Trump leaks, on their face political and unprecedented, were nonetheless justified whistleblowing, akin perhaps to Felt's leaks or to leaks about illegal surveillance programs or about illegal interrogation practices at CIA black sites. Put another way, it is possible that the benefits of the leaks, considered narrowly, outweigh the evil inherent in breaching the first two taboos above. The situation the leaks are a response to is itself extraordinary to the point of being unprecedented. The acting attorney general of the United States, Sally Yates, believed that Flynn, the new National Security advisor, was compromised by the Russians and vulnerable to blackmail, and so warned the White House, which seemed to take no steps in response to the information.[47] More broadly, a number of very odd circumstances suggested unusual and potentially corrupt connections between the Trump campaign and administration and the Russian government, about which the FBI had been conducting a counterintelligence investigation since the summer of 2016. All of this came in the context of the unprecedented Russian DNC hack designed, our intelligence agencies tell us, to help Donald Trump win the election. And then once in office, President Trump himself engaged in vicious and in many instances false attacks on the intelligence community and Justice Department investigators.

Do these unprecedented circumstances justify the unprecedented Deep State leaks? As I write in September 2017, we don't have enough information, or adequate consensus about how to judge illegal leaks, to assess costs and benefits here. The lines crossed by the Deep State leaks against Trump were thought to be absolute ones until 2017. But we have never faced a situation in which the National Security advisor, and perhaps even the president of the United States, presented a credible counterintelligence threat involving one of our greatest adversaries. Perhaps the facts will develop to give us enough clarity about the Russia-Trump connections to be able to make a better judgment along the lines of the judgment history has made about Mark Felt's leaks. Though perhaps we will never have adequate informational clarity, and thus won't be able to reach consensus on whether the leaks were justified.

But however those matters develop, the whole ordeal has already done great damage to both the presidency and the national security bureaucracy. One important question going forward is whether the taboo on leaking the content of foreign intelligence collections is broken, and to what degree, and what the consequences of that breach are. As Deep State officials get a taste for the power that inheres in the selective revelation of such information, and if the leaks are not responded to with severe punishments, it is easy to imagine the tools that brought down Flynn being used in other contexts by national security bureaucrats with different commitments and interests.

Even the most severe critics of President Trump should worry about this subtle form of antidemocratic abuse. As Adam Klein asked: "If you welcomed these leaks because they hastened Flynn's departure, would you be comfortable with selective leaks of US-person intercepts becoming a routine weapon in political catfights? With an unelected 'permanent state' wielding this power to undermine or intimidate politically accountable officials? With political appointees using it to sideline rivals or attack political opponents?"[48] It was very hard and very damaging to eliminate the various forms of surveillance abuse that prevailed in the pre-Church days. The actions of the Deep State in the early Trump days, exacerbated by the president's own actions, threaten to take us back to that time.

The big loser in all this will probably be the national security bureaucracy itself and, to the extent it is weakened, the security of the American people. Even if it turns out that Flynn and others close to Trump were in the bag for the Russians, many people will for a long time view the anti-Trump leaks as political abuse of intelligence to harm political enemies. This perception will be deepened by the Trump administration's relentless and often false attacks on the integrity of the intelligence community, including its false suggestion that the original collection that incidentally captured Flynn's communications, as opposed to the leaks of such information, was illegitimate.

The Flynn and related leaks didn't just violate the law— they violated the core commitment the intelligence community made in the grand bargain not to politicize, or appear to politicize, the use of surveillance tools or the fruits of their use. The whole intelligence collection system—which has an importance that far transcends its undoubtedly large importance in this discrete context—is vulnerable here for the simple reason that the intermixture of politics with intelligence collection is the intelligence system's Achilles' heel.[49] If surveillance comes to be seen through a domestic political lens, with domestic political winners and losers, the intelligence community will have a very hard time acting with needed public credibility. And that in turn means it will have a harder time doing what it needs to do to keep us safe.

NOTES

1. Hans Morgenthau, "The Impact of the Loyalty-Security Measures on the State Department," *Bulletin of the Atomic Scientists* 11, no. 4 (1995): 134.
2. Exec. Order No. 10,450, 18 Fed. Reg. 2489 (April 27, 1953).
3. Ibid.
4. Ibid. For a later and broader version of a similar idea, see Michael J. Glennon, *National Security and Double Government* (New York: Oxford University Press, 2014).
5. David Remnick, "There Is No Deep State," *New Yorker*, March 20, 2017; "What Is the 'Deep State'?" *The Economist*, March 9, 2017.
6. See Julie Hirschfeld Davis, "Rumblings of a 'Deep State' Undermining Trump? It Was Once a Foreign Concept," *New York Times*, March 6, 2017; Steven A. Cook, "The Deep State Comes to America," *Foreign Policy*, February 24, 2017.
7. For broader definitions of *Deep State* that contain critiques of the concept from which I have learned much, see Rebecca Ingber, "The 'Deep State' Myth and the Real Executive Branch Bureaucracy," *Lawfare*, June 14, 2017, https://lawfareblog.com /deep-state-myth-and-real-executive-branch-bureaucracy; Jon D. Michaels, "Trump and the 'Deep State,'" *Foreign Affairs* 96, no. 5 (September/October 2017): 52.
8. The FBI's precursor, the Bureau of Investigation, was created in 1908. Hoover led the BOI beginning in 1924.
9. See generally US S. Church Committee, Intelligence Activities and the Rights of Americans, S. Rep. No. 94–755 (1976).
10. Id.
11. I follow John Brehm in using the term *sabotage* to describe an agent who acts contrary to the interests or instructions of the

principal because she has divergent preferences. See John Brehm and Scott Gates, *Working, Shirking, and Sabotage: Bureaucratic Response to a Democratic Public* (Ann Arbor: University of Michigan Press, 1999); see also Jacob Gersen and Adrian Vermeule, *Delegating to Enemies, Columbia Law Review* 112, no. 8 (December 2012): 2193.

12. A related move was to feed the president tendentious information to influence his decision in a particular direction.

13. Ronald Kessler, *The Secrets of the FBI* (New York: Crown Forum, 2012), 38.

14. See generally U.S. S. Church Committee.

15. Church Commission [US S. Church Comm., supra note 9.] Id.

16. Id.

17. Id.

18. See Jack Goldsmith, *Power and Constraint* (New York: W. W. Norton & Co., 2012), 83–84.

19. Goldsmith, supra note 15, 87–89. Id.

20. See Jack Goldsmith, "The Irrelevance of Prerogative Power, and the Evils of Secret Legal Interpretation," in Clement Fatovic and Benjamin A. Kleinerman, eds., *Extra-Legal Power and Legitimacy: Perspectives on Prerogative* (New York: Oxford University Press, 2013); Jack Goldsmith, "Toward Greater Transparency of National Security Work," remarks delivered at ODNI Conference, May 6, 2015, http://jackgoldsmith.org/toward-greater-transparency-of -national-security-legal-work/.

21. Remnick, "There Is No Deep State."

22. See David E. Pozen, "The Leaky Leviathan: Why the Government Condemns and Condones Unlawful Disclosures of Information," *Harvard Law Review* 127, no. 512 (2013): 545. I draw here on Pozen and my discussion in *Power and Constraint*, 215–23.

23. See Pozen, supra note 19, 293–304; Goldsmith, *Power and Constraint*, supra note 17, 218–23.

24. See Jack Goldsmith, "The Latest Erosion of Norms Against Publishing Classified Information," *Lawfare*, April 28, 2015, https://lawfareblog.com/latest-erosion-norms-against-publishing -classified-information.

25. See Matt Apuzzo, "Times Reporter Will Not Be Called to Testify in Leak Case," *New York Times*, January 12, 2015.

26. And there are of course other reasons for constraint, including First Amendment concerns, political backlash, graymail, and the like.

27. But there are complications even here. What if Snowden (in his "virtuous" domestic whistleblowing activities), or Mark Felt (in bringing down Nixon), was acting on behalf of a foreign power? That is, what if a foreign intelligence agent leaks US government information that is *motivated* to harm the US government but that in fact *results* in virtuous, democracy-enhancing consequences? I explore these complications, which will become more pronounced in a world in which journalists receive secure anonymous leaks, in Jack Goldsmith, "Journalism in the Doxing Era: Is Wikileaks Different from the *New York Times*?" *Lawfare*, January 16, 2017, https://www.lawfareblog.com/journalism-doxing-era-wikileaks -different-new-york-times.

28. See Eric Lichtblau, *Bush's Law: The Remaking of American Justice* (New York: Pantheon Books, 2008).

29. Jack Goldsmith, "Secrecy and Safety," *New Republic*, August 12, 2008.

30. Goldsmith, *Power and Constraint*, supra note 17, 52–55.

31. Jack Goldsmith, "Three Years Later: How Snowden Helped the U.S. Intelligence Community," *Lawfare*, June 6, 2016, https:// www.lawfareblog.com/three-years-later-how-snowden-helped-us -intelligence-community.

32. See, e.g., James Warren, "Snowden and the NSA: Behind the Scenes," *U.S. News & World Report*, May 18, 2016, https://www .usnews.com/opinion/articles/2016–05–18/civil-liberties-and -national-security-expert-on-edward-snowden-and-the-nsa (interview with Geoffrey Stone).

33. In response to the fallout from Snowden, President Obama issued PPD-28 to address concerns about privacy protections for non-US citizens abroad, but this document did not bring material changes to US law or practice. See Presidential Policy Directive—Signals Intelligence Activities, January 17, 2014, https://obamawhite house.archives.gov/the-press-office/2014/01/17/presidential -policy-directive-signals-intelligence-activities. The broader point is that Snowden's leaks of information about surveillance programs outside the United States directed at non-US persons cannot be characterized as whistleblowing to actions illegal under US law.

34. See Barton Gellman, "Edward Snowden, After Months of NSA Revelations, Says His Mission's Accomplished," *Washington Post*, December 23, 2013, at https://www.washingtonpost.com/world /national-security/edward-snowden-after-months-of-nsa-revelations -says-his-missions-accomplished/2013/12/23/49fc36de-6c1c-11e3 -a523-fe73f0ff6b8d_story.html?utm_term=.afb795ce3bb1; Amy Davidson Sorkin, "Did Edward Snowden Break His Oath?" *New Yorker*, January 5, 2014, http://www.newyorker.com/news/amy -davidson/did-edward-snowden-break-his-oath.

35. See, e.g., Glenn Greenwald et al., "Edward Snowden: The Whistleblower Behind the NSA Surveillance Revelations," *The Guardian*, June 11, 2013 ("I'm willing to sacrifice all of that because I can't in good conscience allow the US government to destroy privacy, internet freedom and basic liberties for people around the world with this massive surveillance machine they're secretly building"); James Bamford, "Edward Snowden: The Untold Story," *Wired*, August 2014 (explaining Snowden's concerns about overbroad US surveillance in China).

36. President Trump did, however, retweet a reference to the "Deep State." See Julia Manchester, "Trump Promotes Hannity's 'Deep State' Monologue," *The Hill*, June 16, 2017, http://thehill.com /media/338241-trump-shares-hannity-tweet-on-monologue -calling-for-leakers-to-be-jailed.

37. Greg Miller et al., "National Security Adviser Flynn Discussed Sanctions with Russian Ambassador Despite Denials, Officials Say," *Washington Post*, February 9, 2017, https://www .washingtonpost.com/world/national-security/national-security -adviser-flynn-discussed-sanctions-with-russian-ambassador -despite-denials-officials-say/2017/02/09/f85b29d6-ee11-11 e6-b4ff-ac2cf509efe5_story.html?utm_term=.a2ea59c0dd85.

38. Maggie Haberman et al., "Michael Flynn Resigns as National Security Adviser," *New York Times*, February 13, 2017, https:// www.nytimes.com/2017/02/13/us/politics/donald-trump -national-security-adviser-michael-flynn.html.

39. Pamela Brown et al., "Sources: Russians Discussed Potentially 'Derogatory' Information About Trump and Associates During Campaign," CNN, May 30, 2017, http://www.cnn.com/2017/05 /30/politics/russians-trump-campaign-information/index.html.

40. Gloria Borger et al., "Russian Officials Bragged They Could Use Flynn to Influence Trump," CNN, May 19, 2017, http://www .cnn.com/2017/05/19/politics/michael-flynn-donald-trump -russia-influence/index.html.

41. Adam Entous, Ellen Nakashima, and Greg Miller, "Sessions Discussed Trump Campaign-Related Matters with Russian Ambassador, U.S. Intelligence Intercepts Show," *Washington Post*, July 21, 2017, https://www.washingtonpost.com/world/national -security/sessions-discussed-trump-campaign-related-matters -with-russian-ambassador-us-intelligence-intercepts-show/2017/07 /21/3e704692–6e44–11e7–9c15–177740635e83_story.html?utm _term=.729c2d9e76ab.

42. Ellen Nakashima, Adam Entous, and Greg Miller, "Russian Ambassador Told Moscow That Kushner Wanted Secret Communications Channel with Kremlin," *Washington Post*, May 26, 2017, https://www.washingtonpost.com/world /national-security/russian-ambassador-told-moscow-that -kushner-wanted-secret-communications-channel-with -kremlin/2017/05/26/520a14b4–422d-11e7–9869 -bac8b446820a_story.html?utm_term=.127b7a5196d6.

43. The closest precedent I can find is when Bill Gertz in 1999 reported that "national security intercepts indicated that Chinese secret agents had notified China that the American bombing of the Chinese embassy in Belgrade during the NATO war on Yugoslavia had not been accidental, as the United States claimed, but had been deliberate." See Jack Nelson, "U.S. Government Secrecy and the Current Crackdown on Leaks," Shorenstein Working Paper Series 24 (2002), https://shorensteincenter.org/wp-content /uploads/2012/03/2003_01_nelson.pdf. These were foreign intelligence intercepts, but they might not have been FISA-approved and they did not reveal US-person information.

44. Gloria Borger et al., "Russian Officials Bragged They Could Use Flynn to Influence Trump, Sources Say," ("Russian officials bragged in conversations during the presidential campaign that they had cultivated a strong relationship with former Trump adviser retired Gen. Michael Flynn and believed they could use him to influence Donald Trump"); Jim Sciutto et al., "British Intelligence Passed Trump Associates' Communications with

Russians on to US Counterparts," CNN, April 14, 2017, http://www.cnn.com/2017/04/13/politics/trump-russia-british -intelligence/index.html ("British and other European intelligence agencies intercepted communications between associates of Donald Trump and Russian officials and other Russian individuals during the campaign and passed on those communications to their US counterparts, US congressional and law enforcement and US and European intelligence, sources tell CNN"); Shane Harris, "Russian Officials Overheard Discussing Trump Associates Before Campaign Began," *Wall Street Journal*, July 12, 2017, https://www .wsj.com/article_email/russian-officials-overheard-discussing -trump-associates-before-campaign-began-1499890354-lMyQjA xMTI3MjE5MjExMzI0Wj/ ("Investigators are re-examining conversations detected by U.S. intelligence agencies in spring 2015 that captured Russian government officials discussing associates of Donald Trump. . . . In some cases, the Russians in the overheard conversations talked about meetings held outside the U.S. involving Russian government officials and Trump business associates or advisers"); Michael Schmidt et al., "Trump Campaign Aides Had Repeated Contact with Russian Intelligence," *New York Times*, February 14, 2017, https://www.nytimes.com/2017/02/14 /us/politics/russia-intelligence-communications-trump.html ("The intercepted calls are different from the wiretapped conversations last year between Michael T. Flynn, Mr. Trump's former national security adviser, and Sergey I. Kislyak, Russia's ambassador to the United States"); cf. Ken Rudin, "What to Make of the Alleged Jane Harman/AIPAC Quid Pro Quo," NPR, April 20, 2009, available at http://www.npr.org/sections/politicaljunkie/2009/04 /alleged_harmanaipac_chat.html.

45. Timothy H. Edgar, *Beyond Snowden: Privacy, Mass Surveillance, and the Struggle to Reform the NSA* (Washington, DC: Brookings Institution Press, 2017).

46. See Adam Klein, "It's Not About Mike Flynn," *Lawfare*, February 17, 2017, https://www.lawfareblog.com/its-not-about -mike-flynn; Eli Lake, "The Resistance Cheers Tactics Trump Will Likely Use Against Them," Bloomberg, March 17, 2017, https:// www.bloomberg.com/view/articles/2017–03–17/the-resistance -cheers-tactics-trump-will-likely-use-against-them; Timothy

Edgar, "Michael Flynn May Want to Call the ACLU," *Lawfare*, February 14, 2017, https://lawfareblog.com/michael-flynn-may -want-call-aclu.

47. On calls for resistance, see Oona Hathaway and Sarah Weiner, "Dissenting from Within the Trump Administration," *Just Security*, January 17, 2017; Jennifer Nou, "Bureaucratic Resistance from Below," *Notice & Comment*, November 16, 2016; Evan Osnos, "Resisting Trump from Inside the Government," *New Yorker*, November 21, 2016. On the early evidence, see Justin Caffier, "How Federal Civil Servants Are Waging Bureaucratic War Against Trump," *Vice News*, February 13, 2017; Juliet Eilperin et al., "Resistance from Within: Federal Workers Push Back Against Trump," *Washington Post*, January 31, 2017; Gregory Krieg, "Going Rogue: Bureaucrats Find Ways to Resist Trump," CNN, February 2, 2017; Andrew Restuccia et al., "Federal Workers Turn to Encryption to Thwart Trump," *Politico*, February 2, 2017; Michael D. Shear & Eric Lichtblau, " 'A Sense of Dread' for Civil Servants Shaken by Trump Transition," *New York Times*, February 11, 2017; Abigail Tracy, "An Anti-Trump Resistance Movement Is Growing Within the U.S. Government," *Vanity Fair* (online version), February 1, 2017.

48. Matthew Rosenberg, "6 Takeaways from Monday's Senate Hearing on Russia," *New York Times*, May 8, 2017, https://www.nytimes .com/2017/05/08/us/politics/sally-yates-james-clapper-russia -hearing.html.

49. See Klein, "It's Not About Mike Flynn," supra note 45.

50. Jack Goldsmith and Benjamin Wittes, "The 'Grand Bargain' at Risk: What's at Stake When the President Alleges Politics in Intelligence," *Lawfare*, April 4, 2017, https://www.lawfareblog .com/grand-bargain-risk-whats-stake-when-president-alleges -politics-intelligence.

HOW WE LOST CONSTITUTIONAL DEMOCRACY

TOM GINSBURG AND AZIZ HUQ

Washington, DC, November 2024

For the second time in three election cycles, a populist billionaire has won an Electoral College majority to become president of the United States. Drawing a cue from her recent predecessors, she has campaigned in fiery tones, demonizing liberals, threatening to shut down the universities that shelter them and to lock up the ghetto thugs and radical Islamic terrorists they defend. She promises to restore American pride and power and to take back our country from radical ruination. After a feckless four years of divided government, in which crime upticked, the economy stagnated, and America's place in the world seemed to decline, the country's citizens respond to the president-elect's unequivocal promise of law and order. And, as she happens to own the largest media conglomerate in the country, that message finds its way to many ears.

Upon taking office, the new president seizes a moment of unified government to systematically consolidate power over other branches and civil society. Unlike her predecessors, she does not antagonize the courts. Instead, she hand-picks allies for key judicial vacancies and looses an army of Ivy League–trained lawyers to draft each executive order, and to explain how her innovations are consistent with the framers' original understandings. In response, judges double down on existing doctrines that command deference to the executive's policy choices, enable the use of coercion, and impede scrutiny of the motives behind such action. A cottage industry of legal scholarship mushrooms celebrating the "efficiency" and "optimality" of this new judicial restraint.

As her party in Congress bickers, substantive legislation continues to be rare, and executive orders have become the modal form of new law. Even when constitutionally commanded, the congressional role has withered. The appropriations and budgeting processes are largely driven by the president's agenda. On the regulation front, Congress enacts an umbrella statute known as the Authorization of Regulatory Force and Adjustment (affectionately known as "ARFA") that delegates to the president the power to "take all necessary and appropriate steps he or she deems necessary" to streamline regulations "notwithstanding any prior laws passed by Congress." Citing the White House's unique democratic mandate and credentials, the Supreme Court upholds this delegation.

Using its newfound regulatory power, the executive branch consolidates many government functions into the

White House, creating a system of policy "czars," including a gaggle of so-called princelings, who are close friends and family of the president herself. Congress repeals the Hatch Act and enacts the Holman Rule into law. The latter, formerly an 1876 House budget rule that allowed federal employees' salaries to be reduced to $1, is aggressively used to purge non-loyalists from the bureaucracy. Citing theories of the "unitary executive" and "presidential administration," the president claims the same power as a matter of inherent authority, and soon federal agencies are almost exclusively populated by those personally loyal to the new commander in chief.

On another front, the president urges her congressional majority to change the terms of the Federal Elections Campaign Act so that members of the two major parties alternate years serving as chair of the Federal Elections Commission, such that the president's party holds the chair during even years. Coincidentally, all national elections are held in even years. Meanwhile, the Internal Revenue Service steps up audits of media companies that compete with the president's company, along with not-for-profits providing legal services to regime opponents. Periodically, the national security agencies anonymously leak transcripts of opposition politicians' compromising communications—often containing salacious details of extramarital affairs or sexual peccadillos.

Outside of government, the president's media empire also turns on individual civil servants and the residual few federal judges not aligned with the White House. Those who resist her policies or her growing cult of personality are flagged in a nightly Twitter blast about the "Enemies of the

People." A sympathetic judiciary relaxes First Amendment constraints on libel and slander awards, and also permits punitive damages in such cases. Two national newspapers on the East Coast are forced into bankruptcy by litigation costs and awards of damages.

Three years later, a lone terrorist commits a suicide attack at an NFL game. On the evening of the attack, the president stands in the stadium's still-smoldering entranceway to announce a new raft of restrictions on social media and "un-American" religious associations. She further explains that she will seek a constitutional amendment repealing the Twenty-second Amendment, which limits the president to two terms in office. State-level gerrymandering has given her a comfortable two-thirds majority in both houses of Congress. Privately, some members of her party are dismayed, but they are too intimidated by the president's power and media empire to openly resist. The amendment sails through the otherwise demanding ratification process. A year later the president joins Franklin Delano Roosevelt as the only persons to serve more than two terms in office, sworn in on a Bible held by her princeling son-in-law and presumptive heir.

DYSTOPIAN FICTIONS OF THE KIND WE HAVE JUST SKETCHED HAVE their guilty pleasures. We squirm with recognition at Offred's plight or quiver in admiration of Winston's resistance. But dystopian fictions, like their utopian counterparts, have a serious end: just as Margaret Atwood, in writing *The Handmaid's Tale*, sought to rely solely on repressive measures she had culled from human history, our less eloquent exercise has relied on legal and institutional changes that can be observed in one or another national context in which some backsliding away from democratic values has already occurred. Indeed, the real reason we begin with this unhappy tale is to ask what is it, precisely, that prevents the same steps from unfolding in the United States? And would what we have described amount to a failure of democracy?

Two years ago, many might have responded that the scenario we have sketched was too far-fetched to be imaginable. The United States has the world's oldest democratic constitution still in force. Beyond the relatively thin text of the document, there were norms of political practice, settled conventions within federal institutions, and robustly independent courts that would inhibit any attempt to permanently consolidate power. Despite the Civil War, two world wars, and countless economic and security emergencies, national elections have never been postponed. Britain, by contrast, canceled elections during World War II. To be sure, there have been dark moments. President Abraham Lincoln unilaterally suspended the writ of habeas corpus in May 1861, as war with the South was beginning. As Geoffrey Stone's magisterial history of the First Amendment documents, antiwar activism was effectively criminalized in World War I, changing the parameters of the political sphere in important ways. Human and civil rights have been violated during many other crises, and we have a dismayingly long history of disenfranchising, excluding, and subordinating racial minorities. However, despite all this, we lack a history of *wholesale* corrosion of the three main pillars of our democratic institutions—elections, the rule of law, and freedoms of speech and association. As a result, we lack the historical experience needed to evaluate the current risk to key national institutions.

One reaction to this history would be to ascribe the US Constitution a measure of prophylactic power. The thesis would be that democracy has thrived in the United States because of the distinctively effective design of the Constitution in buffering that practice from external and internal threat. The argument would gain strength from observing that the rest of the world has not been so lucky. In the past decade, an increasing number of seemingly stable, reasonably wealthy democracies have retreated from previously robust democratic regimes toward autocracy. These states are literally all over the globe. They range from Eastern Europe (Hungary and Poland) to the Mediterranean (Turkey) to Latin America (Bolivia and Venezuela). Once-anticipated democratic gains in Russia and China have failed to materialize. Meanwhile, a hoped-for "fourth wave" of democracy in the Arab Spring's wake has dissipated into bitter civil war or charismatic authoritarianism.

Democratic backsliding is far less rare than political scientists used to believe. In recent scholarship, we have identified thirty-seven instances in twenty-five different countries in the postwar period in which democratic quality declined significantly, even though a fully authoritarian regime didn't emerge. That is, roughly one out of eight countries experienced measurable decay in the quality of their democratic institutions—without fully collapsing into dictatorship.

Scholars used to argue that democracy, once attained in a fairly wealthy state, would become a permanent fixture. As the late Juan Linz put it, democracy would become "the only game in town." That prediction turned out to be merely an aspiration, rather than a reality.

As a result, the global trajectory for democracies—as opposed to partial or complete autocracies—does not look positive, as the following chart shows. Although we are not yet at a moment in which democracies are rare, as in the 1970s, it is quite possible that what Samuel Huntington called the "Third Wave" of democratization has peaked. The recent de-democratization trend is worrisome.

REGIME TYPES IN THE THIRD WAVE

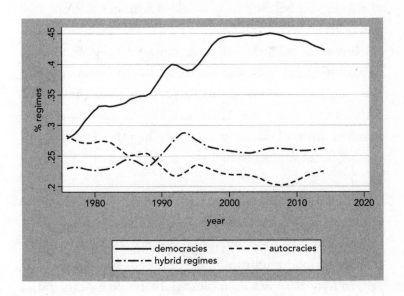

Adapted from Freedom House data 2016

Of course, we should not take for granted the assumption that experiences in other parts of the world matter for the United States. At least since the time of Alexis de Tocqueville, commentators have argued that our country has a distinct and robust democratic tradition and our people a uniquely democratic temperament. Indeed, the phrase "American exceptionalism" was first used in US communist circles in the 1920s in the course of efforts to explain the apparent immunity of US democracy to the lure of proletarian revolution in the wake of World War I. American exceptionalism has since become something of a national credo, in the fashion of the earlier notion of manifest destiny. It is hence all but obligatory, at least in the context of public political debate, to say that the founders created a marvelous system of checks and balances that would defeat any attempt at a power grab.

But a careful study of other countries' experiences, in light of the legal resources contained in our own Constitution, suggests that such complacency is unwise. The United States is not exceptional. It is instead vulnerable to the most prevalent form of democratic backsliding: the slow and tortuous descent toward partial autocracy.

IN ONE REGARD, THOSE WHO WORRY ABOUT AN OVERREACTION TO President Trump are correct. A sudden and dramatic end to democracy in the United States, for example through a military coup, is highly unlikely. Coups, of course, still happen. In May 2014, for example, the Thai military suspended that country's constitution and ended democratic rule. A year earlier, the Egyptian military ousted then-president Mohamed Morsi in favor of General Abdel Fattah el-Sisi. By contrast, an attempted coup against Turkish president Recep Tayyip Erdoğan in 2016 failed, although it did paradoxically precipitate an acceleration of that country's rush toward autocratic consolidation.

But despite these high-profile examples, coups are in fact increasingly rare. A 2011 study of democratic backsliding identified fifty-three historical cases of democratic decline.[1] Out of those, only five involved coups or other sudden collapses into authoritarianism. What's more, since the 1950s coups have become increasingly infrequent.[2] And they usually take place in a context quite different from the American situation. Full-on democratic collapse tends to occur in recently established, relatively impoverished democracies, in which civilian control of the military is tenuous. None of those conditions apply in the US (despite economic problems such as rising inequality).

An alternative to the military coup is the rapid asphyxiation of democracy using emergency powers. Deployment of such powers is not uncommon. From 1985 to 2004, 137 countries invoked state-of-emergency procedures at least once. Commentators who worry about President Trump's behavior after a terrorist attack have something like this in mind. It is certainly true that the Constitution lacks the careful restrictions on emergency powers of the sort that other countries' constitutions employ.[3] The latter typically place crisp constraints on the length and scope of extra-constitutional behavior, and they name the constitutional actors who must sign off on the emergency measures. Contrary to the arguments of Carl Schmitt and his legatees, these exceptional powers have not necessarily proved unworkable or inimical to ordinary politics.

But the US Constitution contains no such provisions. Instead, American presidents and judges have inferred vague emergency powers into many of the Constitution's key clauses and phrases—such as Article II's reference to the president as "Commander in Chief." The latter—which might have been understood principally as a means of assuring civilian control of the military—is also understood as a basis for the president's power to respond to "sudden" attacks, but also as a more diffuse authority to act unilaterally on national security or foreign policy grounds. Similarly, the president's power to "take Care" that the laws are enforced has experienced a kudzu-like creep as both Democrats and Republicans invoke it to justify expansive executive power outside the emergency context. Coupled to these constitutional claims are broad statutory delegations such as that under the 2001 and 2012 Authorizations for the Use of Military Force. These provide sub-constitutional foundations for aggressive claims of presidential power in the United States and beyond, and have become ingrained in our law. It is simply a contingent matter of judicial doctrine that more specific language is required in the domestic realm.

Paradoxically, what seems like a drafting failure in the Constitution may also work to democracy's advantage. The very fact that government has a great deal of legal discretion in responding to perceived crisis—often to the detriment of important liberty and dignity interests—means that there is far less plausible justification for calling off the regular processes of elections in order to deal with a crisis. But one of the lessons of recent comparative experience is that the *quality* of democracy can decline precipitously even as formal elections continue to be held.

THE MOST IMPORTANT REASON THAT THE SUDDEN COLLAPSE OF DE-mocracy is rare—and a key reason it is unlikely in the US—is that a sudden derogation of democracy *simply isn't necessary*. Would-be autocrats have a cheaper option at hand, one that is far less likely to catalyze opposition and resistance: the slow, insidious curtailment of democratic institutions and traditions.

One reason we expect that democracy will end only by way of a "crisis," or a sudden turning point, is because we are quick to assume that the narrative of political life will track the arc of fictional accounts of political upheaval. Fiction is dominated by dramatic moments of clarification and revelations, victories and defeats. But real life is not like *House of Cards*. There need not be sharp inflexion points. Indeed, it is worth reflecting on the fact that democracy—even in its thinnest sense of mere competitive elections—relies on transparency, legality, impartiality, and constraint. These are promoted by a range of different laws, norms, institutions, and individual loyalties. All of these rarely vanish at once. Their slow evaporation may be ineffable and easily missed.

To understand this form of democratic backsliding, it's important to understand the essential components of a democracy. First, there must be elections, which must be both free and fair. Elections by themselves are not enough: both Russia and China, after all, have elections that formally reflect the choice of the people, but allow only limited choices. Second, democracy needs liberal rights of speech and association so those with alternative views can challenge government on its policies, hold it accountable, and propose alternatives. Finally, democracy can't work if the ruling party has the courts and bureaucracy firmly in its pocket. The rule of law—not just the rule of the powerful and influential—is essential. Take away but one of these attributes, and democracy might wobble. Sap all three, and the meaningful possibility of democratic competition recedes from view.

It is here that comparative experience proves salient. It is possible to examine other countries that have experienced various forms of democratic backsliding to understand the specific legal mechanisms and institutional changes that are employed to unravel democratic practice. By comparing the resulting tool kit of antidemocratic devices to the institutional safeguards of democracy contained in the US Constitution, we obtain some traction on the question of whether our organic document has indeed served an effectual prophylactic purpose.

That comparative experience shows that would-be autocrats find it critical first to control the public narrative, often by directly attacking or intimidating the press. Libel suits—Vladimir Putin, for example, recriminalized libel, after it had been decriminalized in 2011 under Dmitry Medvedev—drummed-up prosecutions, and vise-like media regulation accomplish the same ends. A mogul who controls powerful media, such as Italy's Silvio Berlusconi, has an extra advantage of being able to crowd out other voices from the national stage. Contrary to hopes expressed in the early days of the Internet's development, new forms of social media may have made it easier rather than more difficult to obtain a practical hegemony over the terms of national debate.

Conjuring or overemphasizing a national security threat creates a sense of crisis, allowing would-be autocrats to malign critics as weak-willed or unpatriotic. The underlying crisis can be more or less real, and may or may not impact the jurisdiction in tangible ways to affect the tenor of domestic politics. In Hungary, for example, Viktor Orbán has carefully invoked the Islamist terrorism and the migration crises to cement his popular standing, notwithstanding the fact that Hungary is not in the crosshairs of either crisis. There are other common rhetorical moves that can be loosely characterized as "populist" in character. Leaders who wish to roll back democratic institutions, for example, tend to depict those institutions' defenders as representatives of a tired, insulated elite engaged in self-dealing to the detriment of the people. In contrast, such leaders portray themselves as embodying the uniquely authentic voice of the people. Here, Trump is illustrative, and we cannot resist citing a claim he made in a May 2016 political rally that captures the core of this logic: "The only thing that matters," he said, "is the unification of the people—because the other people don't mean anything."

A second element of democratic backsliding is a systematic effect to dismantle the plurality of national institutions. In particular, institutions tasked with maintaining the rule of law, or that provide a foothold for oppositional politicians, are targeted quickly. Comparative experience suggests that an independent judiciary and institutional checks such as legislative oversight of administrative activity can prove significant barriers to democratic backsliding. Hence, we often see would-be autocrats trying to pack the courts or intimidate judges into getting with the program. When the state bureaucracy insists on rule-of-law norms, they too must be bullied into submission. Weakening civil-service tenure protections is an underappreciated way to accomplish this. When government workers hired on the basis of merit are elbowed out and replaced by loyal partisans, this not only removes one potential source of opposition to the executive branch but it also enables a would-be autocrat to direct formidable prosecutorial and investigative apparatuses against political foes. The recent fraud conviction of Putin opponent Alexei Navalny shows how such tools can be used against an opponent who threatens to amass power through electoral popularity.

Finally, political competition must be stanched, even if elections proceed in some form as a way of enabling leaders to claim a mantle of legitimacy. Modifying presidential term limits is a common move, but so too are changes to the ground rules of elections in order to permanently lock in temporary majorities.

To witness the full panoply of these measures being deployed against democracy, there are no better contemporary case studies than Hungary and Poland. In a startlingly short time frame, populist governments in both countries have straitjacketed independent courts; dismantled independent checks on political power; used regulation to muzzle the media or stack it with cronies; and conjured supposed security threats from immigrants and minorities as a justification for centralizing power and dismantling checks. In Hungary, the Fidesz government used constitutional amendments to entrench its slim (53 percent) majority beyond easy electoral challenge by changing the composition and operation of a previously independent electoral commission. The result was that in 2014, it won two-thirds of the parliamentary seats with 45 percent of the vote. Fidesz also changed the composition of the Constitutional Court and created a new National Judicial Office. It also strengthened the prime minister's control of supervisory bodies such as the Electoral Commission, Budget Commission, Media Board, and Ombudsman offices. Incumbent officials were removed to make way for Fidesz loyalists, who have facilitated the rise of what Orbán calls—intending the description as praise—"illiberal" or "non-liberal" democracy.

The Polish Law and Justice Party ("PiS"), elected in October 2015, began its tenure by selecting five new judges for the Constitutional Court, while refusing to swear in three other judges who had been properly appointed by the previous government. Two months later, the PiS-controlled parliament enacted an amendment to the Constitutional Tribunal Act requiring a two-thirds majority on the court in order for its decisions to be binding. In the same month, the parliament also enacted a new media law dismissing the boards of all public-service broadcasters and vesting the treasury minister with authority to replace them with pro-PiS leadership. That new leadership subsequently purged journalists who were insufficiently enthusiastic about the government's agenda.

Hungary and Poland are hardly unique. In Turkey, President Erdoğan leveraged the 2016 coup attempt to deepen his massive purge of almost every state institution, leaving regime loyalists firmly in control. As of this writing, more than 135,000 soldiers, judges, police officers, university deans, and teachers have lost their jobs, in some cases without due process. While some of these dismissals may have been formally legal, they appear to have extended far beyond the ranks of actual opponents of the regime. Erdoğan's AK Party has also suspended and manipulated media licenses, arrested journalists on national-security grounds, and adopted a new constitution in which he will serve as the center of the entire political system, with minimal accountability.

In Venezuela, the Chávez regime notoriously aggregated executive power, limited political opposition, attacked academia, and stifled independent media—a classic example of "de-democratization" under the color of law. Some moves were especially creative. When a political opponent won at the municipal level, the Chávez regime responded by gutting the powers wielded by the new mayor and granting them to a new alternative institution.

A hallmark of these examples of democratic backsliding is that many of the power grabs are legal in and of themselves. Central among these legal measures is the early disabling of internal monitors of governmental illegality by the aggressive exercise of (legal) personnel powers. Often, there are related changes to the designs of institutions, which might be brought about through legislation. Ironically, the law is deployed to undermine legality and the rule of law more generally. Relatedly, it is quite telling that many of the new breed of populist autocrats are lawyers by training. This includes Lech Kaczyński (Poland), Viktor Orbán, and Vladimir Putin. All have teams of (often American-trained) lawyers, willing and able to further their entrenchment in power.

The cumulative effect of many small weakening steps is to dismantle the possibility of democratic competition, leaving only its façade. It is a death by a thousand cuts, rather than the clean slice of the coup maker. This is what makes the slow road from democracy so alluring to seekers of power, and so dangerous for the rest of us. Because it can be masked with a veneer of legality, it can be cloaked with plausible deniability. It is always possible to justify each incremental step.

SO COULD IT HAPPEN HERE? LOOKING TO THESE RECENT EXAMPLES suggests that the US Constitution may be good at checking coups or the antidemocratic deployment of emergency powers, but it is not well suited to stall the slow decay of democracy. Our eighteenth-century Constitution singularly lacks the provisions necessary to slow down a would-be autocrat bent on the slow dismantling of democracy.

To be sure, the cumbersome process of constitutional amendment makes it difficult for a president who wishes to amass more formal power. But other much-cited checks and balances have been profoundly overstated. The institutional checks on national political power rest on theoretical assumptions that have proved in practice rather fragile. James Madison thought that the divergent "ambitions" of the legislative and executive branches would cause those institutions to balance one another. But he failed to anticipate the rise of a two-party political system at the national level. The national party system has reshaped incentives. Congressmen today may have little reason to investigate or otherwise rein in an aggressive president of their own party. That today's Republicans are not eager to investigate President Trump's financial dealings, or his contacts with Russia, is entirely predictable from an institutional standpoint. And this tendency would be even more pronounced in a world in which individual legislators owed their seats to the president, which might be the case were a billionaire to throw around campaign cash—or accusations of disloyalty—liberally.

Other constitutions give minority parties rights to demand information and make inquiries, but the US Constitution does not. Too many of our election rules depend on the good faith of the party in power.[4] As the omnipresence of gerrymandering shows, good faith may not be enough. After the 2010 redistricting in Wisconsin, the Republican Party was able to win 60 of 99 seats in the state legislature, despite winning less than half of the statewide vote. Meanwhile, North Carolina Republicans tried a strategy that was straight out of Hugo Chávez's playbook when their party's candidate lost the governor's race. They cut the governor's staff by 80 percent, eliminated his ability to name trustees of the state university, and required that cabinet appointees be approved by the legislature. They also restructured the elections board so that they would hold the chairmanship during all statewide elections. Although these moves were rejected by the courts, there is no reason to expect that they would not be invoked again in other states, perhaps to greater success.

As the North Carolina example shows, the federal courts are critical in upholding the rule of law and defending democracy. But there is a growing acceptance in American jurisprudence of "deference" to the political branches. That ideology, in combination with aggressively partisan appointments—Trump is in a position to fill 112 federal judicial vacancies, out of 870 seats—could erode public confidence in judges' ability to stand up to government overreach, and thus lead to democratic retrogression. Certainly, after a period of eight or more years with one party in the White House, it is hard to see how the courts could be much of a check on democratic backsliding.

Moreover, the notional independence of even the Supreme Court is more dependent upon "norms" than on constitutional rules such as tenure protection and salary guarantees. And norms can change. In a less polarized time, the US Senate would have held confirmation hearings for Merrick Garland, President Obama's last Supreme Court nominee. Yet by playing hardball, Republicans may end up reshaping how laws are interpreted for decades to come. One implication is that the nomination and confirmation processes are likely to be more politicized, with more partisan candidates being proposed and appointed, and the federal courts becoming correspondingly less legalistic, more disparaging of interests other than those of the dominant coalition, and more heedless of the risk of democratic backsliding.

Other nations, unlike the United States, place judicial appointments beyond political control. Whether such judges are more independent or robust as defenders of democracy is an empirical question, but at a minimum, such systems reduce the ease with which politicians can tinker with personnel.

Similarly, in the United States, the civil service—which scholars understand as a bulwark against autocracy—is protected largely by tradition, in lieu of constitutional rules. That is why the Republican move to lay off federal workers and reduce the benefits of those who remain is so significant, as is a gratuitous revival of the Holman Rule in 2017. In addition, US attorneys also serve "at the pleasure" of the president, and it is largely restraint—not always exercised—that prevents presidents from punishing them or rewarding them for partisan legal attacks. Other constitutions, moreover, create independent ombudsman's offices to monitor corruption or human-rights compliance as supplements to the judiciary that make up for the latter's institutional weaknesses. Not so ours. Instead, institutions such as the Office of Government Ethics are staffed by the president, and ultimately vulnerable to capture or marginalization.

What of constitutional rights? While the First Amendment (currently) limits the misuse of libel law, it does not hedge the risk of partisan media regulation by the FCC or other agencies. Media companies seeking to keep regulators' favor now have lots of reasons to trim the sails of their political coverage. And the First Amendment, for good or ill, arguably protects sources of outright propaganda—sites spreading lies about politicians, for example—which could in tandem with presidential attacks on the media lead citizens to distrust all news sources.

There is, in short, nothing particularly exceptional about the American Constitution—at least in any positive sense. Because of its age, the Constitution doesn't reflect the learning from recent generations of constitutional designers. If anything, it is more vulnerable to backsliding than the regimes that failed in Poland, Hungary, Venezuela, Turkey, and elsewhere. As a result, whether or not the United States moves away from its best democratic traditions doesn't rest on the Constitution or on simple fidelity to constitutional rules. Those will quite plainly not be enough. Nor will it be enough to belabor the technical legal merits or demerits of specific executive actions, or their opponents' responses. To do so misses the forest for the trees. In particular, those who insist on formal legality at the expense of considering the motives and immediate effects of an executive action do the republic a great disservice.

Rather, the degree to which democratic norms and practices are lost in the United States over the next four years will depend on how both politicians and citizens react. The quality of our democracy will depend on what happens on the streets, what happens in legislative backrooms (especially on the Republican side), and, most important, what happens at the polls. But it won't depend, in any simple way, on the Constitution. And at least in this regard, there is nothing exceptional about our current predicament. The quality of our democracy is entirely contingent—on the personnel in the courts, on the configuration of forces in Congress, and on the willingness of our public to exercise independent judgment in a bitter media environment. One hopes these forces will remain robust over the next decade, but it is not hard to imagine a scenario in which they do not. We would, in short, do well to reject feel-good talk about American exceptionalism and embrace some of the founders' bracing and necessary trepidation about the future.

NOTES

1. Gero Erdmann, "Decline of Democracy: Loss of Quality, Hybridisation and Breakdown of Democracy," in Gero Erdmann and Marianne Kneuer, eds., *Regression of Democracy?*, *Comparative Governance and Politics* special issue 1 (2011).

2. Jonathan M. Powell and Clayton L. Thynne, "Global Instances of Coup from 1950 to 2010: A New Dataset," *Journal of Peace Research* 48, no. 2 (2011): 249.

3. Christian Bjørnskov and Stefan Voigt, "The Determinants of Emergency Constitutions," https://papers.ssrn.com/sol3/papers.cfm?abstract_id=2697144.

4. David Pozen, "Constitutional Bad Faith," *Harvard Law Review* 129, no. 4 (2016): 885, 907.

ON "IT CAN'T HAPPEN HERE"
NOAH FELDMAN

Sinclair Lewis's resonant title phrase "It Can't Happen Here" implicates at least four basic clusters of key questions, each connected to one of the component words:

First, what is the "it" that cannot happen? Authoritarianism? Extra-constitutional government? Rights suppression? Some combination?

Second, is "can't" a statement of probabilities, or some absolute condition of impossibility? Assuming the former, how improbable must the bad outcome be for Lewis's phrase (ironically intended, to be sure) to hold true as a proposition?

Third, what would count as "happening"—in the past or future? There's a rich body of dystopian literature picturing different "it"s. But perhaps our existing reality is actually more like one of the "it" outcomes than we believe.

Fourth, perhaps most pungently, where is "here"—the United States of 2017? Some other specific global locale? A mature, evolved democracy? Put another way, what are the aspects of a given polity that would prevent the undesirable outcome specified by the "it"?

This chapter is structured by these clusters of questions. It argues, roughly, that the contingent features of durable liberal democracy in mature, rich capitalist democracies in the twenty-first century are fairly robust to revolutionary change, but that incremental changes have and will continue to redefine our conception of what counts as liberal democracy—almost imperceptibly.

I. IT

For Lewis, publishing in 1935, the "it" was fascism on the Italian and German models. The political environment was structured by pervasive worries about the weakness of liberalism and parliamentarism as political models and capitalism as an economic model. These weaknesses were of course linked—just as the then-contemporary alternatives of state socialism and corporatist fascist authoritarianism were linked.

Today the economic aspect of the feared "it" has faded as a consequence of the global dominance of capitalism in the early twenty-first century. The Chinese state-centered capitalist model marks an alternative form of capitalism, to be sure. But the "it" is now conceived largely in political terms.

While that focus is reasonable, it's important not to make the cardinal mistake of thinking that a political fear should be considered only in political terms. To the contrary, the possibility of political change is just as enmeshed as ever in economic structures and forces. Political economy, not politics alone, is the correct conceptual frame for asking about what can and cannot happen politically.

Thus, capitalism in its particular contemporary Western consumerist form must be understood as a major and limiting factor for what sort of political regime could emerge in existing democracies. The point is not that these fundamental economic structures would guarantee the continuation of liberal democracy as it presently exists. Rather, the reality of political economy suggests that existing economic structures constrain and limit political possibilities—and vice versa. Economic and political institutions exist in a delicate and complex dynamic interplay.

The "it," then, could not plausibly involve a radical transformation of existing economic institutions in the short to medium term. That requires a turn to the structures of politics and political ideology to enable a fruitful conversation on what the "it" might be. In the process, the essential starting point is an acknowledgment that we don't have a precise terminology or mode of analysis for existing political arrangements in the contemporary West, including the United States.

The phrase *liberal democracy* is not a bad starting point. But it's worth recalling that neither *liberal* nor *democratic* are words that derive from, say, the US Constitution. Liberal democracy is therefore at its descriptive best no more than an attempt to make sense of evolving political-institutional developments that in the US took their present form no earlier than 1964–65 and the passage of the Civil Rights Act and Voting Rights Act. Before that, such democracy as existed in the US did not extend to many of the country's African-Americans. And *liberalism*—that much-contested term—looked remarkably different before the civil libertarian decisions of the Warren Court.

To make matters worse, *liberal democracy* floats in contemporary discourse back and forth between a linguistic descriptor and a normative ideal deployed to achieve some form of political-moral judgment. These two aspects of the phrase cannot be easily or stably kept apart. It's almost impossible to speak about liberal democracy without assuming some descriptive content. But it's simultaneously almost impossible to speak about liberal democracy without holding up some abstract idea, the content of which is necessarily subject to normative debate.

I mention all this because to say "it can't happen here" is to posit that what exists now is somehow essentially different from "it." Yet if we can't fully specify what exists now, we can't easily say that "it" differs. Our form of analysis depends, then, on an essentially comparative claim: that "it" differs in relevant respects from what we now have—so much so that "it" becomes something definitively new.

The trouble here is that current political institutions do differ in fundamental ways from those that came before. It's just that the generally gradual nature of the transformation of political institutions in a stable democracy tends to mask the scope and nature of the transformation. We may say today that the power of the presidency, for example, is greater than at any previous sustained moment in US history. But Arthur Schlesinger Jr. said the same in 1973 when he published *The Imperial Presidency*—and he was almost certainly correct then. So is the power of the presidency in 2018 an "it" that has happened here? The answer can come only from a nuanced comparison.

That comparison also requires recognition that many aspects of the US constitutional system were importantly contested from the moment they came into existence after ratification, or even before. To stick with the question of presidential power, it seems altogether plausible that James Madison would look on contemporary presidential power as a gross distortion of his design, a distortion so great that it could be characterized as an "it" for him. But it seems equally plausible that Alexander Hamilton, who openly advocated British-style monarchy at the Constitutional Convention in Philadelphia in 1787, would see the contemporary presidency as a logical and perhaps inevitable outgrowth of the original design.

A similar analysis could be performed for nearly any imaginable evolution of our existing political institutions. Could our free speech norms be radically transformed into a far less permissive, speech-protective social and legal practice? If so, civil libertarians would certainly claim that we had become a new kind of "it." But defenders of the transformation would point back to earlier eras in the history of the First Amendment, in which contemporary legal-constitutional norms were almost entirely absent.

Regular, contested elections would seem to be an essential component of our political scheme. But if some new political regime maintained those elections while transforming the practices that made them contested, would that count as an "it"? Certainly US elections today look radically different from those that existed in the nineteenth or most of the twentieth century. The preservation of forms gives us a sense of gradual continuity, even where the content of the social practice has been radically transformed.

Thus, if the "it" is fascism, perhaps it remains fair to say that "it" can't happen here. But if the "it" is the gradual and not-so-gradual transformation of political institutions and practices, not only can "it" happen—"it" has happened, repeatedly. Power has been more and less concentrated over the course of US political history. Changed modes of mass public communication have been more or less susceptible to changed distribution of power.

So although we can have a serious discussion about whether the US could experience the kinds of political changes that have occurred or are occurring presently in Hungary, Poland, and Turkey, the conversation is in a sense misleading. The characteristic mode of American political transformation has been more subtle and gradual—but no less transformative over time. Even our ideal of "liberal democracy" represents a form of government starkly different from the republicanism embraced by (some of) the framers. The US will assume some new governmental form in the future—without anyone acknowledging that "it" has ever happened.

II. CAN'T

Can't is a strong word. But it can't mean "can't," at least not in the context of "it can't happen here." Impossibility is too strong a condition to apply to the vagaries of human political affairs.

Can't therefore must mean something like "highly unlikely according to some probability calculus." That calculus, of course, will be almost totally idiosyncratic and unquantifiable. No data set of countries that have undergone democratic transitions and then reverted to nondemocratic forms of government can credibly be said to tell us how likely some similar reversion would be to occur in the US or in other mature Western democracies. The problem of extrapolating from the data to a distinct political-economic and institutional setting is simply too great.

The point isn't to disparage the form of political scientific analysis that tries to isolate certain features of governmental systems, to evaluate transformative events in a quantifiable fashion, to build data sets, and to use them for predictive purposes. This is a perfectly respectable and defensible academic enterprise—subject always to the epistemological limits imposed by the methodology.

Those include, first and most significantly, the smallness of the *n*. This is a serious and pervasive problem in the quantifiable political science of international comparisons. When studying events like the process of democratization and the decompensation or collapse of democratic states, the numbers are necessarily small.

Second, and more frequently overlooked, is the inherent danger of retrofitting or mining data in the difficult process of identifying the features that are supposed to determine outcomes. The natural thing to do in performing such work is to compile a data set that includes a reasonably large number of factors that might be expected to produce outcomes. The data set in hand, the researcher then runs various progressions to see which factors would seem to be explanatory.

Yet as a substantial body of recent statistical work indicates, this method poses serious problems for the epistemological validity of the associations that emerge. To oversimplify, in the presence of a large enough body of factors, some will likely show more than random—even statistically significant—"effects" that are in fact nothing more than coincidence.

Third is the perennial problem of omitted variables, particularly those associated with specific historical periods. To compile a large enough data set to say anything that seems meaningful, a researcher would have to look across at least a century of examples. Yet the causal factors associated with, say, the interwar period or the era of the Cold War are bound to be markedly correlated across cases. That potentially confounds generalizations that aren't based on external factors such as great power weakness or great power intervention.

What emerges from these caveats is that in asking what "can't" means, we may ultimately mean nothing more or less than that we are making a seat-of-the-pants assessment of likelihood, unmoored to meaningfully quantifiable analysis.

That's all right, of course. The probabilities of many, indeed most, complex political events are not susceptible to being assessed with scientific rigor.

At the same time, we should keep in mind that low-probability events do on occasion come to pass. Thus, to say it can't happen here isn't to say that it absolutely can't. Confidence must not be confused with certainty.

III. HAPPEN

What would it mean for "it" to "happen"? The very word *happen* hints at some contingent, even accidental, chain of events. Yet the fiction writers who have spent the most time dreaming up dystopian scenarios of democratic collapse have frequently imagined that concrete individuals caused the outcomes. That's particularly true when the imagined scenario is one driven by populism. Because populist movements sometimes feature demagogic leaders, it's easy to conclude that those leaders are the necessary precondition for their movements.

It isn't just Hitler or Mussolini who helped create this often unexamined assumption. Viktor Orbán in Hungary and Recep Tayyip Erdoğan in Turkey are two immediate, contemporary examples of powerful leaders under whose government democratic norms have been consistently and actively eroded without either of them entering fascist territory.

Yet a moment's reflection should dispel the idea that a single figure, however charismatic, can topple democratic norms and institutions. The leaders who have substantially reversed democratic progress have all, without exception, relied on institutions, including political parties and para-militaries.

Without exception, the leaders' own nongovernmental or quasi-governmental institutions have engaged in complex processes of institutional capture, taking over and in the process transforming existing state institutions. This is the most crucial element of what "happens." The state's institutions may arguably have to be weak in some relevant sense for the party or junta or movement to capture those institutions and turn them to new uses. But the state itself need not be weak. Indeed, takeover is likely to be a more valuable and effective tool precisely when the state is strong.

The reason for the value of a strong state is the key next step here: when the would-be autocrat or authoritarian grasps the reins of state power and then uses it to marginalize other nongovernmental or quasi-governmental competitors for power. This is the crucial consolidation mechanism that facilitates democratic reversal.

The state is the prize, to be sure. But it is also the mechanism for maintaining the prize.

This observation yields the hypothesis that two factors are especially important to watch when determining whether "it" can or can't happen. One is the capacity of state institutions to be captured by political forces who can then subvert those institutions for the purposes of excluding and even eliminating competition. The other is the durability and ability of competing non-state institutional actors to withstand state-directed attempts to marginalize or defeat them.

Durable, independent, and confident state institutions are more likely to be able to withstand and resist capture than newer, dependent, and insecure institutions. Well-established bureaucracies are interesting examples of durable, independent, and confident institutions. It's a mistake to imagine such bureaucracies as well-oiled machines that can be easily turned to achieve the purposes of an antidemocratic regime. That may occur, of course—but it's likely to occur only when the bureaucracy broadly approves of the policy direction being taken by the new government.

Think of the World War II–era German army, a prime example of a durable, independent, and confident state institution. The Wehrmacht effectively served Hitler's interests in its initial invasions of the East and West, largely because the officer corps understood these undertakings as consistent with at least some version of German national interest. That same officer corps eschewed the ideology and politics of Nazism. And as the war progressed and Hitler made vast and significant strategic blunders, the Wehrmacht became a site of (modest) resistance to Hitler's projects.

Of course, the capacity and independence of such bureaucratic institutions is not an unmitigated good. Under normal democratic conditions, we often fear the power and independence of bureaucracies that resist democratically elected officials. Independent courts are just one dramatic example. In the extreme case, such as in Egypt, a "Deep State" may exercise bureaucratic powers to resist and subvert democratic change.

These risks associated with independent state institutions, however, precisely reveal the huge significance of such institutions in predicting whether liberal-democratic subversion can occur. Where bureaucracies including courts and militaries are accustomed to operating according to legal and cultural norms, radical change is far less likely to occur. If "it" can't happen in contemporary Western democracies, much of the explanation lies with these state institutions.

Today, such institutions are pervasive in Western democracies, and are themselves pervaded by cultures of regularity, legality, and independence. These features are present, I would argue, to an unprecedented degree. They make it extraordinarily unlikely that it could happen here.

These institutions, I want to point out, are not classically democratic nor classically republican. To an important degree, they represent the fusion of the modern bureaucratic state with liberal ideals. In this fusion, they are perfectly capable of resisting popular democratic transformation.

I'm not speaking in unmitigated praise of these institutional forces. I am simply noting their tendency to resist radical change that violates their core set of values, beliefs, and institutional interests. Bureaucracy has its vices. But those vices have corresponding virtues.

The other crucial institutional determinant is surely the ecosystem of non-state institutions capable of resisting efforts at state takeover. These institutions include most importantly the press and political parties, but also civil society groups that are capable of organizing action whether using traditional political and legal means or social media.

It's frequently been argued that robust civil society institutions are crucial for the democratization process. I'm suggesting, I hope not controversially, that these institutions probably play an even greater role in resisting antidemocratic change than they do in producing democracy in the first instance.

It's noteworthy, I think, that civil society resistance to antidemocratic change can have a paranoiac bent. Civil society actors are the first and most public to say dramatically that democratic structures are in danger. In contrast, bureaucratic resistance is likely to be quiet, slow, and to a degree uncoordinated. But that's at least in part because the civil society actors think of themselves as sentinels. And part of their job is to create a public atmosphere of concern that might motivate state actors—such as leakers—to engage in acts of resistance.

It may be worth acknowledging that even so cautious a thing as a collection of essays on the theme of "it can't happen here" has a modestly paranoid edge to it. That could be true even if the essays argue, as this one roughly does, that in fact it can't happen here. But this mild paranoia is justified by what I've described as the sentinel function of civil society. And university teachers count as participants in durable, independent, and confident non-state or quasi-state institutional bureaucracies.

Assessing the ecosystem of civil society institutions in the contemporary US and Western Europe, it seems to me that they are as powerful and capable of offering meaningful resistance as any in world history. Of course, that doesn't mean these institutions could survive a direct onslaught by the state. But the civil society institutions exist in a complex interplay with state actors, who to an important degree take their cues from civil society institutions.

IV. HERE

For purposes of this essay, "here" could refer to just the contemporary United States—not Western European or other developed democracies. Indeed, in Lewis's title, the "here" is arguably intended to contrast the US precisely with Western Europe, where fascism and Nazism emerged despite at least some democratic practice and precedent. For Americans, the phrase "it can't happen here" thus implies, subtly or not so subtly, a version of American exceptionalism. It can happen elsewhere and to others, but not to us.

I want to resist this impulse to American exceptionalism. It's not that the US is situated exactly like other mature or developed democracies. It isn't, for reasons of both contingent history and self-perception. Rather, an exceptionalist conception of the possibilities of democratic undoing might blind Americans to important lessons that can be gleaned from elsewhere.

Consider Canada. It seems altogether implausible to think that Canada would be any more susceptible to antidemocratic forces than would the US. The reason is not a shared constitutional history, for the two constitutional traditions are not deeply overlapping. Nor is it the accident of geographical contiguity (witness Mexico) or even the highly non-accidental fact of cultural interpenetration.

Rather, what puts the US and Canada on similar footing is the presence in both of the independent, durable, and confident institutions of government that together stand in the way of democratic reversal. And in both cases, these institutions are of relatively long duration.

The same is true of most Western European democracies, I believe. Those that have sustained liberal democracy since the 1950s mostly share these features. And some, like Spain, which embraced liberal democracy rather later, seem to share them as well, probably because of the strong Spanish state that emerged under Francisco Franco's dictatorship and survived into the country's democratic period. Even Italy and Greece, with all their histories of political turmoil, their weaker states, shakier civil society institutions, and weak economies, seem highly unlikely to devolve away from democracy.

But perhaps this judgment is overly confident, given that Eastern European democracies seem so substantially less stable. I have already briefly mentioned Hungary and Poland, both apparently well on the way to some form of democratic reversal. To be sure, emerging into democracy post-1989, after the fall of communism, means these democracies are of shorter duration. But the problem seems to lie not merely in the passage of time, but in the relative lack of independence and confidence in state institutions and the weaker civil society ecosystem.

Poland, of course, democratized in part because of civil society entities such as *Solidarność*. But in retrospect, labor union activism under communism wasn't enough to press democracy on Poland. That took the external shock of Soviet collapse. Then democracy was adopted for lack of any serious competitor.

Consequently, it could be argued that the rapidity of democratization in Eastern Europe has impeded the development of the robust civil society ecosystem necessary to resist de-democratization. Sometimes, years of struggle in the democratization process, as in for example South Korea or Taiwan, may serve as an incubator for oppositional civil society. Both Taiwan and South Korea, incidentally, are democracies of only recent coinage, yet both seem more capable of resisting a democratic undoing than Eastern European democracies.

Latin American democracies are something else again, always assuming they can even be classified in a single category, which is itself a bit doubtful. In no case, with the possible exception of Brazil, does it seem to me that democratic undoing is unthinkable. Political economy combines with state weakness and a lack of powerful civil society institutions, except for political parties.

The point of this extremely thin, indeed meager set of comparisons is simply to highlight that it is not solely long tradition or political culture that makes it true that "it can't happen here" in the US. Taiwan and South Korea don't have long democratic traditions. Neither does Spain. Depending on how you measure, even Germany can't be treated as having a long history of democracy. What's more, these countries all have very different political cultures from one another, and from the US.

Put another way, the veneration of the US Constitution that pervades American political culture is a useful and valuable tool for resisting democratic decompensation. But it isn't necessary, or even determinative. As I've suggested, constitutional tradition has evolved very greatly, and the features that protect against a democratic reversal are not for the most part grounded in the fundamental structures of the Constitution as written.

Instead, it's the unwritten constitution of the contemporary US—a set of ideas and practices that encompasses political economy, institutional independence, and non-state/nongovernmental institutions—that eases my mind. I hope, too, that it should ease yours.

CONCLUSION

In this essay I have tried to avoid any sort of triumphalism. The fact that, in my view and under my definitions, it can't happen here isn't proof of any sort of institutional superiority. It isn't proof of unbroken constitutional tradition. It also isn't an unalloyed good, resting as it does on institutional virtues that have significant corresponding vices.

Nor should my conclusion be taken to mean that we don't need to remain vigilant, even mildly paranoid, about the risks of democratic reversal. As I've suggested, for civil society, at least, the sentinel function calls for some aggressive outrage.

Yet in the end, I also want to say that too much dystopianism, too frequently or easily deployed, has its own costs. It's important to distinguish policies we don't like from policies that attempt a fundamental transformation of political institutions. That's true for purposes of conserving critical resources. But it's also true for purposes of drawing public attention and debate.

In today's Western liberal consumerist democracies, citizen engagement can't be taken for granted. It must be husbanded and preserved, treated as a resource to be deployed when the stakes are high and the polity is in some danger. Our "it" is not what it was. Nor is our "here."

AUTHORITARIANISM IS NOT A MOMENTARY MADNESS, BUT AN ETERNAL DYNAMIC WITHIN LIBERAL DEMOCRACIES

KAREN STENNER AND JONATHAN HAIDT

INTRODUCTION

Western liberal democracy seems to be in the grip of a momentary madness, or so the story goes. All across the West, publics we might have hoped were evolving in linear fashion into more perfect democratic citizens have "suddenly" been overcome by a "wave" of "far-right" fervor. They bristle with nationalism and anti-globalism, xenophobia, and isolationism. There are calls to ban immigration, to deport "illegals," and to abandon asylum obligations. Migrants and refugees are seen as threats to national security: as terrorists in waiting or in the making. Significant public resources are to be diverted to their surveillance and to thwarting the evils they would otherwise surely perpetrate. Beyond their depiction as "the enemy within," they are deemed an existential threat to culture and national identity, competitors for jobs, and a brake on national prosperity. Leaders are exhorted to favor their own countrymen over "aliens" and outsiders, and to shield them from the brutal forces of global trade with protectionism.

These unexpected public demands seem to travel with an angry rejection of the leaders and institutions that pulled these "politically incorrect" options from the policy menu. There is a fundamentally antidemocratic mood afoot that has lost patience, in particular, with the strictures of political correctness. In these conditions, formerly reviled parties and movements that once languished on the fringes have become viable—acceptable if not quite respectable. The newfound popularity of these parties—some with past or present ties to Nazi ideology—is fueled by perceptions that the political mainstream has lost touch with those they are meant to represent. "Self-serving" political elites, leaders viewed as remote from regular folk but "pandering" to minorities, seem to feed into a growing sense that "this is not my government" and "these are not my people." This may well be the animating spirit at the heart of what has come to be called "far-right populism."

While the origins of these developments are open to question, the purported outcomes have unquestionably been shocking to many. Donald Trump ascended to the American presidency. Partisanship and ideology aside, it is hard to imagine that Trump's temperament and experience equip him for leadership of the free world. Britain voted to exit the European Union in a history-changing referendum. And the French flirted dangerously with Le Front National. While (to many commentators' palpable relief) Marine Le Pen was ultimately held to "just" 35 percent of the presidential vote, this can be seen as a victory over far-right populism only compared with what might have been. The same can be said regarding the recent performance of the Freedom Party's Norbert Hofer in Austria's presidential election. In both cases, the far-right populist candidate came close to winning the presidency of a major Western nation, and note, in neither case facing off against a contender from the traditional "left" or "right." Geert Wilders's Party for Freedom was blocked from the Dutch governing coalition, despite placing second, only via the determined collusion of all his mainstream opponents. Recent general elections in Germany and Austria have likewise seen a marked "populist" surge that upended "normal" politics. Whatever these political brands might once have represented, "left" versus "right" is being overturned in a new game of "insiders" versus "outsiders" . . . or so it seems.

POPULISM AS A PERSON–SITUATION INTERACTION

So what is this far-right populism? And where has it "suddenly" come from? From its alleged suddenness, many analysts have arrived at explanations that are redolent of sudden ill health. By this account, far-right populism is a momentary madness brought on by recent environmental stressors (the global financial crisis, the decline of manufacturing, the inevitable dislocations of globalism) and exploited by irresponsible leaders who deflect the patients' anxieties onto easy scapegoats (migrants, refugees, terrorists) for their own political gain. Central to this diagnosis is the notion that the patients' fears are irrational and can be alleviated by more responsible treatment and the reduction of stress (by boosting the economy or increasing social supports). With appropriate interventions and the removal of toxic influences, it is thought that our populists will eventually "snap out of it" and come back to their senses.

The social scientific literature on populism crosses many disciplines, and the concept is frequently and casually deployed in both academic and popular commentary. We cannot do justice to it here. Many accounts converge on the idea that populism is a kind of "zeitgeist" in which the pure/real/true people are seen to be exploited by a remote/corrupt/self-serving elite (e.g., Mudde 2004: 560). In what is perhaps the most explicit and detailed definition, populism is seen as "pit[ting] a virtuous and homogeneous people against a set of elites and dangerous 'others' who are together depicted as depriving (or attempting to deprive) the sovereign people of their rights, values, prosperity, identity, and voice" (Albertazzi and McDonnell 2008: 3). From our perspective, the addition of these details—regarding the goodness and sameness of the ingroup, and the outgroup's intent to undermine their values and identity—serves mostly to reinforce our sense that populism per se is really more "zeitgeist" than political ideology or enduring predisposition. On its own, it seems to us more a complaint about the current state of the world (a perception of contemporary conditions) rather than a vision of the good life. It gains substance and meaning only when fleshed out and prefixed by something else, like *far-right* populism: what Mudde and Kaltwasser (2017) would call a "host ideology." Only then do we know *both* what our populists actually want (virtue and homogeneity: the one right way for the one true people) and how they presently feel (that elites and dangerous "others" are thwarting those desired ends).

Broken down in this manner, we can see that the present phenomenon of far-right populism fits easily into the framework of a "person-situation interaction" that is at the heart of social psychology. This is the notion that *Behavior* is a function of the *Person* (stable personality and enduring traits) interacting with their current (ever-shifting) *Environment*: $B = f(P, E)$. More pointedly, it is neatly encompassed by an interaction that Stenner (2005) labeled the "authoritarian dynamic": *intolerance of difference = authoritarian predisposition x normative threat.* In this essay, we contend that the political shocks roiling Western liberal democracies at present—which in reality began with rumblings in the 1990s—are more appropriately and efficiently conceived as products of this authoritarian dynamic.

THE "AUTHORITARIAN DYNAMIC": A PARSIMONIOUS ACCOUNT OF "FAR-RIGHT POPULISM"

In the opening paragraphs of this paper, we took care to draw out two distinct but seemingly entangled components of the current wave of far-right populism. These were (i) a multifaceted demand for less diversity and difference in society (the "far-right" component: a particular conception of the good life) and (ii) a critique of the faithless leaders and institutions currently failing to deliver this life (the "populism" component), presumably due to their political correctness and fidelity to values remote from what The People actually want. Tangled up together, the two components fuel the populist fervor that now besets the West. From the perspective of Stenner's "authoritarian dynamic," this "far-right populist" tangle simply represents the activation of authoritarian predispositions (in the roughly one-third of the population who are so inclined) by perceptions of "normative threat" (put most simply: threats to unity and consensus, or "oneness and sameness"). The predictable and well-understood (not sudden or surprising) consequences of activating this authoritarian dynamic—of "waking up" this latent endogenous predisposition with the application of exogenous normative threat—are the kinds of strident public demands for greater oneness and sameness that we now hear all around us. Stenner explicitly noted that the theory of the authoritarian dynamic was intended to explain "the kind of intolerance that seems to 'come out of nowhere,' that can spring up in tolerant and intolerant cultures alike, producing sudden changes in behavior that cannot be accounted for by slowly changing cultural traditions" (Stenner 2005: 136).

In the remainder of this paper we will outline the theory of the authoritarian dynamic, briefly review available evidence, and then examine whether this alternative account provides a more compelling and simpler explanation of populism across the seemingly diverse cases of Trump, Brexit, and the National Front. We take advantage of an extraordinary data set collected by EuroPulse in December 2016 that gives us deep insights into voting for populist candidates and causes in the United States, Britain, and France.

THE AUTHORITARIAN DYNAMIC

HOW AUTHORITARIANISM IS DIFFERENT FROM CONSERVATISM

Stenner (2005, 2009a) identified three distinct psychological profiles of people who are typically lumped together under the unhelpful rubric of "conservative," and who tend to vote for candidates designated as "right-wing." The latter is a largely content-free self-placement, whose meaning is inconsistent across cultures and times. On this so-called right wing of politics, Stenner distinguished between what she called "laissez faire conservatives," "status quo conservatives," and "authoritarians." It is vital to keep this distinction in mind because it is only the authoritarians who show persistent antidemocratic tendencies and a willingness to support extremely illiberal measures (such as the forced expulsion of racial or religious groups) under certain conditions (i.e., normative threat).

Laissez faire "conservatives" are not conservative in any real sense. They typically self-identify as classical liberals or libertarians. They strongly favor the free market and are usually pro-business, seeking to thwart "socialist" or "left-wing" efforts to intervene in the economy and redistribute wealth. Psychologically speaking, they have nothing in common with authoritarians (Haidt 2012). Authoritarians—those who demand authoritative constraints on the individual in all matters moral, political, and racial—are *not* generally averse to government intrusions into economic life. Empirically, laissez faire conservatism is typically found to be either unrelated to authoritarianism or else inversely related to it, and not implicated in intolerance or populism to any significant degree.

AUTHORITARIANISM VERSUS "STATUS QUO CONSERVATISM"

Status quo conservatives are those who are psychologically predisposed to favor stability and resist rapid change and uncertainty. They are in a sense the true conservatives: the heirs of Edmund Burke. Status quo conservatism is only modestly associated with authoritarianism and intolerance, and only under very specific conditions. It tends to align with intolerant attitudes and behaviors only where established institutions and accepted norms and practices are intolerant. In a culture of stable, long-established, institutionally supported and widely accepted tolerance, status quo conservatism and authoritarianism will essentially be unhitched, and status quo conservatism will lend little support to intolerant attitudes and behaviors.

Contrast status quo conservatism then with authoritarianism: an enduring predisposition to favor obedience, conformity, oneness, and sameness over freedom and difference. Bear in mind that we are speaking here of a *psychological* predisposition and not of political ideology, nor of the character of political regimes. (Note also that we make no claims about the psychological predispositions of Donald Trump,

Marine Le Pen, or any other political leader. Authoritarianism is an attribute of the follower, not necessarily of the leader, and one does not need to be an authoritarian to successfully deploy authoritarian rhetoric and attract authoritarian followers.) Authoritarianism is substantially heritable (McCourt et al. 1999; Ludeke, Johnson, and Bouchard 2013) and mostly determined by lack of "openness to experience" (one of the "Big Five" personality dimensions) and by cognitive limitations (Stenner 2005); these are two factors that reduce one's willingness and capacity (respectively) to tolerate complexity, diversity, and difference.

In contrast to status quo conservatism, authoritarianism is primarily driven not by aversion to *change* (difference over time) but by aversion to *complexity* (difference across space). In a nutshell, authoritarians are *"simple-minded avoiders of complexity more than closed-minded avoiders of change"* (Stenner 2009b: 193). This distinction matters for the challenges currently confronting liberal democracy because in the event of an "authoritarian revolution," authoritarians may seek massive social change in pursuit of greater oneness and sameness, willingly overturning established institutions and practices that their (psychologically) conservative peers would be drawn to defend and preserve.

To avoid tautology with the dependent variables we are trying to explain—a problem that plagued earlier research on *The Authoritarian Personality* (Adorno et al. 1950)—Stenner (2005) usually gauges "latent" authoritarianism with a low-level measure of fundamental predisposition: typically, respondents' choices among child-rearing values.

CAN IT HAPPEN HERE?

For example, when asked what qualities should be encouraged in children, authoritarians tend to prioritize obedience, good manners, and being well behaved over things like independence, curiosity, and thinking for oneself. Pitting this "bare bones" measure of authoritarianism against *any* variety of "conservatism," and the whole roster of sociodemographic variables—including education, income, gender, class, and religiosity—Stenner (2005: 133; 2009a: 152) has shown via the *World Values Survey* that authoritarianism is the principal determinant of general intolerance of difference around the globe.

WHAT AUTHORITARIANISM DOES[1]

Authoritarianism inclines one toward attitudes and behaviors variously concerned with structuring society and social interactions in ways that enhance sameness and minimize diversity of people, beliefs, and behaviors. It tends to produce a characteristic array of *functionally related* stances, all of which have the effect of glorifying, encouraging, and rewarding uniformity and disparaging, suppressing, and punishing difference. Since enhancing uniformity and minimizing diversity implicate others and require some control over their behavior, ultimately these stances involve actual coercion of others (as in driving a black family from the neighborhood) and, more often, demands for the use of group authority (i.e., coercion by the state).

In the end, then, suppression of difference and achievement of uniformity necessitate autocratic social arrangements in which individual autonomy yields to group authority. In this way, authoritarianism is far more than a personal distaste for difference. It becomes a normative worldview about the social value of obedience and conformity (versus freedom and difference), the prudent and just balance between group authority and individual autonomy (Duckitt 1989), and the appropriate uses of (or limits on) that authority. This worldview induces bias against different others (racial and ethnic outgroups, immigrants and refugees, radicals and dissidents, moral "deviants"), as well as political demands for authoritative constraints on their behavior. The latter will typically include legal discrimination against minorities and restrictions on immigration, limits on free speech and association, and the regulation of moral behavior (e.g., via policies regarding abortion and homosexuality, and their punitive enforcement).

WHEN AUTHORITARIANISM DOES THIS

Stenner's theory of the "authoritarian dynamic" tells us exactly *when* authoritarianism does these things, making it a useful tool for understanding the current wave of populism. As noted earlier, the authoritarian dynamic posits that intolerant behavior is a function of the interaction of an enduring psychological predisposition with transient environmental conditions of normative threat. Stenner contends that in the absence of a common identity rooted in race or ethnicity (the usual case in our large, diverse, and complex modern societies), the things that make "us" an "us"—that make us *one and the same*—are common authority (oneness) and shared values (sameness). Accordingly, for authoritarians, the conditions most threatening to oneness and sameness are questioned or questionable authorities and values, e.g., disrespect for leaders and institutions, authorities unworthy of respect, and lack of conformity with or consensus in group norms and beliefs. This is what Stenner has termed "normative threat," or "threats to the normative order."

Stenner (2005) demonstrated the prevalence and significance of this authoritarian dynamic with many different kinds of data, showing that the intolerance produced by authoritarianism is substantially magnified when respondents:

- *perceive* that the public and political elites are ideologically distant, or that leaders on all sides have let them down (see Stenner 2005: 57, from the *Durham Community Survey, 1997*)
- are *experimentally* exposed to seemingly real news coverage about "leaders unworthy of our trust," or "fractured public opinion" where "no one agrees on anything anymore" (see Figure 1 below, from the *Cultural Revolution Experiment 1995*, reported in Stenner 2005)
- are being interviewed *at a time* of high variance in public opinion (e.g., during some particularly fractious week in US history, as determined by the actual variance in survey responses to the *General Social Survey 1972–2000*; see Stenner 2005: 314)
- are living *in a place* (e.g., some nation of the world) marked by high variance in public opinion (see Stenner 2005: 314, from the *World Values Survey 1990–1995*).

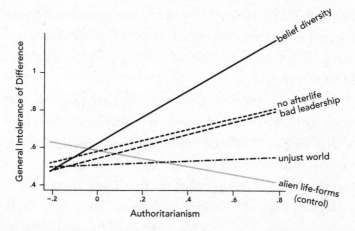

FIGURE 1. Effects of authoritarianism on general intolerance of difference given experimental manipulation of threat. Reprinted from Stenner (2005).

In every case, normative threat dramatically increased the influence of authoritarianism on general intolerance of difference: racial, political, and moral. The latter constitute the authoritarian's classic "defensive arsenal," concerned with differentiating, defending, and glorifying "us," in conditions that appear to threaten "us," by excluding and discriminating against "them": racial and ethnic minorities, immigrants and refugees, political dissidents, radicals, and moral "deviants." Notice that the activation of the authoritarian dynamic by collective threat in *one* domain will typically boost the display of these classic attitudes and behaviors across *all* domains. Thus, should fears about Muslim immigration activate authoritarian predispositions, this will usually provoke authoritarians to a whole panoply of sympathetic "vibrations," which might include strident demands to limit rights and protections for "domestic" racial/ethnic minorities, to restrict free speech and assembly, and to deploy state authority to write moral strictures into public policy, e.g., to roll back gay rights and "crack down" on criminals.

Without a theoretical framework that pulls all these seemingly disparate behaviors together—as functionally related elements of the authoritarian's classic defensive stance—contemporary analysts can be left puzzling over (for example) why support for the death penalty and for the public whipping of "sex criminals" should turn out to be the strongest "predictors" of a vote in favor of Brexit (Kaufmann 2016). The authoritarian dynamic offers such a framework, which here we will test using recent EuroPulse data on populist voting across the US, UK, and France.

THE EUROPULSE DATA SET AND OUR ANALYSIS PLAN

DATA: EUROPULSE DECEMBER 2016

The EuroPulse survey is conducted each quarter by Dalia Research (Germany). Dalia uses a proprietary software platform to reach respondents through web-enabled devices as they interact with a wide range of websites and apps. Dalia seeks out users fitting the required profile for the task and offers them access to premium content in exchange for survey completion.[2] This should reach a more representative slice of the relevant population and interview them under more natural conditions than is possible (for example) issuing email invitations to that atypical portion of a population that has sufficient interest, time, and energy to register for research panels and complete surveys on any topic for modest material rewards.

One of the world's largest omnibus surveys, EuroPulse is conducted across all twenty-eight EU countries, in twenty-one different languages. Four times a year, the EuroPulse survey interviews a census representative sample of 10,000 Europeans to track public opinion on a variety of topics. In the unique instance of the EuroPulse survey conducted over December 2–11, 2016—just a few weeks after US voters elected President Trump on November 8—Dalia added a representative US sample to the EuroPulse mix. Their stated purpose was to enable researchers to detect any commonalities in populist support across the US and Europe (including voting for Brexit in the UK and for the National Front in France), publicly issuing a "Research Challenge" to that effect.

EXCLUDING NON-WHITES FROM ANALYSES

The EuroPulse-plus-US data set of December 2016 included 12,235 respondents: n=1,052 in the US sample, and n=11,283 across the European Union. However, given the nature of our research questions, we excluded non-whites from the current investigation, leaving n=661 in the US (which also excluded Hispanics) and n=10,500 across the EU. As explained elsewhere (Stenner 2005), this is not to say that authoritarianism is necessarily expressed in a fundamentally different manner depending on race/ethnicity, or majority/minority status, than among whites across Europe and the US. It is just that the demarcation of ingroups and outgroups, and delineation of the norms and authorities to which one owes allegiance, might vary. We would not expect, for example, any authoritarianism among African-American leaders of the Black Lives Matter movement to propel them toward a vote for Donald Trump, nor North African Muslim immigrants in France to be attracted (by any predisposition to authoritarianism) to the National Front. Excluding non-whites left us a sample of 11,161 respondents from twenty-nine countries, with 3,202 of those of special interest in our present search for a common dynamic in populist voting across the US (n=661), UK (n=1,256), and France (n=1,285).

DEPENDENT VARIABLE: POPULIST VOTING

The dependent variable throughout our analyses—our principal outcome of interest—was the probability of voting for populist candidates and causes. For the US sample, this was reflected by respondents' self-report (in early December) of having voted for Donald Trump in the presidential election just a few weeks prior. For the UK, the dependent variable was respondents' self-report of having voted a few months earlier in the British referendum of June 23 in favor of leaving the European Union. For our French sample, populist voting was indicated by self-reports of intended vote in the upcoming election, which would be the presidential election of April/May 2017.

There is mostly good correspondence between these self-reports and the real incidence of both vote turnout and vote choice in these elections, although our starting sample does seem to over-represent Americans who turned out to vote, and to under-represent Britons voting to leave the European Union, probably due to some combination of selection and social desirability bias (Karp and Brockington 2005). Survey respondents are disproportionately likely to vote, and people tend to over-report engaging in civic behaviors such as voting. Similarly, it may be that those groups that leaned toward exiting Europe were disinclined subsequently to broadcast that, as well as generally less disposed to answering surveys.[3]

In any case, only those who said they voted (or intended to vote, in the case of France) were retained in the following analyses, leaving final sample sizes of 451, 858, and 1,045 for the US, UK, and France, respectively. Our dependent variable was scored "1" for a vote in favor of Trump, Brexit, or Le Pen, and "0" otherwise. We analyzed each of these three vote choices separately, since they reflect very different decision contexts. But we synthesized our findings across the three countries, since our main goal was ultimately to identify commonalities in the forces driving populist voting across liberal democracies.

MAIN EXPLANATORY VARIABLE: AUTHORITARIAN PREDISPOSITION

We followed our previous practice in forming a "bare bones" measure of authoritarianism from respondents' choices among pairs of child-rearing values. As always, we sought a measure that reflected something more akin to a deep-seated, enduring political "personality" than a current policy attitude; that could do so across widely varying cultures with different ingroups and outgroups, dissidents and deviants; and that did not make specific reference to objects, actors, or events that featured in current political contests and might be the very subjects of our inquiries.

We formed our measure of authoritarian predisposition from responses to the following four EuroPulse items: "Which is more important for a child to have? Independence / Respect for elders? Obedience / Self-reliance? Consideration for others / Good behavior? Curiosity / Good manners?" Responses considered authoritarian (each scoring "1") were respect for elders, obedience, good behavior, and good manners. Alternatively, preference for children being independent, self-reliant, considerate, and curious reflected the inverse of authoritarianism (each scoring "0").[4] Any inability or refusal to choose between a pair of values ("don't have an opinion") was considered a neutral response (scoring "0.5"). After summing these four components, re-scoring the resulting scale to be of one-unit range, and centering its midpoint on "0" (to ease interpretation of interaction coefficients), our final measure of authoritarian predisposition ranged across nine points from –0.5 to +0.5.

According to this measure, about a third of white respondents across these twenty-nine liberal democracies proved to be authoritarian to some degree, in the sense of passing the neutral midpoint of the scale and leaning toward authoritarianism in their value choices. Specifically, 33 percent were authoritarian, 37 percent were non-authoritarian, and 29 percent were "balanced" or neutral.[5]

KEY INTERACTION CONDITION: NORMATIVE THREAT

We constructed an overall measure of "normative threat" from several key sentiments found in the EuroPulse survey. We sought to reflect three core components of threat to the normative order: loss of societal consensus, loss of confidence in leaders, and loss of confidence in institutions.

First, the closest sentiment we could find in the EuroPulse survey to perceived loss of consensus was the express feeling that one's country was "going in the wrong direction" (either *very wrong* or *somewhat wrong*) in response to the question *"Over the past 5 years, has [the United States / the United Kingdom / France] gone more in the right or wrong direction?"*

Second, we measured general loss of confidence in leaders by means of strong agreement with the statement *"Government is controlled by the rich elite,"* which readers might recognize as an item sometimes deployed in measures of populism. (Recall our earlier assertion that so-called populist sentiments might more simply be understood as perceptions of normative threat.)

Third, we wanted to measure loss of confidence in government institutions in a way that captured both dissatisfaction with the current government and disillusion with democratic government more generally. To this end, we combined ordinal scale responses to two questions: *"How satisfied are you with the way democracy works in your country?"* (which ranged across four points from *"very satisfied"* up to *"not at all satisfied"*), and *"What is your opinion of the government in [the United States / the United Kingdom / France]?"* (which ranged across five points from *"very positive"* to *"very negative"*). Summing these two equally weighted components created a finely graduated nineteen-point measure reflecting "dissatisfaction with democratic government."

Finally, our overall measure of normative threat standardized and summed these three equally weighted components and re-scored the result to be of one-unit range. This overall scale (deployed in all subsequent analyses) ranged across seventy-five points from "-.5" to ".5," centered on a midpoint of "0."

OTHER EXPLANATORY VARIABLES:
ECONOMIC EVALUATIONS

An adequate test of the explanatory power of the authoritarian dynamic in this domain must necessarily also control for the economic "distress" that is traditionally cited as fueling populist sentiments and voting behavior. A number of scholars have noted recently that economic factors actually seem rather weak and inconsistent predictors of populism and intolerance, particularly compared with value conflict and cultural "backlash" (see Inglehart and Norris 2017). Stenner (2005) previously found that, to the extent that economic factors did predict expressions of intolerance, the effect tended to be confined to negative retrospective evaluations of the national economy, which might be felt as a kind of collective threat by authoritarians (although the effects of such threats were rarely as powerful or consistent as the classic normative threats). In contrast, Stenner found that personal economic distress tended to either be inconsequential or actually *diminish* the impact of authoritarianism on intolerance, perhaps by distracting authoritarians from their problematic concern with the fate of the collective, thereby "improving" their behavior.

Fortunately, the EuroPulse survey measured the standard array of economic evaluations, including four items asking for retrospective and prospective evaluations of both the national economy and one's own household finances, as follows:

> Retrospective evaluation–national economy: "How
>   do you think the general economic situation
>   in [the United States / the United Kingdom /
>   France] has changed over the past 12 months?
>   (It has . . . got a lot better, got a little better,
>   stayed the same, got a little worse, got a lot
>   worse, I don't know)."
> Prospective evaluation–national economy: "How do
>   you expect the general economic situation in [the
>   United States / the United Kingdom / France] to
>   change over the next 12 months? (It will . . . get
>   a lot better, get a little better, stay the same, get a
>   little worse, get a lot worse, don't know)."
> Retrospective evaluation–household finances:
>   "Compared to 12 months ago, your household
>   financial situation is . . . (a lot better, a little
>   better, the same, a little worse, a lot worse, don't
>   know)."
> Prospective evaluation–household finances: "How
>   do you expect the financial position of your

household to change over the next 12 months?
It will . . . (get a lot better, get a little better, stay
the same, get a little worse, get a lot worse, don't
know)."

As noted, these discrete evaluations (whose pairwise correlations here ranged from .20 to .54) have typically been found to exert varying influence on intolerant and populist sentiment, and were thus left as separate variables in our model.

MODELS AND METHODS

We employed logistic regression to analyze each of our dichotomous measures of populist voting as a function of the authoritarian dynamic—the interaction of authoritarian predisposition with our overall measure of normative threat.

Note that each of these models also originally included as controls the four discrete items reflecting economic evaluations, as well as the interactions of those evaluations with authoritarianism. With sample size trimmed by the elimination of non-whites and non-voters, it was important not to overload the models, particularly in view of their estimation via logistic regression. Thus, if any of these evaluations or their interactions proved statistically insignificant, they were removed from the model in question. The full models and raw results (logit coefficients) from which the findings presented here in the text are derived are reported in Appendix F, Table 1, at www.KarenStenner.com under "Repository" (including results for the economic control variables). The conditional coefficients (marginal effects) calculated from those raw results are also reported there in Appendix F, Table 2.

Here in the text itself, we present succinctly in Table 1 (below) only our core findings regarding the impact of the authoritarian dynamic, as conveyed via changes in the predicted probability of voting for populist candidates and causes, given different predispositions to authoritarianism, and varying conditions of normative threat.

**TABLE 1. PROBABILITY OF VOTING
FOR POPULIST CANDIDATES AND CAUSES:**
Trump, Brexit and Le Pen (2016–2017)

		Pr(Voting for Trump)	Pr(Voting for Brexit)	Pr(Voting for Le Pen)
Effects of independent variables (X):	Under interaction conditions:	Increasing X changes Pr(Y) from:		
Authoritarianism	*if high normative threat*	.07 → .87*	.30 → .93*	.11 → .84*
	if mid normative threat	.21 → .63*	.38 → .68*	.07 → .31*
	if low normative threat	.48 → .31	.47 → .27	.05 → .04
Normative Threat	*if authoritarian predisposition*	.31 → .87*	.27 → .93*	.04 → .84*
	if balanced predisposition	.39 → .41	.36 → .70*	.04 → .44*
	if non-authoritarian predisposition	.48 → .07*	.47 → .30	.05 → .11

*Note: Predictions derived from logistic regression analyses in Appendix F, Table 1 at www.KarenStenner.com under "Repository"; * significant at p < 05.*

Before turning our focus to the authoritarian dynamic, we note first that authoritarianism did indeed prove to be the main "background" determinant of populist voting across all three countries in our investigation. That is to say, there was no socio-demographic variable whose impact on populist voting exceeded that of our basic "child-rearing values" measure of authoritarianism: not education, income, religion, gender, age, or urban/rural residence. We found that the impact of authoritarianism was substantial even under ordinary conditions—among those not feeling particularly threatened (or reassured)—increasing the probability of a populist vote by about .42, .30, and .24 in the US, UK, and France, respectively (see Appendix F, Table 2, upper panel).

Put more simply, even given middling perceptions of normative threat in their polity, Americans ranged from about a .21 to a .63 probability of voting for Trump as authoritarianism went from its lowest to its highest levels (see Table 1, page 197). Similarly, highly authoritarian Britons had about a 68 percent likelihood, and their non-authoritarian peers about a 38 percent chance, of voting to leave the European Union when perceptions of normative threat were unremarkable. And under those same conditions, about 31 percent of highly authoritarian French voters would likely opt for Le Pen, compared to only about 7 percent of their non-authoritarian compatriots.

A NOTE ON INTERPRETATION OF RESULTS

Note that all the statements directly above simply represent alternative ways of describing the results presented in the upper panel of Table 1 (page 197), across the row labeled "if mid normative threat." This seems the appropriate place to pause and ensure we have clarity first on some important issues of methodology and terminology. For us, the "impact" of any independent variable (e.g., authoritarianism) is the difference in expected outcomes (e.g., in the likelihood of voting for Trump) between those scoring at the extremes (highly authoritarian versus non-authoritarian) of that explanatory variable. Technically, it is the change predicted in the dependent variable for a one-unit increase in the independent variable, e.g., the change in the probability of populist voting in response to a one-unit increase in authoritarianism. Recall we scored all our variables such that a "one-unit increase" always entails moving across the full range (from lower to upper bound) of the explanatory variable, e.g., it is the difference between the very non-authoritarian and the highly authoritarian. The change that such an increase induces in the likelihood of populist voting is, in our terminology, the "impact" of that explanatory variable.

Crucially, we expect that this impact will vary under different conditions, e.g., given conditions of normative threat or reassurance. This varying impact is reflected by the varying magnitude and direction of the conditional coefficients we report in Appendix F, Table 2, and likewise by the steepness and direction of the slopes in the associated Figures 2 and 3 (below). The reader can refer to Appendix F, Table 1 for the full results from which these conditional coefficients and slopes were derived.

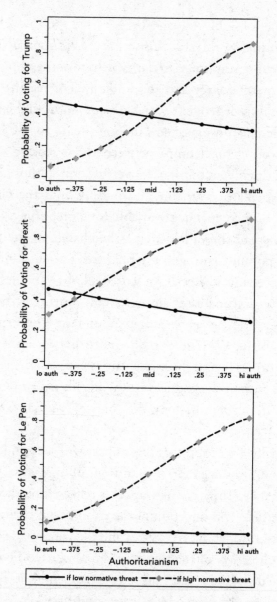

FIGURE 2: Impact of authoritarianism on voting for populist candidates and causes, for those who perceive low versus high normative threat.

RESULTS

IMPACT OF AUTHORITARIANISM ON POPULISM, GIVEN VARYING NORMATIVE THREAT

Figure 2 (opposite) depicts the impact upon voting for populist candidates and causes of moving across the full range of the authoritarianism measure (from very non-authoritarian up to highly authoritarian) as the variable with which it interacts—normative threat—is held, in turn, at very high and low levels. These different slopes graphically reflect what we have called the authoritarian dynamic: they represent the varying effects of authoritarianism under conditions of normative threat and reassurance.

The three constituent panels of Figure 2 reflect the probability of voting for Trump, Brexit, and Le Pen, respectively. All these *authoritarianism x normative threat* interactions proved to be very substantial and highly significant (see Appendix F, Table 1). As anticipated, the impact of authoritarianism was greatly magnified (steepened) under conditions of normative threat. For example (see Figure 2, upper panel), we found that authoritarianism increased the probability of voting for Trump by about .80 under conditions of high normative threat, with the likelihood of a Trump vote ranging from only about 7 percent (for non-authoritarians) to about 87 percent (for authoritarians) among disillusioned respondents who saw their government as controlled by rich elites and their country headed in the "wrong direction." Note that the steepness of these slopes and their end points (both specified above) align, respectively, with the marginal effects reported in Appendix F,

Table 2, and with the marginal probabilities presented here in Table 1 (page 197).

Much the same pattern was evident for the UK (see Figure 2, middle panel), where we found that authoritarianism increased the probability of voting to leave the European Union by about .64 given conditions of high normative threat, with the likelihood of favoring Brexit ranging from about 30 percent (for non-authoritarians) to about 93 percent (for authoritarians) when leaders, governments, and democracy itself were all found sorely wanting (see Table 1, page 197). Likewise regarding the electoral appeal of the National Front in France (see Figure 2, lower panel). Here we found that authoritarianism increased the probability of voting for Le Pen by about .75 given high normative threat, with the likelihood of a vote for the National Front ranging from about 11 percent (among non-authoritarians) to about 84 percent (among authoritarians) given wholesale loss of confidence in democratic government and leadership (see Table 1, page 197).

Notice that throughout Figure 2, this impressive impact of authoritarianism is effectively flattened to virtually nothing under conditions of great normative reassurance, i.e., when people are sure their country is headed in the right direction and feel confident in the workings of democracy, positive about the government, and unconcerned about elite machinations. Although the marginal effects are not statistically significant in the case of reassurance, we see at least a hint in these pictures that under these reassuring societal conditions, authoritarians might even be repelled by populist movements, seemingly lending more of their support to mainstream parties and leaders when the normative order seems intact and functional, and worthy of their allegiance.

Keep in mind it is *not* that people become less authoritarian under these conditions, only that their authoritarianism produces less manifest intolerance. Their inherent predispositions remain intact but latent, awaiting only the sounding of the next societal alarm—about immigrant hordes, moral decay, political disarray—to kick back into action and haul out the defensive arsenal.

IMPACT OF NORMATIVE THREAT ON POPULISM, GIVEN VARYING AUTHORITARIANISM

Some of this becomes clearer still when viewed from a different angle. Figure 3 (page 204) simply takes that same *authoritarianism x normative threat* interaction and depicts it from the other side, this time showing how the impact upon populism of normative threat (of moving from the lower bound of the scale, reflecting great reassurance, up to the upper bound, indicating extreme threat) depends on the predispositions of the perceiver: whether authoritarian or non-authoritarian.

When considered from this alternative perspective, the potential political power of the authoritarian dynamic is readily apparent. In the lower panel of Table 1 (page 197), we see that increasing feelings of normative threat intensified attraction to populism even among those of "balanced" disposition (at least outside the US), who were driven a considerable way toward voting for Brexit and nearly halfway

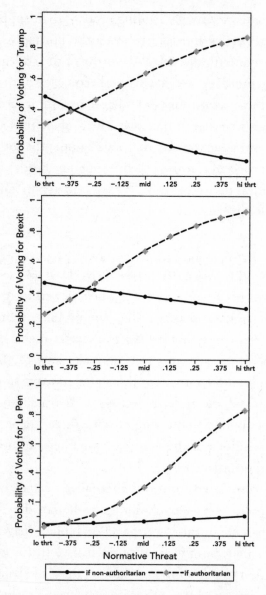

FIGURE 3. Impact of normative threat on voting for populist candidates and causes, for those who are low versus high in authoritarianism.

to accepting the National Front as feelings of normative threat soared. But this impact of normative threat on populist voting was basically *doubled* for those of authoritarian disposition. As anticipated, it was authoritarians—heavily invested in the normative order that fills their world with oneness and sameness—who were by far the most reactive to normative threat (see Figure 3). For example, we calculated that rising normative threat increased authoritarians' probability of voting for Trump by about .58 (see Appendix F, Table 2), boosting their likelihood of a Trump vote from about 31 percent, among those feeling reassured about the polity, up to about 87 percent, for those convinced their world was coming apart (see Table 1, page 197).

We detected the same forces at work in the UK sample (see Figure 3, middle panel), where we found that mounting threats to the normative order drove authoritarians toward leaving the European Union, boosting their likelihood of favoring Brexit from about 27 percent, when feeling roundly reassured, up to about 93 percent, once highly threatened (see Table 1, page 197). An even starker picture was painted for France (see Figure 3, lower panel). Here we saw the accumulation of normative threat increase authoritarians' probability of voting for the National Front by about .80, lifting their prospects of tapping Le Pen for the presidency from as little as 4 percent, given constant reassurance, to as much as 84 percent, in the face of intense normative threat (see Table 1, page 197).

Finally, our evaluation of the evidence is not complete until we consider how normative threat affects those at the lower bound of the authoritarian spectrum. Across two decades of empirical research, we cannot think of a significant exception to the finding that normative threat tends either to leave non-authoritarians utterly unmoved by the things that catalyze authoritarians or to propel them toward being (what one might conceive as) their "best selves." In previous investigations, this has seen non-authoritarians move toward positions of greater tolerance and respect for diversity under the very conditions that seem to propel authoritarians toward increasing intolerance. In a nutshell, authoritarians act more like authoritarians, and non-authoritarians more like their antithesis, under these conditions. As authoritarians move to shore up their defense of oneness and sameness, non-authoritarians may redouble their own efforts on behalf of the "open society." Based now on this latest evidence, it seems that non-authoritarians' "activation"—in defense of freedom and diversity over obedience and conformity—includes rejection of populist candidates and causes that fail to share this vision of the good life.

Certainly this appears to hold at least for non-authoritarians in the contemporary United States: see Figure 3, upper panel, for a stark depiction of this "classic" polarization under conditions of normative threat. It is sobering indeed to ponder the self-fueling properties of this dynamic—where perceptions of normative threat produce increasing polarization that in turn further exacerbates normative threat—which is surely implicated in our debilitating contemporary "culture wars" (see also Hetherington and Weiler, 2009).

ECONOMIC FACTORS WEAK AND INCONSISTENT

The one empirical task that remains is to compare the impact of the authoritarian dynamic on support for populist candidates and causes with that of economic "distress," variously conceived. As noted at the outset, the notion that populist attitudes and behaviors are driven, in some way, by economic distress is one of the most common accounts offered for the current "wave" of populism in the wake of the GFC, the decline of manufacturing, and the inevitable dislocations of globalism. It is a highly "rational" account of the populist phenomenon, with economics and materialism at its core, and analysts offering these kinds of accounts sometimes go to considerable lengths even to reframe manifestly nonmaterial explanations in materialistic terms. For example, there is the argument that anti-immigrant sentiment is not really (or only) about immigration, but instead (or additionally) a means of expressing economic fears and displacing them onto the immigrants (refugees, minorities, guest workers, terrorists-in-the-making) who are purportedly stealing the natives' jobs and draining communal resources that ought to be reserved for the locals.

Our own investigation finds the evidence in support of the notion that populism is mostly fueled by economic distress to be weak and inconsistent, however that distress is conceptualized. Preliminary analyses confirmed that the four economic evaluations available in the EuroPulse data (retrospective and prospective evaluations of the national economy and household finances) represented distinct sentiments, and ought to be entered separately in our model.

In terms of both the magnitude and direction of their effects, these four variables exerted widely varying influence on populism (in contrast to the various components of normative threat), as a review of the economic results in Appendix F will confirm. This persisted even without controlling for authoritarianism and normative threat, and regardless of whether the model included interactions between authoritarianism and the various economic components.

We found that the effects of these economic evaluations were either weak and inconsistent or, sometimes, large and counterintuitive. Evaluations of household finances seemed mostly inconsequential as predictors of populist voting (which accords with the generally modest effects discerned for income). Perceptions of (past) national economic decline had some mixed effects (including, in the case of France, in interaction with authoritarianism), but certainly seemed to propel some voters toward Trump. Yet even that finding sits side by side with a seemingly counterintuitive result, with positive evaluations of the economic *future* apparently associated with support for both Trump and Brexit (see Appendix F). Of course, the direction of causality remains unclear. Given that these hopeful sentiments were measured *after* the vote in each case, it is quite possible that having voted for Trump/Brexit, these voters consequently felt more optimistic about the future. It is plausible that a vote for Trump may have reflected in some part dissatisfaction with past economic progress *together with* hope for a future economic turnaround. If so, this would make America's choice of a billionaire businessman for president an expression not just of unleavened economic fear and disappointment but also at least a touch of economic hope and optimism for the future.

In any case, what we found is that there is no real pattern to be discerned in regard to economic influences across either the different economic components or the different polities. This would accord with the inconsistent findings typically reported by others, and with the general state of uncertainty regarding whether we are truly confronting a "wave" of populism (and whether it is surging or has stopped), and also with the continuing disagreement over the direction of causality between anti-immigrant sentiment and professions of economic distress. We refer here to the dispute over whether our "populists" are typically starting with (real or imagined) perceptions of financial/economic threat and projecting that onto easy targets like immigrants, or whether they are starting with their opposition to immigration and—due to the constraints of political correctness—merely expressing that as economic distress (viz., "the immigrants are stealing our jobs"). We think the totality of evidence tends to favor the latter, a theme we will return to below.

DISCUSSION: IMPLICATIONS FOR LIBERAL DEMOCRACIES

DEMOCRACY DOES NOT BREED DEMOCRATS

Trump ascended to the American presidency, Britain exited Europe, and the French flirted with the National Front because Western liberal democracies have now exceeded many people's capacity to tolerate them—to live with them, and in them. This is hard to accept until one comes to terms with two critical realities. First, people are not empty vessels waiting to be filled with appreciation and enthusiasm for democratic processes. It is perhaps ironic that tolerance of difference is now threatened by liberal democrats' refusal to recognize that many of their fellow citizens are . . . different. We all come into the world with distinct personalities, which is to say, predisposed to want, need, and fear different things, including particular social arrangements. Presumably, societies with a diverse mix of complementary characters tended to survive and adapt to changing environments in human evolution. Notwithstanding some ancient migration bottlenecks, these different personalities—authoritarian and libertarian, open and closed, risk-seeking and risk-averse, to name but a few—have over time distributed themselves all around the world. This means there are plenty of would-be liberal democrats languishing in autocracies, and many authoritarians struggling along under "vibrant" liberal democracies.

Second, there is remarkably little evidence that living in a liberal democracy generally makes people more democratic and tolerant. This means that most societies—including those "blessed" with democracies—will *persistently* harbor a certain proportion of residents (by our calculations, roughly a third) who will always find diversity difficult to tolerate. That predisposition, and those limitations, may be largely immovable. And this is the most important implication: if we are right about normative threat serving as a critical catalyst for these characters, then the things that multiculturalists believe will help people appreciate and thrive in democracy—

experiencing difference, talking about difference, displaying and applauding difference—are the very conditions that encourage authoritarians not to the heights of tolerance, but to their intolerant extremes. Democracy in general, and tolerance in particular, might actually be better served by an abundance of common and unifying rituals, institutions, and processes.

IS ANYBODY LISTENING?

Democratic enthusiasts and multiculturalists sometimes make the mistake of thinking we are at an enlightened point in human history (Fukuyama 1992) when all these different personalities—daily experiencing the joys of increasing liberty and democracy—are evolving in a fairly predictable and linear fashion into more perfect democratic citizens. This is why the populist "wave" strikes many observers as a momentary madness that "comes out of the blue," and why the sentiments that seem to fuel these movements are often considered merely the products of frustration, hatred, and manipulation by irresponsible populist leaders—certainly not serious, legitimate preferences that a democracy must attend to.

When authoritarians raise concerns about, say, the rates or sources of immigration, they are not actually saying, "I'm scared I might lose my job," but in fact, "This is making me very uncomfortable and I don't like where our country is headed." Moreover, "Nobody will let me say so, and only [this Trump-like figure] is listening to me." Our sense is that if Trump had not come along, a Trump-like figure would have materialized eventually. It may be the case that many Republicans would have voted for anyone marketed under the Republican brand. And Hillary Clinton may well have won if FBI director James Comey had not made his ill-timed announcement. And it seems likely that Russian interference tilted the outcome. But one must still explain why a Trump-like figure was even within reach of the presidency, *and* why Trump-like figures are popping up all over, *and* why the outrageous statements that critics thought would surely destroy their candidacies seem to be the very things that most thrill their supporters and solidify their bases.

Trump publicly inviting Russia to hack into Clinton's private emails was shocking to many from a number of perspectives, but perhaps the most prominent was the lack of horror expressed by many of his supporters at what might conceivably be characterized as treason. When being interviewed about his foreign policy, Trump assured us that he himself would happily "take out the families" of suspected ISIS terrorists: essentially, making a public declaration of his willingness to commit war crimes. Far from provoking horror, Trump's many astonishing statements—all indelibly infused with classic authoritarian sentiments and stances—were greeted with a kind of exhilaration by his supporters. It became clear that a large portion of the American people felt the nation's political leaders had not just failed them but actually did not represent them. Here "represent" goes well beyond mere political representation to something more primitive, like "belonging." In essence: "You are not us." In this state of mind, it no longer seemed beyond the pale to publicly invite a dangerous and long-standing adversary to spy on the country's leaders, or extol the effectiveness of war crimes for nipping terrorism in the bud. The gleeful reactions of Trump's supporters to his "strongman" posturing attested to their anger and bitterness regarding the "political correctness" of the "liberal elite," and the pleasure they seemed to derive from watching someone who sounds like "us" finally sticking it to "them."

IMMIGRATION POLICY AND DEMOCRATIC DISCOURSE

Clearly, immigration policy is the flashpoint for populism and offers a critical starting point for any new efforts at civil peace. If citizens say they're concerned about the rate of immigration, we ought to at least consider the possibility that they're concerned about the rate of immigration, and not merely masking a hateful racism or displacing their economic woes onto easy scapegoats. Common sense and historical experience tell us that there is some rate of newcomers into any community that is too high to be sustainable—that can overwhelm or even damage the host and make things worse for both old and new members. It is also common sense that some newcomers are more difficult to integrate than others—especially when there are clashing values and lifestyles. Some might, accordingly, need to be more carefully selected, or more heavily supported and resourced to encourage and aid their assimilation. All these things must be considered when formulating a successful immigration policy (Haidt 2016). Ignoring these issues is not helpful to either the hosts or the

CAN IT HAPPEN HERE?

newcomers. It is implausible to maintain that the host community can successfully integrate any kind of newcomer at any rate whatsoever, and it is unreasonable to assert that any other suggestion is racist.

As noted, we already have some idea of what the requirements for social cohesion are in many other contexts. There are surely types and degrees of affinity between host and newcomers, rates of entry, and methods of supporting their assimilation and inclusion that facilitate successful integration into the community. Frank consideration of these matters is the key to broad acceptance of immigration policy and vital to the continued health of our liberal democracies. For all the reasons we have canvassed, these things are not currently known, but are knowable. It is essential for free societies to discuss these issues openly, and a matter of great urgency that we empirically investigate these parameters and settle the matter with hard evidence. Most obviously, if we were able to discuss these kinds of questions openly, they could simply be incorporated into mainstream political debates and effectively managed by normal political processes, cutting much of the fuel for intolerant social movements. Another important benefit of better immigration policies is that the resulting improvements in social inclusion and cohesion are likely to reduce the prospects of radicalization and terrorism, since these phenomena may be driven, in large part, by the dis-integration of perpetrators from their families and communities.

DEMOCRACY'S CORE DILEMMA,
AND A CRITICAL CROSSROADS

Although we have paid great attention here to the role played by normative threat in the populist phenomenon, one critical thing to note about authoritarians is that they are *not* especially inclined to perceive normative (or indeed, any other kind of) threat—they are just especially reactive when they do. If anything, authoritarians, by their very nature, want to believe in authorities and institutions; they want to feel they are part of a cohesive community. Accordingly, they seem (if anything) to be modestly inclined toward giving authorities and institutions the benefit of the doubt, and lending them their support until the moment these seem incapable of maintaining "normative order." As our observation of the mechanics of the authoritarian dynamic made clear, authoritarians are highly reactive *and* highly malleable. Depending on their assessment of shifting environmental conditions, they can be moved from indifference, even positions of modest tolerance, to aggressive demands to "crack down" on immigrants, minorities, "deviants," and dissidents, employing the full force of state authority. This is to say, the current state we find ourselves in can easily be made much worse, or much better, by how we come together and respond to this now in terms of attending to people's needs for oneness and sameness; for identity, cohesion, and belonging; for pride and honor; and for institutions and leaders they can respect. This should take the place of demeaning and ridiculing authoritarians, ignoring their needs and preferences (which is an undemocratic way for a democracy to treat a third of its citizens), and simply waiting for them to "come back to their senses." It is condescending to say that no sane, reasonable person could want the things they want, therefore they must be unhinged or else are being manipulated.

But this is no momentary madness. It is a perpetual feature of human societies: a latent pool of need that lurks just beneath the surface and seems to be activated most certainly by things that constitute the very essence of liberal democracy—things such as

> ... the experience or perception of disobedience to group authorities or authorities unworthy of respect, nonconformity to group norms or norms proving questionable, lack of consensus in group values and beliefs, and, in general, diversity and freedom "run amok" ... (Stenner 2005: 17).

Liberal democracy has now exceeded many people's capacity to tolerate it. And absent proper understanding of the origins and dynamics of this populist moment, well-meaning citizens, political parties, and governments are likely to respond to these movements in ways that serve only to exacerbate their negative features and entirely miss their possibilities. The same warning goes out to all of Western Europe and the English-speaking world post-Brexit. Worst of all, we might miss the real opportunities for a thoughtful, other-regarding reconciliation of two critical parts of our human nature: the desire to liberate and enable the individual, and the impetus to protect and serve the collective.

We have shown that the far-right populist wave that seemed to "come out of nowhere" did not in fact come out of nowhere. It is not a sudden madness, or virus, or tide, or even just a copycat phenomenon—the emboldening of bigots and despots by others' electoral successes. Rather, it is something that sits just beneath the surface of any human society—including in the advanced liberal democracies at the heart of the Western world—and *can be activated by core elements of liberal democracy itself.*

Liberal democracy can become its own undoing because its core elements activate forces that undermine it *and* its best features constrain it from vigorously protecting itself. So it seems we are not at the "end of history" (Fukuyama 1992). The "last man" is not a perfected liberal democrat. Liberal democracy may not be the "final form of human government." And intolerance is not a thing of the past; it is very much a thing of the present, and of the future.

REFERENCES

Adorno, Theodor, Else Frenkel-Brunswik, and D. J. Levinson. 1950. *The Authoritarian Personality.* New York: Harper and Row.

Albertazzi, Daniele, and Duncan McDonnell. 2008. *Twenty-First Century Populism. The Spectre of Western European Democracy.* United Kingdom: Palgrave Macmillan.

Duckitt, John. 1989. "Authoritarianism and Group Identification: A New View of an Old Construct." *Political Psychology*, 10(1): 63–84.

Fukuyama, Francis. 1992. *The End of History and the Last Man.* New York: Free Press.

Haidt, Jonathan. 2012. *The Righteous Mind: Why Good People Are Divided by Politics and Religion*. New York: Pantheon Books.

———. 2016. "When and Why Nationalism Beats Globalism." *The American Interest*, 12:1, July 10.

Hetherington, Marc J., and Jonathan D. Weiler. 2009. *Authoritarianism and Polarization in American Politics*. New York: Cambridge University Press.

Inglehart, Ronald, and Pippa Norris. 2016. "Trump, Brexit, and the Rise of Populism: Economic Have-Nots and Cultural Backlash." *HKS Working Paper No. RWP16–026*.

Karp, Jeffrey A., and David Brockington. 2005. "Social Desirability and Response Validity: A Comparative Analysis of Overreporting Voter Turnout in Five Countries." *Journal of Politics*, 67(3): 825–40.

Kaufmann, Eric. 2016. "Brexit Voters: NOT the Left Behind." *Fabian Review*, June 24.

Ludeke, Steven, Wendy Johnson, and Thomas J. Bouchard, Jr. 2013. "Obedience to traditional authority": A heritable factor underlying authoritarianism, conservatism and religiousness. *Personality and Individual Differences*, 55(4): 375–80.

McCourt, K., Bouchard, T. J., Jr., Lykken, D. T., Tellegen, A., and Keyes, M. 1999. "Authoritarianism revisited: Genetic and environmental influence examined in twins reared apart and together." *Personality and Individual Differences*, 27: 985–1014.

Mudde, C. 2004. The Populist Zeitgeist. *Government and Opposition*, 39: 541–63.

Mudde, C., and C. R. Kaltwasser. 2017. *Populism: A Very Short Introduction*. New York: Oxford University Press.

Stenner, Karen. 2005. *The Authoritarian Dynamic*. New York: Cambridge University Press.

———. "Three Kinds of 'Conservatism.'" *Psychological Inquiry* 20, no. 2/3 (April–September 2009a): 142–59.

———. "'Conservatism,' Context-Dependence, and Cognitive Incapacity." *Psychological Inquiry* 20, no. 2/3 (April–September 2009b): 189–95.

NOTES

1. This section draws on arguments and evidence first presented in Stenner (2005, 2009a, 2009b). The reader is referred to the originals for further details and discussion.

2. In terms of collection methodology, Dalia's platform approaches millions of potential respondents through a network of over 40,000 apps and websites, whose users are anonymously profiled across key demographic attributes and selected according to census statistics. Data are collected online via desktop, laptop, tablet, and smartphone, and then weighted according to population structures and census statistics to obtain a representative sample.

3. Ultimately, just 55 percent of eligible Americans actually voted in the 2016 presidential election (compared to the 68 percent of our US sample who reportedly turned out), with 46 percent of those voting for Trump (compared to 44 percent in our sample). In Britain, 72 percent of those registered turned out to vote in the referendum, which exactly matches our British sample's self-reported turnout. But as noted, our sample seems to underrepresent the "exit" vote, with 52 percent voting to leave the European Union in reality, compared to 43 percent in our sample. Our figures do closely align in the French case, where 78 percent of those who were eligible voted in the first round of the recent presidential election (compared to the 80 percent of our French sample who said they intended to vote). And 21 percent ultimately opted for Le Pen in that first round (compared to the 22 percent of our sample who said they intended to do so).

4. Note that this is simply an unobtrusive means of measuring values; it need not reflect either how respondents were raised or how they are raising their own children.

5. We stress that the people we classified as being of authoritarian predisposition did not always describe themselves as right of center. In fact, when required to "describe [their] political views on a left-right scale," 42 percent of these authoritarians chose one of the "left-wing" options, while 58 percent chose one of the right-wing options. Among those we classified as non-authoritarian, 55 percent placed themselves left of center and 45 percent placed themselves right of center.

STATES OF EMERGENCY
BRUCE ACKERMAN

There is something about the presidency that loves war talk. Even at its most metaphorical, martial rhetoric allows the president to invoke his special mystique as commander in chief, calling the public to sacrifice greatly for the good of the nation. Perhaps the clarion call to pseudo-war is just the thing the president needs to ram an initiative through a reluctant Congress. Perhaps it provides rhetorical cover for transforming the courts into rubber stamps. Or perhaps it serves as a grand occasion for ego gratification.

Or all of the above. We are not dealing with a constitutional novelty. Almost two centuries ago, Andrew Jackson was famously making war on the Bank of the United States, indulging in legally problematic uses of executive power to withdraw federal deposits from The Enemy, headed by the evil one, Nicholas Biddle.

To be sure, the "war on terrorism" isn't as much of a stretch, say, as the "war on poverty" or the "war on drugs."

Classical wars traditionally involve sovereign states attacking one another's territorial integrity, and it may seem a small matter to expand the paradigm to cover non-state actors engaging in similar assaults: is there really such a big difference between December 7th and September 11th?

The panic-driven responses of the Bush and Obama administrations only begin to suggest the dangers of equating the two events. The torture chambers at Guantánamo and elsewhere have largely been reserved for foreigners. Yet the presidential embrace of war talk could have also legitimated the sweeping detention, torture, and summary execution of countless Americans on the massive "watch lists" compiled by the security services. This danger is not merely hypothetical—there have been notorious cases involving citizens and legal residents. Nevertheless, their actual number has been relatively small.

I hardly wish to minimize the terrible crimes against humanity committed by the American government over the past fifteen years. Worse yet, its utter failure to make a serious effort to hold the responsible officials accountable only serves to compound our national disgrace. Nevertheless, we should recognize that this dark chapter in American history has not yet led to an all-out presidential assault on liberal democratic life in the United States itself.

There may be worse yet to come. Recent terrorist incidents have not involved the deaths of thousands, as at the Pentagon and Twin Towers, or even hundreds, as at the Oklahoma City Federal Building. They have involved small numbers of deaths inflicted by a small number of attackers—whose weapons are primitive, but who often demonstrate their media savvy by choosing symbolically central locations for their assaults. These incidents have sufficed, however, to catalyze draconian revisions in antiterrorist legislation in both Britain and France, as well as increasingly tough talk by Europe's sensible centrist politicians. What to expect, then, of Donald Trump on the terrible day when Americans learn that five or ten or twenty thousand have been slaughtered in some new disaster?

Make no mistake: we live in an age in which smaller and smaller numbers of terrorists can buy more and more destructive weapons at lower and lower prices. The state is losing its monopoly on mass destruction, and it will be impossible to preempt all future attacks. This is not, I should emphasize, a problem that has anything in particular to do with the threat posed by ISIS or its counterparts. There are 330 million people living in America, and it takes only a few hundred extremists with a few million dollars to obtain weapons that could devastate a major American city. The question is not whether our security services will preempt some of these attacks—they will. It is whether they will prevent all of them—they won't.

We may be lucky. When the tragedy occurs, the sitting president may turn out to be a sober defender of our democratic traditions. But as *The Federalist Papers* remind us, "[e]nlightened statesmen will not always be at the helm," and we would be wise to seize the moment and consider how we might create a new statutory framework to control a full-scale presidential assault on our liberal democratic tradition.

From this perspective, the transparent demagogy of President Trump may well represent the last realistic political opportunity to take this question seriously. Within a few short months, Trump's terrorist-tweeting has already generated a bipartisan congressional initiative by Senators Jeff Flake and Tim Kaine to frame a new Authorization for Use of Military Force that would allow the House and Senate to reassert their constitutional authority over unilateral presidential war-making abroad. While this is important, it is no less important to frame an appropriate congressional response to the prospect of the abuse of presidential powers at home.

It would be a mistake for Congress to rely on the Supreme Court to do the job for it. Suppose President Trump responds to a massive attack with a massive roundup of domestic terrorists. It would probably take a year or so before a legal challenge would reach the Supreme Court. Based on the Justices' performance since September 11, it isn't at all clear how they would respond: while a majority has sometimes upheld basic principles of due process in dealing with terrorism, they have failed to fashion effective modes of relief for obvious victims of injustice. Worse yet, they have never formally overruled their infamous World War II decisions—*Korematsu* only one of several—upholding the long-term detention of Japanese-Americans by the commander in chief. Unless they do so, it will be tough to forge effective constraints on the president's power to make war on his fellow citizens. Despite these caveats, it is too soon to dismiss the Court as a paper tiger. Depending on the course of future appointments, the majority may well emerge as a significant force at its moment of truth.

But I wouldn't count on it. Paradoxically, Trump's huffing and puffing, together with his demagogic behavior, may jolt serious Democrats and Republicans in Congress to take seriously the prospect of a draconian response to the next major attack—and seize the moment to consider a new statutory framework that would increase the chance of preserving our democracy before it is too late. The new initiative should explicitly reject the claim, made most explicitly by Jay Bybee and John Yoo for the Bush administration, that the commander in chief has the unilateral power to make never-ending war on the home front. It should instead create a new system of checks and balances based on a different, and commonsense, notion: that a major terrorist attack will predictably create a "state of emergency," warranting extraordinary measures over the short term—so long as decisive steps are taken to guarantee that they won't endure beyond the period of their obvious necessity.

These basic principles are already a familiar part of the legal terrain. The newscasts constantly report declarations of emergency by governors responding to natural disasters—and though this is less familiar to ordinary citizens, presidents regularly declare emergencies in response to foreign threats. The challenge is to adapt these principles to deal with the distinctive features of the problem raised by the increasing ease with which relatively small terrorist networks can obtain weapons of mass destruction.

First and foremost, the new framework should impose

strict limits on unilateral presidential power. While President Trump has forsworn daily briefings, he will undoubtedly hear his national security advisor let him know of the latest looming threats by terrorist networks lurking somewhere in this great land of ours. These threats should never be enough for him to trigger a state of emergency. Instead, only an actual attack on the scale of September 11 creates the distinctive "second-strike problem" that justifies extraordinary action.

The problem is simply this: On the one hand, the major attack has taken the security services by surprise—otherwise, they would have seized the key actors in the terrorist network. On the other hand, the fact that the terrorists have managed to pull off a major attack vastly increases the risk that they are in a position to follow up with a second attack unless decisive steps are taken immediately to preempt the threat. Putting both hands together, the emergency rationale goes like this: Given the ignorance of the security forces, the only way to minimize the chances of a second strike is to detain terrorist suspects on the basis of reasonable suspicion, rather than the higher standards required for criminal prosecution. If they must convince judges that they have probable cause to target particular terrorists, this will give the network enough time to strike again and escalate the panic further—eroding public confidence that the crisis will ever end.

The commonsense case for a state of emergency is, then, compelling. But it comes with a commonsense caveat: there is every reason to expect that the security agencies will systematically abuse the extraordinary powers they have been granted. Since they are unable to pinpoint the key actors in the terrorist network, they will be obliged to rely on "watch lists" they have prepared before the event, which identify tens of thousands of Americans who have been identified as potentially involved in problematic activities. As a consequence, the only way they can disrupt the terrorist network in the short term is to use these watch lists as the basis for massive detentions. Yet while such a step might—or might not—be effective, only one thing is clear. Most of the prisoners behind bars will be entirely innocent.

Given these obvious risks, Trump should be authorized to act unilaterally only for the time it takes for Congress to consider whether a "state of emergency" is truly justified—say, a week or two. Unless the president can persuade a majority of both chambers to approve his initial declaration, the state of emergency should immediately lapse. Even if they do approve, this vote should be valid for only two months—and the matter should then return to Congress to determine whether conditions have sufficiently returned to normal to require the security services to establish that they have "probable cause" for each and every one of their arrests. On this second round of reappraisal, moreover, it shouldn't be enough for a simple majority to go along with Trump's demands for further antiterrorist sweeps. The president must persuade a supermajority of 60 percent of both chambers that extraordinary measures are justified. This supermajoritarian threshold should continue to increase with further presidential requests. When Trump returns after two more months, he must gain a 70 percent majority; and he will confront an 80 percent threshold every time he returns for a further renewal.

This "supermajoritarian escalator" puts the ongoing exercise of emergency power in control of the minority party in Congress—precisely the group that will be especially alive to the danger that Trump will use his extraordinary powers to further his political ambitions. Especially as election day approaches, they will be especially skeptical of presidential requests for renewal—unless, of course, the terrorist network is continuing to wreak havoc. Rather than depending on judges as the principal check on the abuse of presidential power, the new statute should rely on the political branches to play a central role in creating a democratic system of checks and balances.

Yet courts will also have critical oversight functions to play. As we have seen, the emergency statute should authorize short-term detention on reasonable suspicion, without insisting on probable cause. But given the probable innocence of most of those swept into prison, this is only acceptable on a short-term basis. Once a suspect has been held, say, for forty-five days, the government can continue his confinement only by presenting evidence in court of a kind generally required for this purpose. Moreover, even at the beginning of the emergency forty-five-day period, the security services must inform the court of the reasons why their targets have acted suspiciously, detailing the data provided in their "watch lists" with appropriate provisions for confidentiality. It should never be enough simply to lock a person up on the arbitrary hunch by somebody-or-other in the security hierarchy. Similarly, the statute should provide for an independent civilian authority, supervised by the courts, to prevent torture and other inhumane techniques at detention centers.

But it is not enough to rely on proactive measures by judges and civilian watchdogs during the emergency. The statute should also grant financial compensation to everybody whose fundamental rights have been abused by the emergency sweeps. This includes, most obviously, detainees who have been thrown into jail on the basis of an arbitrary hunch. It should include also the mass of individuals whose names have appeared on "watch lists" but who are never charged with a crime in connection with the attack. They have not only sacrificed their personal liberty for the public good. While trapped in overcrowded cells, they may well have lost their jobs and generated traumatic anxiety among their families and friends. This is fundamentally wrong. The statute should instead provide all innocent victims of the emergency a weekly payment of $3,000—three times the median weekly income for an American family. This award will not only respond to their material losses; it will also help them deal with the stigma that will otherwise be associated with the fact of their incarceration. By paying them generous compensation, the government will be demonstrating that these victims of the watch list should not be treated as presumptive terrorists by the rest of society—but that they have instead been called to sacrifice their personal lives as part of a broader effort by American citizens to sustain their republic at a challenging moment in its history.

I FIRST PROPOSED A "STATE OF EMERGENCY" REGIME IN THE IMMEDI-ate aftermath of September 11—and my initiative generated a broad-ranging discussion that has had some practical impact both here and abroad.[1] But more recently, serious attention to the problem has declined, and this essay is an attempt to revive the conversation. Much that was said during the first round of debate remains important—clarifying critical issues of statutory design as well as fundamental questions dealing with the place of emergency legislation in the larger constitutional order. But I hope that I have persuaded you that recent events have made it more, not less, imperative to confront these questions once again.

In placing emergency legislation back on the action agenda, we will be redeeming a tradition that goes back to the Philadelphia Convention. In writing the original Constitution, the founders paid very little attention to the nature and scope of fundamental rights—leaving it to the first Congress to fill this gap with a series of amendments. But they made an exception when it came to states of emergency—which they treated in a fashion that parallels the dualistic approach taken here. On the one hand, Article One insists that the guarantee against arbitrary arrest and conviction is indeed foundational; on the other, it recognizes that emergency conditions may justify temporary limitations. To put this dualism in the founders' words: "The privilege of the writ of habeas corpus shall not be suspended, unless when in cases of rebellion or invasion the public safety may require it."

The eighteenth-century language invites us to reflect more deeply on our twenty-first-century problem. As I have emphasized, it is of high importance to limit emergency powers to those occasions on which a terrorist organization has successfully engaged in an attack on the scale of September 11. In terms of the founding text, I suggest that such an act of organized violence represents a modern-day version of "rebellion"—in which the extremist group, either secular or religious, seeks to overthrow the very foundations of our constitutional democracy. Our twenty-first-century challenge is to respond in the spirit of the founders—and adapt the principles of checks and balances so that emergency powers may be invoked when "the public safety may require it." At that same time, we must prevent the exercise of extraordinary authority from destroying the very constitutional order the declaration of emergency purports to protect.

Are we equal to the challenge?

NOTES

1. See, e.g., Bruce Ackerman, "The Emergency Constitution," *Yale Law Journal* 113, no. 5 (March 2004): 1029–1091; David Cole, "The Priority of Morality: The Emergency Constitution's Blind Spot," *Yale Law Journal* 113, no. 8 (June 2004): 1753; Laurence Tribe and Patrick Gudridge, "The Anti-Emergency Constitution," *Yale Law Journal* 113, no. 8 (June 2004): 1801; Bruce Ackerman, *Before the Next Attack* (New Haven: Yale University Press, 2006); Bruce Ackerman, *The Decline and Fall of the American Republic* (New Haven: Yale University Press, 2010), 166–74.

ANOTHER ROAD TO SERFDOM: CASCADING INTOLERANCE

TIMUR KURAN

In one of the most influential books of the twentieth century, *The Road to Serfdom*, Friedrich Hayek warned against the dangers of state control over the economy. He was writing during World War II, a time when collectivists on the left were extinguishing private property and those on the right were empowering the state with expanding rights of ownership and management. The horrors of Stalin, Hitler, and Mussolini were widely apparent. These were not aberrations caused by madmen, argued Hayek. Rather, they resulted from placing undue faith in the capacity of government to engineer utopia. Although the democracies fighting these regimes were by and large free of the conditions that produced collectivist horrors, that was no reason for complacency. The United States could institute tyranny inadvertently, through well-intended calls on government to solve social problems.[1]

There is another road to serfdom, whose fount is not collectivist economic ideology. Although it may culminate in resource centralization, its starting point is the selective suppression of communications. The suppression comes from leaders harboring undue faith in their own sense of the good society, or from citizens who entrust leaders with extensive powers to direct the "right" messages. To block ostensibly harmful acts and expressions, such efforts at control limit the free exchange of ideas. One consequence of their vigilance is the distortion of knowledge in the public domain. Another is the curtailment of social experimentation, which depends on the sharing of thoughts. Limits on expression also impoverish people's understandings of social processes. Politicians exploit the resulting combustion of hostility, panic, and ignorance through policies that may seem responsive to grievances but are ultimately counterproductive. By pandering to intolerant constituents and stoking fear and anger, they enable the rise of a leader with autocratic ambitions. Using state resources, that leader may then reinforce and deepen the prejudices instrumental in his own ascent.

Vladimir Putin of Russia and Recep Tayyip Erdoğan of Turkey offer cases in point. Each identified and then exploited strains of intolerance to solidify political and economic power, ultimately using his followers' sense of victimization to stoke hostility toward anyone who stood in his way. The victims of such tactics include people who, by helping to cleanse public discourse, galvanize the very processes responsible for turning legitimate democratic power into dictatorship.

Donald Trump's meteoric rise to power has advanced certain preconditions of a similarly autocratic regime in the United States. But could the world's most powerful country really become a dictatorship? The American political system incorporates checks and balances designed to protect individual liberties, sustain the coexistence of lifestyles, and keep groups from acting on intolerance.[2] These safeguards came into play as soon as Trump took power and began issuing executive orders. His successive "Muslim bans" of early 2017, which suspended visits from certain majority-Muslim countries, were blocked by courts until the Supreme Court allowed the partial implementation of a tempered version. Several of his aides with suspected ties to authoritarian governments were forced to resign, and Congress is investigating the Trump campaign's ties to Russia.[3] When in August 2017 he failed to condemn violence by white supremacists, he was widely denounced by a very wide spectrum of leaders, including top officials of his own party.[4] Nevertheless, the effectiveness of American democratic institutions cannot be taken for granted. For one thing, intolerance may make people rationalize selective suspensions of constitutional and political protections. For another, the very fact of Trump's electoral success points to systemic vulnerabilities of which he is more a symptom than a cause. If Trump were to disappear from American politics, sliding toward dictatorship would remain a danger. Another person with contempt for democratic values and procedures—Republican, Democrat, or Independent—could capture the presidency through support from intolerant constituents.

INTOLERANT COMMUNITIES

Whereas in Hayek's feared trajectory liberties are lost because of government expansion, in the present case the engine of illiberalism is communities situated in civil society—the portion of the social system outside of direct government control. These communities include associations similar to those that Alexis de Tocqueville considered vital to American democracy.[5] Sustained primarily by shared interests, these associations constrain individual behaviors by promoting common understandings of right and wrong. They also limit what individuals may say or do to each other with impunity. Intolerant communities differ from idealized Tocquevillean associations partly in degree, then. They are communities whose hallmark is an unusually strong sense of proper behavior. They differ in kind because of their self-righteous determination to hold outsiders to their own standards, which they consider above criticism. Insofar as they get involved in politics, intolerant communities threaten democratic governance. They lay the foundations for tyranny by creating constituencies prepared to suspend the rule of law for some higher purpose.

Intolerant communities thrive in the presence of other intolerant communities, especially those intolerant of them. They exclude aggressively because they themselves are excluded. They hate because they are hated. They censor because their own views are dismissed, mocked, and suppressed. Clashes between intolerant communities undermine freedom of association, extinguish individualities, and incapacitate democratic institutions. Through these channels they facilitate the rise of dictatorship.

Members of an intolerant community do not consider themselves *intolerant* in any negative sense, because no one is obliged to tolerate intolerance. They define their vigilance not as the denial of others' freedoms but as drawing boundaries that are essential to human civilization. "We are protecting victims," they will say, or "we are preventing victimization." Just as the highway patrol enforces rules vital to road safety, so, in their own minds, they merely enforce rules that protect the good life for all. Intolerant communities differ, then, from a Tocquevillean association in terms of compatibility between their own self-definition and the definitions of others. In Tocqueville's America, the social functions of a parent-teacher association were not in dispute, and they drew no objections. By contrast, what an intolerant community accomplishes is a matter of huge disagreement, as is its legitimacy.

Another possible difference concerns group membership. Unlike the members of a Tocquevillean association, people who identify with an intolerant community do not necessarily recognize themselves as members. Outsiders define their membership and also ascribe to them motives and influences that may well be spurious. Thus, individuals may be treated as part of an intolerant community simply because of where they work (for instance, a university) or where they live (Appalachia). Disagreements may exist, then, regarding the boundaries of a particular intolerant community.

Intolerant communities compete for members through methods akin to those of political parties. Like the propaganda departments of parties, they promote ideologies that focus attention on particular grievances, interpretations of history, and policy instruments. They also provide social status to their members and treat nonmembers with contempt. Finally, they claim to speak for entire categories of people—women, Christians—when in fact the groups include many who hold very different views. Insofar as an intolerant community is successful, a combination of indoctrination and fear expands its membership.

In any given society, multiple intolerant communities may vie for dominance. Often, this competition sustains an equilibrium whereby they coexist in rough balance. As I suggest below, in mid-2017 the polarized politics of the United States exhibits just such an equilibrium. At the most basic level, the US has two intolerant communities, each an alliance of overlapping subcommunities that are divided themselves. Each intolerant community has distinct grievances, worldviews, and justifications for silencing others. No single term does justice to the many motives driving the alliances. Precisely because they do not recognize their own existence, they have no self-adopted names.

Given the heterogeneity of these two communities, and their diverse internal disagreements, attempts at naming are precarious. But labels offer useful analytic shorthands, provided one keeps in mind what they conceal. On that basis,

I shall characterize one community as "identitarian" and the other as "nativist." The identitarian coalition loosely connects groups that define themselves according to some form of identity, mostly gender, ethnicity, or sexual orientation. The nativist coalition encompasses groups suspicious of economic globalization, technological innovation, cultural change, and cross-border labor mobility.

In national politics, the identitarians are generally aligned with the left and the nativists with the right. But neither group defines itself exclusively or even mainly in terms of the political spectrum running from left to right. The left-right spectrum dates from the Industrial Revolution, when the principal social conflict concerned the division of economic output between labor and capital.[6] Over time, left and right developed entrenched positions on a wide range of social conflicts. Some of these other conflicts have gained salience through postindustrial technological changes. For identitarians, identity-based matters are more central to the quality of life, and nativists say the same about cultural continuity and the scope of economic freedoms. It is critical that distinct conflicts are involved. The difference makes it harder to achieve compromises than in a system based on the left-right spectrum. Indeed, it is easier to make trade-offs in a single dimensional space that measures the division of the economic pie than in a multidimensional space. Even communication is difficult when adversaries disagree on the nature of the social conflict. Absent a common understanding of what needs to be discussed, no one will gather around a table to sort things out.

Our central question can now be restated. Put bluntly, it is whether one of the two intolerant communities might wipe out the other. This would entail the submission of one to the other's wishes by accepting, if only tacitly, its worldview and favored policies. Members of the defeated community would stop expressing their own grievances. They would pretend to share the victor's interpretations of events. Public discourses would reflect the victor's prejudices; they would get saturated with claims that the vanquished community considers contemptible. Observing other societies, one sees that shocks to a social system—business cycles, job-replacing technologies, loss of institutional safeguards—can upset an equilibrium, inducing realignments that then feed on themselves. One type of intolerance starts growing at the expense of the other. Turkey's authoritarian transition exemplifies just such a process. The possibility of an analogous transition in the United States is the question at hand.

IDENTITARIAN INTOLERANCE

The intolerance of American movements based on a sub-identity is widely known as political correctness, a term coined in the 1980s as a pejorative.[7] These movements claimed to dignify, protect, and advance constituencies that were, and in many cases remain, underrepresented in certain lucrative and esteemed professions. Originally, the alliance aimed to serve African-Americans and other ethnic minorities, women, gays, and lesbians. In the intervening years, the scope of the alliance has expanded. It now includes a broader set of sexual minorities known as LGBTQAI and, increasingly, also new immigrants from underdeveloped countries. Depending on the context, the presumed male-factors of these sub-identities are whites, males, and hetero-sexuals. These groups are ostensibly committed, sometimes subconsciously, to safeguarding privileges rooted in history.

The identitarian alliance makes itself felt most promi-nently on college campuses and in entertainment. Its causes include multiculturalism, the sexual revolution, curriculum diversification, and affirmative action based on identity rather than economic status. Such causes face opposition, which identitarians struggle to silence through political correctness. As they see it, policing speech and behaviors offensive to their constituents enhances study and work en-vironments; it levels an economic, social, and intellectual playing field that has long been tilted in favor of whites, men, and heterosexuals.[8] In the 2010s, political correct-ness shifted emphasis from suppressing hate speech targeted at its constituents to creating safe spaces that shelter them from discomforting acts and expressions. The task requires curbing microaggressions, which are intrinsically trivial acts that cause unintentional harm. Examples include a smile perceived as an affront, a question treated as an act of ex-clusion, boredom attributed to stereotyping, and an idea treated as insensitivity. Microaggressions can be limited by issuing trigger warnings whenever a topic potentially upset-ting to an oppressed constituency is on the agenda. Con-sider an assignment to read a novel on the tribulations of an immigrant family. A trigger warning would let victims of anti-immigrant speech avoid the relevant content.[9]

The critics of identitarian political correctness consider it a system of oppression that shields unjust, inefficient, and even counterproductive identity-based policies from public scrutiny. It institutionalizes mistrust, intolerance, and hatred of others, they say, while hiding behind egalitarian slogans to create new bastions of privilege. In blocking frank and open discussion of identitarian agendas, political correctness also limits the exposure of identitarian intolerance.[10] Identitarians respond that their rules of expression merely protect oppressed groups against hurt and aggression. As such, they amount not to intolerance but to its negation.

During the 2016 presidential campaign, identitarians heavily supported the Democratic candidate Hillary Clinton. In itself, that fueled speculation that if elected she would promote political correctness. She validated suspicions through a passing comment now remembered as the biggest gaffe of her campaign: the description of half of her opponent's supporters as a "basket of deplorables."[11] Her wording dehumanized tens of millions of Americans. She was taken to mean that in addition to rejecting the policy positions of her opponent's supporters, she despised their values and lifestyles. In other words, the characterization aligned her with political correctness while epitomizing its widely despised intolerance. By energizing her opponents, the comment may well have cost her the close election.

CONSERVATIVE AND NATIVIST INTOLERANCE

The appearance of the political correctness concept reflected resistance to the agenda that it was meant to advance. Loose-

knit coalitions opposed to identitarian causes were forming, many centered in conservative churches. Televangelists
such as Oral Roberts, Jerry Falwell, and Pat Robertson and
talk-radio hosts such as Rush Limbaugh and Glenn Beck
were ringing alarm bells about the prevailing social and political trends. The most worrying transformations involved
feminism, abortion, affirmative action, drug abuse, growth
in government, environmental regulation, and restrictions
on religious practices. On these issues, TV networks, leading newspapers, government agencies, career politicians in
Washington and state capitals, the higher-education community, Hollywood, and labor unions all tended to be on
the wrong side. They had united behind family-weakening,
secularizing, repressive, and immoral policies inimical to the
fabric of American society.[12]

In the mid-1990s, Fox News, a new cable network, became this opposition's face on television.[13] Fox News also
championed the interests of business, including both small
and large enterprises. Hence, it helped to sustain the political alliance at the core of the Republican Party, that between
economic and political conservatism. No such alliance is
free of tension; on any given matter, constituents may have
conflicting goals. In this case, the coalition proved sustainable for a while, as the Republican Party's electoral fortunes
waxed and waned. Big business interests paid lip service to
Republican cultural goals, and cultural conservatives put
up with economic policies favoring mega-corporations and
wealthy individuals. The advent of the Tea Party movement
following the 2008 presidential election was the first sign

of a serious split.[14] The Tea Party charged the Republican leadership with hidden political correctness. It also focused attention on the shared interests of the Democratic Party leadership, which has tended to represent highly educated voters, and the big-money wing of the Republican Party.

Donald Trump's political surge owes much to his unprecedented ability to mesmerize the media through outrageous behavior and insults. But also critical was his savvy exploitation of tensions within the two-party system. His candidacy for the Republican nomination provided a huge outlet for the anger of constituencies that have done relatively poorly in recent decades. It gave them hope as he railed against both Democrats and Republicans who benefit disproportionately from rapid technological change and advancing globalization. They succeed, he said, by "rigging the system" in their favor. In the eyes of his followers, such political rhetoric legitimized demonization of the bipartisan "establishment." The passions that Trump aroused are apparent in video clips of his campaign rallies. His fans waited for hours just to hear him speak in person.[15]

What the Trump administration gives to his supporters apart from rhetoric and bravado remains to be seen. His naming of a billionaire-packed cabinet suggests that on the economic front his supporters will be disappointed, as does the initial half-year of his term. What is certain is that Trump's supporters feel more empowered to speak their minds and also to intimidate, silence, and chase away people whom they consider misguided. Just as conservatives feel the need to speak cautiously on university campuses known for identitarian activism, so in distressed towns that voted heavily for Trump self-identified "progressives" know that the climate of opinion is hostile to their own viewpoints. Some Trump supporters are willing to pursue extralegal means for achieving their objectives. The Charlottesville demonstration of August 12, 2017, provides an illustration; the marchers included armed white supremacist groups. In the eyes of such supporters, Trump has legitimized law-breaking through his diatribes against the establishment-rigged system. He has done so also by flaunting the law routinely, whether in ignoring conflicts of interest, inviting Russia to interfere with American elections, questioning the loyalty of immigrant citizens, or dismissing external commitments of the United States.[16]

Just as political correctness demonizes its detractors as racist, misogynist, and homophobic, so Trump's crowds disparage his critics as un-American and crooked. Supporters of nation-building abroad, free trade, and amnesty for undocumented aliens should all be treated with disdain. And they are all the more deserving of opprobrium insofar as they exhibit political correctness. Throughout his campaign, Trump lambasted political correctness as a cancer destroying America and promised to fight it. Friend or foe, everyone in his audiences knew what he meant. He would not coddle undeserving minorities, put foreigners ahead of Americans, or keep the United States in trade treaties that ship jobs abroad. He would not cozy up to Hollywood bosses whose products rarely show evangelicals or conservative whites in a positive light. Furthermore, in reversing established social policies, he would remind America-hating elites that most Americans reject their values.

There is no widely accepted name for the intolerance of the movement centered around Trump. "Trumpism" sees use, but so does the "new political correctness," "patriotic correctness," and "populist correctness."[17] "Nativist intolerance" offers the advantage of conveying the movement's emphasis on "putting America first." Like political correctness, this is a descriptor concocted by a critical outsider. Its practitioners overlap with conservatives who practice "conservative correctness."[18] Their attitudes come in many shades. My nomenclature represents an analytical shorthand that sets aside many nuances.

MUTUALLY REINFORCING INTOLERANCES

Interactions among the rival intolerances are complicated by the fact that neither situates itself along the traditional left-right axis. They are at odds, above all, over the primary axis of conflict in the United States. For identitarians, the fundamental conflict is between groups defined by ethnicity, race, gender, sexual orientation, and citizenship status—factors generally determined at birth. Nativists reject the focus on identity as artificial. For them, the principal fault line of American society runs between ordinary folk, by far the majority, and elites, who control the levers of power. America needs policies that put America first, they say, without slicing Americans into hyper-selfish constituencies. If the mantra of the identitarians is "justice for minorities," that of nativists is "making America great again." Basic disagreement over what needs discussion limits communication between the two sides. It also makes it easier for each to treat the other as deranged, if not subhuman.

Identitarians see the nativist agenda as a reaction to privileges slipping away, as another gasp to undo whatever progress the country has made toward equalizing rights and opportunities across genders, ethnic and racial groups, sexual classifications, and citizenship categories. It proves that the struggle for justice will be long and painful, as they have said all along. The extent of the reaction shows that massive work is required just to maintain the gains of the past half century. The intimidations endured by undocumented immigrants testify to the dangers to minorities, as do mosque burnings, the prevalence of rape, police violence against African-Americans, and rules meant to suppress voting by non-whites. The persistence of these dangers proves the wisdom of censoring sexist, racist, and nationalist expression. They reconfirm that when speech is poorly monitored, offensive discourses spread like cancer. Identitarian intolerance thus derives vitality, even purpose, from nativist intolerance. The big boost that nativists received from Trump's presidency has energized identitarians as well.

For their part, the nativists depend on identitarian activism. Without identitarian policies or associated political correctness, they would be attributing their misfortunes mainly to technology, trade, and immigration. These are all factors resolvable through bargaining within the left-right political spectrum. The identitarian agenda infuriates them by privileging the problems of groups from which they are mostly, if not totally, excluded. An American-born heterosexual white male miner fits none of the victim categories of the identitarians. As he sees it, universities, the mass media, Hollywood, government agencies, and the nonprofit sector ignore his own problems, and they do so because the identitarian worldview blinds them to all but a sliver of human suffering. Adding insult to injury, identitarians also look down at him as uneducated, superstitious, and unpolished—as an inferior creature who does not deserve a hearing. The identitarians may also consider him a villain merely because of his innate persona. Some think that he cannot be a victim of anything, because he belongs to groups that define the establishment. His woes merit no sympathy, identitarians may say, because they represent retribution for past discrimination.

Positions on each side harden, then, because of the other's reactions. Perceived indifference to deep grievances fuels anger, which then undermines empathy for others. An ambitious teenager from a poor family in America's rust belt perceives that the academic establishment is more welcoming to immigrants than to underprivileged Americans like himself; the resulting anger keeps him from appreciating the challenges of being an undocumented college student in the age of Trump. The sense that one cannot speak honestly in milieus dominated by a rival intolerant group leads to disengagement from the problems of others. Imagine a small-town bar that tolerates antigay slurs. The atmosphere makes a gay visitor conceal his sexual identity and keep quiet during a political discussion. That discomforting experience then makes him insensitive to evangelical concerns about declining religious freedoms. Consider, finally, a college student who planned to attend an event featuring a conservative speaker. The speaking invitation is withdrawn under threats of violence from identitarian activists. The episode makes him lose interest in a course on feminist literature. In all such cases, ordinarily equitable people end up embracing double standards. They start denying to groups that they perceive as unsympathetic and insensitive, if not also hostile, rights that they readily grant to members of their own groups. They become intolerant because of others' intolerance.

The political system can reinforce the illustrated polarization. For one thing, polarized voters are more likely to nominate extreme candidates and to take the trouble to vote. For another, politicians whose career success depends on pleasing an extreme constituency are less likely to make compromises.[19] Polarized politicians inflame animosities between citizen blocs that scarcely communicate with one another. Legitimizing intransigence, they also strengthen the logic for pressing one's own causes and dismissing those of the other side. Institutional devices designed to tilt the political playing field, such as gerrymandering and voter-registration restrictions, can complement these effects, partly by narrowing the voter base that the politicians feel obligated to serve, but also by fueling perceptions of partisan mischief.[20]

AVAILABILITY CHAMBERS AS REINFORCERS OF INTOLERANCE

In a polarized environment, people do not willingly step into situations that subject them to rancor. To pick up earlier illustrations, a gay visitor would rather spend time among people who accept his identity; and a student seeking a well-rounded education would rather attend a college hospitable to open-ended political debate. In an ideal world, the menu of options would be sufficiently broad to present gay visitors and college students ideal choices in every possible encounter. Alas, the choices can be quite limited. Some American towns have no gay-friendly bars at all. Most research universities of the United States have student groups who will kick up a storm if an invitation goes out to a speaker whom they find offensive.

Many other settings allow Americans to avoid views, attitudes, and even people whom they find offensive. Cities offer gays abundant opportunities to relax in an LGBTQAI-friendly environment. At least after freshman year, college students can pick compatible roommates. In certain walks of life, then, Americans can sort themselves into groups of like-minded, mutually respecting people. If they so choose, they can socialize only with people who are comfortable with political differences. By the same token, if they are intolerant themselves, they can self-select into suitably prejudiced social and professional groups.

Such groups of politically like-minded people form communication networks known as "echo chambers." [21] The concept refers to surroundings that amplify and reinforce our ideas, beliefs, and information through constant repetition. Idealized Tocquevillean communities served as echo chambers insofar as their members reinforced each other's worldviews through repeated references, often implicit. These worldviews encompassed perceived facts about African-American abilities, the effects of smoking, and the origins of the human species. "Availability chambers" is a superior descriptor, because within groups of like-minded individuals the reinforcement process involves more than exchanging ideas. Understandings get reinforced through a combination of communal and social pressures. Ideas acceptable to the group get "echoed" both because many people share them and because members with doubts refrain from speaking honestly. The joint effect of these two mutually reinforcing processes is that ideas the group appears to deem acceptable become increasingly available in its public communications. The flip side of the high availability of acceptable ideas is the low availability of what is unacceptable. In concentrating their members' attention on acceptable ideas, availability chambers limit their exposure to conflicting facts and arguments.

The concept of availability chambers harkens to availability cascade, which is a self-reinforcing process of collective belief formation. Under an availability cascade, an expressed perception triggers a chain reaction that gives that perception increasing plausibility through its rising availability in public discourse.[22] The process is intermediated by the availability heuristic, a pervasive mental shortcut through which the perceived likelihood of any given event depends on the ease with which its occurrences can be brought to mind. Cognitive psychologists find that individual beliefs regarding truth and falsehood are generally based on the ease with which pertinent examples come to mind. That ease depends on the relative availability of evidence pointing in one direction or the other.

Availability chambers are particularly visible online. Facebook users select their own friends, and Twitter users choose whom to follow. Such social media are conducive, then, to intolerant communities forming and reinforcing their worldviews. People who consider immigrants the source of unemployment interact within chambers consisting of immigration opponents. For their part, people worried about anti-immigrant discrimination self-select into chambers of immigration supporters. Within each chamber, different aspects of the issue get communicated and amplified; different myths get concocted, elaborated, and disseminated; and different entities get demonized. Unsurprisingly, public opinion research finds that online social networks are associated with political polarization.[23]

The same research shows also that online networks boost exposure to materials from their less preferred side of the political spectrum. Though counterintuitive within the analytical framework of an echo chamber, this is entirely plausible once we recognize that intolerant Americans self-select into availability chambers. Members of availability chambers do not simply pass on information about favored policies. They also inform their members about the other side's machinations. To that end, they re-post communications of their opponents, but selectively, in order to heighten the sense of clear and present danger. Thus, news about violence by white supremacists goes viral in identitarian circles, and nativist circles explode with outrage whenever a conservative speaker is prevented from speaking on some campus. In each case, vast numbers of people are held responsible for the excesses of a few.

Members of availability chambers do not simply distort reality by communicating information selectively. They also teach their members to express outrage at the messages of opponents, to despise people with different opinions, and to shame anyone, especially insiders, who might dare to suggest that something in a rival position is worth considering. Teaching members to hate the other side requires communicating information about what opponents are trying to accomplish. In sum, online political networks are not only censoring agents that truncate exposure to political information. They serve also as outrage machines that intimidate and punish anyone who questions their dogma or seems inclined to see some merit in opponents' positions. But in censoring and intimidating, they do not keep their members ignorant about the goals of opponents. Rather, they give their members exaggerated and unrepresentative impressions of rival agendas. Insofar as availability chambers keep views from being heard, they constrain their own members' access to information. Like off-line intolerant communities, their online counterparts are agents of illiberalism toward both outsiders and insiders.

Tensions exist within every network of every intolerant community; no two network members will have identical needs or perspectives. Differences are easy to spot within both nativist and identitarian networks. For instance, the interests of African-Americans at the bottom of the labor market conflict with those of unskilled new immigrants, who depress wages. And in extinguishing low-tech jobs, trade treaties benefit job-losing constituencies through cheaper industrial goods. Intolerant communities deal with such complexities by discouraging their exposure. As within any coalition, whether based on a shared heritage, a shared environment, or a shared political agenda, participants are expected to overlook inconsistencies among the goals of individual members. True, their subcommunities will enjoy some discretion in prioritizing selected elements of the favored policy package. Provided they pay lip service to the community's unity and accept its core principles and goals, they may tailor their positions to special needs. Feminists often include African-American men among the victimizers of American women. Likewise, the proponents of racial justice commonly hold the "white majority" responsible for racial discrimination. Nevertheless, feminists and racial activists maintain harmony within the grand identitarian coalition. They do so by focusing their animus on their common adversaries whenever they join forces.

If one requirement for membership in an intolerant community is shared goals, another is participation in the shaming of villains. That is one reason why so much of their internal discussions convey loathing and why online networks tied to an intolerant community seldom produce constructive ideas for resolving differences peacefully. Network members are expected to enforce their intolerance by persecuting compromisers and by stigmatizing them as ignorant, misguided, selfish, dangerous, and immoral. Failing to display outrage at violators, or neglecting to punish them through denial of opportunities, can cast doubt on one's own intolerance. Members must display hate toward compromisers to prove their own credentials. Consider the identitarian view that discrimination is a core reason for victimization and marginalization. For an intolerant identitarian who subscribes to this worldview, inviting a scholar who focuses on self-destructive behaviors would amount to enabling a campaign to "blame the victim." For intolerant nativists, likewise, gun control of any sort is anathema. Letting someone make a case for banning assault weapons would amount to rewarding a liberal bent on extinguishing the American way of life. The villains here are elites who make streets unsafe through softness on crime and policies responsible for social dysfunction. Such elites must be demonized, along with anyone who seeks to legitimize the liberal agenda.

Loss of expressive freedoms has become a growing source of concern in the United States. The opponents of identitarian policies complain about rules and pressures that hinder honest discourse, and the opponents of nativist policies have analogous grievances.[24] Yet people tend to worry specifically about losing their own voices, not about threats to expressive liberty generally. When identitarian campus activists block a conservative speaker, protests come mostly from conservatives and nativists of various stripes. Similarly, when President Trump bars questions from "fake-news media," objections come largely from groups that voted against him. Moreover, neither side pays much attention to expressive restrictions within its own camp. Yet these restrictions play a key role in turning public discourses into hysterical melees. The internal exchanges of political communities hide complexities, nuances, and variations. They tend to turn ranges of similar views into a single position immune to compromise. Just as a gun rights advocate may also believe in banning the private ownership of assault rifles, so a supporter of affirmative action may believe that without income thresholds, its benefits will go primarily to already privileged applicants. However, for fear of reprisals from their own political soul mates, both will self-censor. Hiding their private preferences and private knowledge about their group's agenda, they will pretend to share its public consensus.

No political network forms an assembly whose members evaluate evidence, weigh the pros and cons of policies, and make reasoned trade-offs in the manner of a collegial research workshop—certainly not if its defining traits include intolerance. Preference and knowledge falsification distort public perceptions of the inclinations and thoughts of their members. They make the typical group member look more homogeneous, more rigid, angrier, and more hateful than in reality. A by-product of concealing doubts and differences is ignorance. Within intolerant networks, falsified communications leave other members in the dark about possible solutions to social problems, or even about the existence of certain problems themselves. In other words, they truncate the public availability of knowledge concerning passionately defended policies. Impoverishing public discourses, they hinder the identification and execution of viable responses to social troubles; and, in the process, they aggravate the very intolerances that inhibit honest communication in the first place.[25]

Participants in politically "extreme" online networks often have "normal" interactions off-line. In fact, most Americans who belong to hate-spewing networks regularly visit "mainstream" news outlets such as CNN, CBS News, and *USA Today.*[26] They thus get exposed to diverse perspectives firsthand. They do not avoid news sites that cover complexities, present bigger pictures, aim for balanced reporting, and feature commentators who appreciate the conflicts among widely held principles of morality. Exposure to contrary opinions does not make an "extremist" politically neutral; judging by the Internet searches of participants in "extreme" online networks, the recipients of mainstream news remain sympathetic, in one degree or another, to positions associated with extremism. Within their online availability chambers, they take positions that their mainstream news sources characterize as extreme. In other words, they take on a radicalized persona.

Once again, this radicalization is not simply a matter of developing extreme ideas. The process is not limited to turning a potentially nuanced communal discourse over competing priorities into rigid and absolute claims about public policy. It also involves heightened intolerance of contrary views. It entails the harassment, shaming, and demonization of people who convey reservations about agendas treated as beyond compromise.

HATRED TRIUMPHANT

Intolerant communities are never satisfied with sharing political power. Precisely because they despise their opponents, they want to drive them out of public spaces, if not to wipe them out. Comments such as "I'm glad he got shot" (referring to a political assassination attempt) convey the extremes that intolerance can reach.[27] Picket signs such as "Death Penalty 4 Fags" offer another grisly example.[28] Intolerant communities also seek to win over people with moderate views, especially those who see matters from multiple perspectives and favor compromises. Through a combination of repression and conversion, they try to expand their social presence, salience, and influence.

By no means is success guaranteed. First of all, rival intolerant communities limit each other's influence by publicizing the other side's incivility and destructiveness. Thus, identitarian communities have framed the Breitbart News Network as a source of malicious stories and destructive policies far outside of mainstream American conservatism.[29] Likewise, nativists have lambasted Black Lives Matter as a movement inimical to the US civil rights tradition and a threat to decent whites.[30] Many tolerant Americans find both the Breitbart News Network and Black Lives Matter to be extreme. Second, the illiberal activities of intolerant communities can antagonize potential recruits; people sympathetic to their core substantive objectives, whether racial justice or protecting domestic jobs, may find their tactics unacceptable. Finally, legal institutions may block an intolerant community's expansion by denying its agenda "mainstream" status. Thus, attempts to constrain American Islam face a huge hurdle: the US Constitution, which protects freedom of religion.[31] Besides, the complex procedures of Congress make it extraordinarily difficult to pass bills fully satisfactory to any given "mainstream" special-interest group, let alone to legislate the agenda of an intolerant community that rival media keep under heavy scrutiny. Furthermore, the federal government shares power with fifty states, which have their own protections for individual liberties. If some school district bans books on evolution or eugenics, other jurisdictions need not follow; and, in any case, state and federal courts are likely to step in, maintaining general access to the controversial literature.

For all these reasons, the political status quo could survive indefinitely without any fundamental change in either the size or practical influence of existing intolerant communities. Shocks along the way could give one community a temporary boost. An Islamist attack might lift nativist support, or a mass shooting of African-Americans might energize identitarians. If such horrors followed a random walk, and the two intolerant communities continued to sow alienation through initiatives that frighten broad constituencies, the present political balance would likely persist. Millions would continue caring more about blocking despised opponents than about alleviating social maladies. Massive dysfunctions, such as schools that fail to prepare students for the global economy, could just fester. Congress could remain deadlocked on many matters, with the extremes of the two parties blocking attempts at compromise. Every new Supreme Court nomination could turn into a life-and-death matter for both sides, repeating the no-holds-barred drama that followed Justice Antonin Scalia's death in 2016.[32]

After all, the US was already a hyper-polarized society before the political ascent of Trump. Depending on the measurement technique, the language of politics has been becoming increasingly polarized since somewhere between the 1970s and early 1990s.[33] In a 2008 YouGov poll, a fifth of both Democrats and Republicans indicated that they would be "somewhat upset" or "very upset" if a son or daughter married someone of the other party.[34] In the 1960s, very few people were offended about the party choice of their relatives.[35] Political scientists of that era repeatedly demonstrated that Americans did not think of parties in ideological terms, as most do now.[36]

If the status quo is awful and the prospect of its perpetuation frightening, it is not the worst possible scenario. Any number of plausible developments could undermine the prevailing equilibrium in American politics and set off a cascade favoring one intolerant community or the other. The possible triggers include emerging technologies. Driverless cars and automated stores will displace millions of drivers and cashiers, swelling the ranks of Americans without marketable skills. Just as China, Mexico, and foreigners are blamed for the loss of industrial jobs, so the unfolding automation could heighten xenophobia and anti-globalism, swelling the numbers of nativists. For another alarming scenario, imagine that the collapse of a pivotal Arab state makes Middle Eastern wars spread to new countries, dragging the US into a Vietnam-style quagmire. The resulting refugee flows would energize nativists, and daily casualty reports would energize identitarians, especially if ethnic minorities suffered disproportionately. Depending on specifics, then, either coalition could be the main beneficiary. Yet another possible destabilizing trigger consists of multiple shocks that sow panic. Several synchronized mass killings by white supremacists might precipitate cascading intolerance against non-identitarians in general.

Social forecasting is risky, especially, it has been said, when it is about the future. No one knows when the prevailing political equilibrium in the US will get disrupted, let alone what would replace it. The social sciences can predict only the mechanisms likely to unfold under particular contingencies. We can thus identify dangers. We can also say why certain events would make intolerance deepen and spread.

Remember that intolerance now gets perpetuated through availability chambers. Within networks that unite political soul mates, people accept falsehoods as true because frequent repetition gives them validity, but also because members with reservations refrain from saying what they really think, from correcting overgeneralizations, and from resisting internal pressures. When a shock compounds the outrage felt toward outsiders, it becomes riskier than ever to promote civility or advance nuanced points. Objections that would have brought scorn in the past are now treated as treasonous. Preference and knowledge falsification spreads. Meanwhile, the just-electrified intolerant community gains because of shared genuine outrage on the part of previously tolerant people and also because people tolerant in private adapt their public faces to the changing political winds. Such transformations could follow, for instance, two back-to-back 9/11s. Anti-Muslim Americans would feel vindicated; and, on that basis, they would feel freer to spew hatred at Muslims. Heretofore vocal defenders of religious freedom, civil rights, due process, and respect for lifestyle diversity would start going quiet. Some would turn against Muslims for opportunistic reasons—say, for career promotion on the back of public hysteria. Crimes associated with Islam would become even more available in public discourses. Communications favorable to Muslims or Islam would now be equated, more commonly than ever, with ignorance or appeasement. The peaceful and constructive sides of American Muslims would become less available still.

Such a scenario is not far-fetched. The US reached its present predicament through the rising availability of discourses motivated by resentment and loathing, and replete with exaggerations, distortions, and outright lies. The forecasted trajectory involves further polarization and a hardening of positions within rival camps until some shock upsets the prevailing balance and allows one coalition to begin crushing the other. The cascade would be reflected in party politics as well. Party factions with ideological affinity to the triumphing intolerance would adopt policies that make their previous pursuits look tame. Turnover in the courts would enable landmark decisions endorsing the trimming of liberties once taken for granted. News outlets committed to balanced journalism would start disappearing—less because of falling readership than because "middle-of-the-road" journalists start radicalizing themselves, perhaps out of conviction, but mostly out of fear. In sum, the institutions protecting Americans from tyranny would disintegrate, forcing them to embrace an illiberal ideology for the sake of personal safety.

What would happen to the small and overlapping associations that Tocqueville considered vital to American democracy? In his time, they were formed freely, they acted autonomously, and generally they respected the liberties of others, African-Americans being the top exception. Although they enforced internal codes of behavior, freedom of association and mobility allowed individuals to escape rules and regulations they found oppressive. Given the ubiquity of hatred now, there is no longer room for Tocquevillean associations. It is not an option to avoid national politics and live the life of one's choice. One cannot interact with society through autonomous associations. Individuals and their associations are both expected to display animus toward the losing form of intolerance. They must treat designated enemies, whether campus liberals or rural whites, as blots on humanity.

FROM INTOLERANCE TO SERFDOM

If that point were reached, the US would be the land of the oppressed. Its people would be living like Václav Havel's paradigmatic victim of communism, the greengrocer who, just to be left alone, keeps on his fruits and vegetables the slogan "Workers of the World Unite!"[37] Through words and deeds, Americans would be voting routinely for agendas that they dread. Shunning evidence of their senses, they would be parroting slogans and forcing others to do the same. They would be persecuting people with whom they actually agree, or at least consider worthy of taking seriously.

Such a political environment offers fertile ground for demagogues promising deliverance from the other side's outrages. By virtue of his (or possibly her) organizational, oratorical, tactical, and strategic skills, one of them becomes the recognized chief of the now-dominant intolerant community. He preserves and expands the coalition through more fearmongering and unrelenting demonization. Insofar as electoral success follows, the group's intolerance begins to benefit from state resources. That then brings into play all the horrors that Hayek attributed to centralized economic governance. State agencies start favoring the victorious side blatantly. Resources are redirected to uses matching the leader's priorities. Programs dear to despised opponents are axed. The leader becomes fiscally unaccountable.

But the leader's fundamental function is not economic redistribution. Rather, it is to harass, humiliate, silence, disempower, and crush the opposition. So it is that Donald Trump, a wealthy businessman with no significant record of helping the poor or the uneducated, came to lead a coalition whose members belong disproportionately to America's disadvantaged. Whereas voters with a college degree backed

Hillary Clinton in the 2016 election by a nine-point margin, Trump outperformed her by an eight-point margin among non–college graduates.[38] The same logic explains why he received enormous support from groups whose values he offends through his lifestyle; evangelicals who frown upon divorce and womanizing provide a case in point.[39] The primacy of hatred over problem solving also illuminates why poor voters stuck with him after he boasted about exploiting loopholes useful only to super-rich tax filers with expensive tax accountants. In their minds, his own financial exploitations are secondary to his nativist platform. Besides, in demonstrating his shrewdness, his financial machinations made him seem all the more capable of outsmarting America's enemies. Nativist voters' relegation of economic matters to secondary status reveals, further, why Trump's electoral fortunes survived incontrovertible evidence of his personal enrichment at the expense of poor Americans.[40]

For nativist voters in 2016, the numerous blots on Trump's record were all forgivable provided he served their overriding goals: to defeat Hillary Clinton, humiliate the identitarian coalition behind her candidacy, and secure the Scalia-vacated Supreme Court seat for a judge who would stand up to identitarians. Trump did not have to be a model of perfection himself. What mattered first and foremost was that he—and only he among all anti-identitarian politicians—could put identitarians in their place and, by hook or by crook, undo their damage.

The composition of Trump's cabinet accords with the primacy of cultural matters over economic inequality and redistribution for his key constituencies. In assembling the wealthiest cabinet in US history, he did not make even a token attempt at giving representation to Americans resembling his core voters economically.[41] The key reason is that his political brand does not require signals of intergroup equity. It even benefits from choices that avoid the appearance of pandering and tokenism, long associated with politicians seeking identitarian support through gender-balanced and ethnically diverse appointments.

Had economic redistribution been a key motivation in the 2016 election, Trump's voter base would have treated his cabinet selections as a punch in the face. On the contrary, some of his wealthiest cabinet officials have received enthusiastic support for their agendas. For example, Secretary of Education Betsy DeVos excites Trump's base for her determination to promote charter schools and private schools. Unsurprisingly, Trump's supporters include people who are displeased with his economic policies. But they favor Trump over his opponents on balance because of his political stands on immigration, religious education, and other issues with cultural resonance.

As of mid-2017, the United States appears far from a bona fide dictatorship. Its institutions designed to prevent tyranny safeguard the liberties of Trump opponents. The press and social media overflow with critical commentary. Major initiatives face resistance from Congress, even from elected officials of Trump's own party. Hyphenated Americans still enjoy legal protections; the government is not making them choose between Americanness and their origins. But the erosion of American democracy continues, and the mutual intolerance at its roots has only intensified. Reasoned and respectful discourse between the two sides remains the exception. Both nativists and identitarians think that the system favors the other side, and they deem each other guilty of double standards. Trump opponents see in his initiatives, appointments, tweets, and even body language mounting evidence of solidifying autocracy. For their part, his supporters think that their hero gets skewered for exercising powers that Barack Obama exploited routinely with impunity. In fact, double standards lie at the core of both nativist and identitarian modus operandi. If a major global crisis were to erupt, identitarians would rush to blame Trump, and nativists would see it as confirmation of mismanagement by global elites. Whoever is in power could use the crisis as an excuse to curtail liberties of the other side. In all likelihood, the governing team's illiberal policies would receive enthusiastic support from millions of people accustomed to considering their opponents subhuman.

Under the Trump administration, the domain of courteous public policy discussions has shrunk further than ever before. His policy zigzags, which are particularly salient in foreign policy, provide another pattern consistent with dictatorship. Although the zigzags could point also to ignorance or inexperience, they betray arbitrariness. Middle Eastern alliances get formed and dissolved in short order through dictatorial decisions whose motives are not always transparent. Likewise, Trump's declared policies on Qatar and health care, and even China, NAFTA, and immigration—

signature issues of his campaign—have made dizzying turns.[42] In democratic regimes, policies change slowly, except after elections or referenda that reveal substantial shifts in voter sentiment. Sluggish adaptation is the norm, because transforming public priorities, legislative procedures, and executive consultations all take time.[43]

In Hayek's dystopia, most people are serfs. As such, they are excluded from policymaking. They produce wealth on command, without any say in either how they work or how the fruits of their labor are spent. They have enslaved themselves by empowering others through government ownership, and they have transferred power to their tormentors in the naive belief that a centralized government makes better decisions than decentralized markets. In the United States today, people have granted enormous power to someone not because they believe in "big government" but, rather, because they consider this transfer essential to crushing their rivals. Nevertheless, the result is serfdom. As in Hayek's dystopia, they have no say over policies, which are not particularly responsive to their needs. Nativist loathing of identitarians gives Trump the political and social leverage to curtail the influences of his opponents; it does not necessarily produce initiatives that benefit his core supporters economically. Even more troubling, the hate-filled social atmosphere that nativist crowds have helped to create makes it difficult for them to go back, should they want a new leader. As individuals, they cannot easily switch sides without enduring the stigma that they helped to produce. They are effectively slaves to the political outcome they helped passionately to construct.

It is tempting to view Donald Trump's presidency as an aberration, and the man himself as the type of politician who gets taken seriously only when many stars line up. The obvious implication is that if Trump were to vanish, American politics would return to normal—to musical chairs between Republicans and Democrats who argue with each other endlessly over mostly symbolic differences. That is wishful thinking. The competing intolerances that made Trump electable would remain, and they might have gained intensity. Besides, on both sides of America's deep political divide, there are politicians ready to take his place as uncompromising punishers of the other side. Their governing styles would almost certainly differ from that of Trump; they would probably not tweet personal insults to critics who get under their skin. For that reason, though, they would probably be more effective at enacting their side's agenda.

A glimmer of hope is that the "mushy middle" in American politics is rediscovering the value of moderation and compromise. For instance, some liberal Democrats who were accustomed to vilifying former Republican presidents, presidential candidates, and legislators are discovering in these leaders virtues that they overlooked. To their eyes, certain Republican leaders now look committed to the core values of American politics and reasonably respectful toward political rivals. For their part, influential Republican leaders are distancing themselves from Trump and participating in bipartisan legislative initiatives. Meanwhile, ordinary Americans of diverse political affiliations show alarm at their country's hyper-polarization.

Whether the "mushy middle" can have a measurable impact on the trends identified in this article is another matter. A successful American movement of moderates requires sustained collective action by citizens willing to speak for moderation and confront rival forms of intolerance. It also requires organization and agreement on leaders. Yet collective action is difficult even under the best of circumstances, when the challenge is only the apportionment of a public good's cost.[44] An added difficulty here is that intolerant communities turn on people open to discussion and compromise. Hence, forming a large and sustainable tolerant community is no easy task in a society seething with intolerance. Many stars must line up for a return to politics based on mutual respect and willingness to seek common ground.

NOTES

1. Friedrich Hayek, *The Road to Serfdom*, ed. Bruce Caldwell from 1944 orig. (Chicago: University of Chicago Press, 2007).

2. For a classic statement, see James Madison, "The Federalist No. 51" (1788) in *The Federalist*, ed. Jacob E. Cooke, (Middletown, CT: Wesleyan University Press, 1961), 347–53.

3. For critical evaluations of the Trump administration's first few months in office, see Deroy Murdock, "100 Days of President Trump: The Good, the Bad, and the Ugly," *National Review*, April 28, 2017; and David Remnick, "A Hundred Days of Trump," *New Yorker*, May 1, 2017.

4. Michael D. Shear and Maggie Haberman, "Trump Defends Initial Remarks on Charlottesville; Again Blames 'Both Sides,'" *New York Times*, August 15, 2017.

5. Alexis de Tocqueville, *Democracy in America*, trans. Harvey Mansfield and Delba Winthrop from 1835 orig. (Chicago: University of Chicago Press, 2000).

6. The left-right spectrum emerged in France, where by 1871

it described party positions. Moving from left to right was considered to correlate also with an emphasis on law and order. See Marc Crapez, "De Quand Date le Clivage Gauche/Droite en France?" *Revue Française de Science Politique* 48 (1998): 42–75.

7. Two books played a central role in popularizing the concept: Alan Bloom, *The Closing of the American Mind: How Higher Education Has Failed Democracy and Impoverished the Souls of Today's Students* (New York: Simon & Schuster, 1987); and Roger Kimball, *Tenured Radicals: How Politics Has Corrupted Our Higher Education* (New York: HarperCollins, 1990).

8. For a compendium of readings that promote some form of political correctness, see Simon During, *The Cultural Studies Reader*, 2nd ed. (London: Routledge, 1999). For the regulation of racist speech, see in particular Charles R. Lawrence III, "If He Hollers Let Him Go: Regulating Racist Speech on Campus," *Duke Law Journal* 39, no. 3 (1990): 431–83.

9. Greg Lukianoff and Jonathan Haidt, "The Coddling of the American Mind," *Atlantic*, September 2015.

10. Paul Berman, *Debating P.C.: The Controversy over Political Correctness on College Campuses* (New York: Dell, 1992); Robert Hughes, *Culture of Complaint: The Fraying of America* (New York: Oxford University Press, 1993).

11. Amy Chozick, "Hillary Clinton Calls Many Trump Backers 'Deplorables' and G.O.P. Pounces," *New York Times*, September 10, 2016.

12. For two analytical works: Kathleen Hall Jamieson and Joseph N. Cappella, *Echo Chamber: Rush Limbaugh and the Conservative Media Establishment* (New York: Oxford University Press, 2008); and Jeffrey K. Hadden and Anson D. Shupe, *Televangelism: Power and Politics on God's Frontier* (New York: Henry Holt, 1988). An account of the strategies of these media by conservative activists: Richard A. Viguerie and David Franke, *America's Right Turn: How Conservatives Used New and Alternative Media to Take Over America* (Chicago: Bonus Books, 2004).

13. David Folkenflik, "The Birth of Fox News," Salon.com, October 19, 2013, http://www.salon.com/2013/10/19/the_birth_of_fox _news/; Stefano DellaVigna and Ethan Kaplan, "The Fox News

Effect: Media Bias and Voting," *Quarterly Journal of Economics* 122 (2007): 1187–234.

14. Ben McGrath, "The Movement: The Rise of Tea Party Activism," *New Yorker*, February 1, 2010; Vanessa Williamson, Theda Skocpol, and John Cogin, "The Tea Party and the Remaking of Republican Conservatism," *Perspectives on Politics* 9 (2011): 25–43.

15. Jeff Sharlet, "Donald Trump, American Preacher," *New York Times Sunday Magazine*, April 17, 2016.

16. Dara Lind, "Donald Trump's Drive for 'Law and Order' Undermines the Rule of Law," https://www.vox.com/policy -and-politics/2017/5/16/15641096/trump-rule-of-law; David Leonhardt, "The Lawless Presidency," *New York Times*, June 6, 2017; Rosie Gray, "Trump Declines to Affirm NATO's Article 5," *Atlantic*, May 25, 2017.

17. "Trumpism": Victor Davis Hanson, "What Exactly Is Trumpism?" *National Review*, January 10, 2017; "new political correctness": Paul Krugman, "The New Political Correctness," *New York Times,* May 26, 2012; "patriotic correctness": John K. Wilson, *Patriotic Correctness: Academic Freedom and Its Enemies* (Boulder, CO: Paradigm, 2008); "populist correctness": Arda Mahdawi, "Populist Correctness: The New PC Culture of Trump's America and Brexit Britain," *Guardian*, February 19, 2017. Because populism can belong to either side of the left-right political spectrum, it limits information about substantive goals.

18. Wilson, *Patriotic Correctness*, chap. 5.

19. Alan I. Abramowitz and Walter J. Stone, "The Bush Effect: Polarization, Turnout, and Activism in the 2004 Presidential Election," *Presidential Studies Quarterly* 36 (2006): 141–54; Nolan McCarty, "The Policy Effects of Political Polarization," in *The Transformation of American Politics: Activist Government and the Rise of Conservatism*, ed. Paul Pierson and Theda Skocpol (Princeton, NJ: Princeton University Press, 2007), 223–55.

20. The direct effect of gerrymandering on polarization is ambiguous; see Nolan McCarty, Keith T. Poole, and Howard Rosenthal, "Does Gerrymandering Cause Polarization?" *American Journal of Political Science* 53 (2009): 666–80. Nevertheless, it is widely viewed as a key source of polarization. See, for instance, Jeffrey Toobin,

"The Great Election Grab," *New Yorker*, December 8, 2003; and Elizabeth Kolbert, "How Redistricting Turned America from Blue to Red," *New Yorker*, June 27, 2016.

21. Cass R. Sunstein, *Echo Chambers: Bush v. Gore, Impeachment, and Beyond* (Princeton, NJ: Princeton Digital Books Plus, 2001); Cass R. Sunstein, *Republic.com 2.0* (Princeton, NJ: Princeton University Press, 2007), especially chaps. 2–3; R. Kelly Garrett, "Echo Chambers Online? Politically Motivated Selective Exposure among Internet News Users," *Journal of Computer-Mediated Communication* 14 (2009): 265–85.

22. Timur Kuran and Cass R. Sunstein, "Availability Cascades and Risk Regulation," *Stanford Law Review* 51 (1999): 683–768.

23. Seth Flaxman, Sharad Goel, and Justin M. Rao, "Filter Bubbles, Echo Chambers, and Online News Consumption," *Public Opinion Quarterly* 80 (2016): SI298–320.

24. Conor Friedersdorf, "The Value of Fighting Attacks on Free Speech Early and Often," *Atlantic*, January 6, 2017; Jonah Goldberg, "Free Speech Isn't Always a Tool of Virtue," *National Review*, June 21, 2017.

25. On the dynamics of preference and knowledge falsification, see Timur Kuran, *Private Truths, Public Lies: The Social Consequences of Preference Falsification* (Cambridge, MA: Harvard University Press, 1995).

26. A mainstream news outlet is one for which the two-party fraction of its readership that voted Republican in the last presidential election is between 0.3 and 0.7. For the three outlets mentioned, the shares are 0.42, 0.45, and 0.47, respectively (Flaxman, Goel, and Rao, "Filter Bubbles," Table 2).

27. Herman Wong, " 'I'm Glad He Got Shot': Nebraska Democrat Caught on Tape Criticizing Rep. Steve Scalise," *Washington Post*, June 23, 2017.

28. Kate Dailey, "Fred Phelps: How Westboro Pastor Spread 'God Hates Fags,'" *BBC News Magazine*, March 21, 2014.

29. Lloyd Grove, "How Breitbart Unleashes Hate Mobs to Threaten, Dox, and Troll Trump Critics," *Daily Beast*, March 1, 2016.

30. David French, "Black Lives Matter Keeps Getting More Radical— Will the Media Care?" *National Review*, August 5, 2016.

31. Establishment clause of First Amendment: "Congress shall make

no law respecting an establishment of religion, or prohibiting the free exercise thereof."

32. Russell Berman, "Democrats Go to War Over Neil Gorsuch," *Atlantic*, March 30, 2017; Ed O'Keefe and Sean Sullivan, "Senate Republicans Go 'Nuclear,' Pave the Way for Gorsuch Confirmation to Supreme Court," *Washington Post*, April 6, 2017.

33. Matthew Gentzkow, Jesse M. Shapiro, and Matt Taddy, "Measuring Polarization in High-Dimensional Data: Method and Application to Congressional Speech," NBER working paper, May 2017.

34. YouGovPolimetrix, "Anglo-Saxon Attitudes: A Survey of British and American Views of the World" (London: *Economist*, 2008).

35. Matthew Gentzkow, "Polarization in 2016," working paper, Stanford University, 2016.

36. Shanto Iyengar, Gaurav Sood, and Yohtach Lelkes, "Affect, Not Ideology: A Social Identity Perspective on Polarization," *Public Opinion Quarterly* 76 (2012): 405–31.

37. Václav Havel, "The Power of the Powerless," in *The Power of the Powerless: Citizens against the State in Central-Eastern Europe*, ed. John Keane, trans. Paul Wilson from 1979 orig. (Armonk, NY: M.E. Sharpe, 1985), 27–28. For an interpretation, see Kuran, *Private Truths*, chaps. 7 and 13.

38. Nate Silver, "Education, Not Income, Predicted Who Would Vote for Trump," *FiveThirtyEight*, November 22, 2016; Alec Tyson and Shiva Maniam, "Behind Trump's Victory: Divisions by Race, Gender, Education," *Pew Research Center Fact Tank*, November 9, 2016.

39. According to exit polls, 81 percent of white evangelicals voted for Trump (Gregory A. Smith and Jessica Martinez, "How the Faithful Voted: A Preliminary 2016 Analysis," *Pew Research Center Fact Tank*, November 9, 2016). For an interpretation, see Molly Worthen, "A Match Made in Heaven," *Atlantic*, May 2017.

40. They include his settlement of a lawsuit against Trump University and his companies' apparent preference for immigrant workers over Americans. For relevant insights, see Ben Shapiro, "Is Donald Trump a Pragmatist?" *National Review*, November 16, 2016; Peter Beinart, "The Anti-Anti-Trump Right," *Atlantic*, February 13, 2017.

41. For estimates, see Larry Buchanan, Andrew W. Lehren, Jugal K. Patel, and Adam Pearce, "How Much People in the Trump Administration are Worth," *New York Times*, April 3, 2017.
42. Stephen Sestanovich, "The Brilliant Incoherence of Trump's Foreign Policy," *Atlantic*, May 2017.
43. A vast political economy literature develops the mechanisms involved. For a sampling, see the essays in Jon Elster, ed., *Deliberative Democracy* (Cambridge, UK: Cambridge University Press, 1998); and Gérard Roland, "Understanding Institutional Change: Fast-Moving and Slow-Moving Institutions," *Studies in Comparative International Development* 38 (2004): 109–31.
44. Mancur Olson, *The Logic of Collective Action: Public Goods and the Theory of Groups*, rev. ed. (Cambridge, MA: Harvard University Press, 1971).

THE RESISTIBLE RISE OF LOUIS BONAPARTE

JON ELSTER

I. INTRODUCTION

The election of Donald Trump as president of the United States has triggered many historical analogies, notably with Mussolini, Hitler, and Berlusconi. Richard Cohen (*Washington Post*, May 3, 2017, p. A 17) suggests an intriguing comparison with Emperor Wilhelm II of Germany, adding, however, that "[m]ore disturbing than the similarities [. . .] are their differences. The kaiser was the product of an archaic monarchical system—the bad luck of the draw. Trump, however, was elected in a democratic process, and yet the result has been distressingly similar." In this chapter I discuss the rise to power of another autocrat, Louis Bonaparte (later Napoleon III), through a democratic process. First, however, I shall comment on the psychology of autocracy. I conclude with some observations on the comparative method.

The title of the chapter is a spin-off from the title of a play by Bertolt Brecht, *The Resistible Rise of Arturo Ui*, an allegorical representation of Hitler's rise to power. Arturo Ui is a gangster who takes over the cauliflower industry (an allegory of the Prussian Junkers) in Chicago by bribery and force. As Ui's rise to power unfolds, there is only *one point* at which he might have been resisted and stopped. This occurs at the very beginning, when Ui bribes a respected politician, Dogsborough (an allegorical reference to General Hindenburg). Ui's further rise to power occurs by brute force, in what seems to be an *irresistible* way. By contrast, I shall show that Louis Bonaparte might have been resisted at *three main branching points*, where his opponents had both the motive and the opportunity to stop him. The central question is *why they failed* to stop him when they could.

To convey some aspects of Arturo Ui's character, let me cite some of the lines that Brecht puts in the mouth of Ui, taken from the translation by Jennifer Wise (1972):

> *It doesn't matter what professors or smart-alecks think;*
> *all that counts is how the little man sees his master.*
>   *I don't muzzle the animal that does my heavy*
> *lifting. I overlook the foibles of my employees.*
>   *Me, I'm a peaceful man. But threats I don't stand*
> *for. You don't trust me blindly no more? Then go.*
> *Nobody's stopping you. You stay, you do your duty*
> *to the utmost. I say who gets what and when: duty*
> *first, rewards later. All I ask of you is trust, trust and*
> *nothing but.*

I'm not exactly loved. My humble beginnings as a poor son of the Bronx are always held against me, "He doesn't even know which fork to use at dinner," they say; "How can we trust him in the world of business?"

Trump observers will nod.

II. THE ROAD TO POWER AND THE USE OF POWER

Wilhelm II was born to rule. He did not have to *do* anything to achieve power. However, the substance of his power was very limited. As Cohen writes, "He was considered a fool and widely ignored within his own government." The French kings from Henri IV to Louis XVI present more interesting cases. The first of these *gained* power in the wars of religion, and consolidated it by converting. Once in power, Henri IV did not keep those who had helped him gain it as his advisors, but looked for administrative competence instead (Babelon 1982, p. 712). After 1945, Charles de Gaulle did the same. By contrast, Louis XIII, Louis XIV, Louis XV, and Louis XVI were *born* to rule, and did rule. They, too, needed advisors, but feared competence.

Before I proceed, let me sketch a character portrait of the narcissistic and megalomaniac ruler. He (or very occasionally she) seeks *glory*, great achievements (by some standard) for his nation that will reflect favorably on himself, because (he hopes) they will be seen as *his* achievements. However, *the desire for great achievements and the desire for taking personal credit for them may be at odds with each other*, if the latter desire induces a choice of inferior advisors, reluctance to listen to their advice, or, on their part, reluctance to offer it.

Consider first *born rulers*, such as Louis XIII, Louis XIV, Louis XV, and Louis XVI. Following the law of averages, they were of medium intelligence and competence (Louis XV stood out, but his intelligence was neutralized by his distrust of himself). Because of the causal efficacy of the Salic law of succession, the French kings were immune to the psychological pathologies of the "bad emperors" in Rome, who were obsessed with fears and suspicions and engaged in wholesale preemptive killings of potential rivals (Veyne 2005, p. 19). They were, however, subject to other, *structurally induced pathologies*. In particular, because they tended not to like the successes of their own agents, they sometimes deliberately chose less competent underlings. When these mostly average individuals were imbued with an inordinate desire for glory, they could not succeed by the route of competence. Instead, they used their equally inordinate power to remove or resist competence in others. Some examples follow.

Louis XIII did accept to work with Cardinal Richelieu—the creator of the modern French state—as his principal minister. Yet "since he could never be happy with him, nor without him, he was never happy" (Petitfils 2008, p. 614). Sometimes, Richelieu invented "arguments without value" against a proposal he wanted the king to accept (Chevallier 1979, p. 289). If we are to believe the character portrait that Saint-Simon (vol. IV, p. 941) sketched after the death of Louis *XIV*, he had what amounted to an inferiority complex. In his judgment, the king was "born with a spirit below the mediocre." He "feared sense (*esprit*), talent, elevated sentiments even in his generals and in his ministers" and "was tired of the superior sense and merit of his former ministers [Colbert and Louvois] and generals [Turenne, Condé]" (vol. IV, pp. 973, 974). Saint-Simon (vol. V, p. 319) also reports a story about how a woman at the Court, Mlle. de Chausserai, obtained all she wanted from Louis XIV "by pretending to be idiotic, ignorant, and indifferent about everything, and give him the pleasant feeling of being entirely superior to her in spirit." Any suggestions had to be made indirectly, to make the king believe that the idea came from him. Moreover, to prevent the appointment of someone to an important position, one could praise the candidate so excessively that the king felt crowded (Saint-Simon, vol. II, p. 556).

Although Saint-Simon's judgment may have been biased by his visceral dislike of Louis XIV, it can be supplemented by other statements. The outstanding diarist Abbé de Véri (vol. 2, p. 225) wrote that "fate gave [Louis XIV] first two competent ministers [Colbert and Louvois] whom he had not chosen and who were only moderately to his taste. When age gave him a pretext for deciding matters himself and choosing his cooperators in the ministry, in the army, and in high office, he made nothing but mistakes and the choices he made according to his preference (*par goût*) were all bad." Although Véri does not explicitly say, as did Saint-Simon, that the king chose incompetent agents *because of* their incompetence, Louis XIV (1806, p. 7) himself made it clear that this was the case: "I thought it was not in my interest to choose men with a more eminent dignity, because, needing to establish my own reputation in all domains, it was important that the public knew, by the rank of those who served me, that I did not intend to share my authority with them, and that they themselves, knowing who they were, should not conceive greater hopes than the ones I chose to give them." Ernest Lavisse (1989, p. 136) writes that Louis XIV "had an *almost childish* fear not only of being, but of 'appearing to be,' governed" (my italics).

Writing about Louis *XV*, the diarist d'Argenson (vol. 4, p. 60) says that he, too, had "the *mutinous spirit of a child*, whose amour-propre makes him ridiculously watchful against the rumor of being governed" (my italics). In fact, one expression of amour-propre is what psychologists call *reactance*, the tendency of agents to reject suggestions or recommendations to perform some action, even when it would be in their interest. According to d'Argenson (ibid.), Louis XV was tainted by this tendency: "If it was discovered that he was going to fight his enemies on the Rhine, that was enough to make him turn his steps towards Normandy; the announcement of anything always made him do the opposite: the announcement of the disgrace of [the officer and diplomat] Bellisle made him a duke, and the announcement of his great favor on the return from [a much admired defense of] Prague caused him and those close to him to appear as being in disgrace." Concerning Louis XVI, Edgar Faure (1961, p. 28) cites a distinction he takes from de Gaulle: he "did not have the *passion for power*, but he did have the *jealousy of decision*." Faure (ibid., p. 428) also refers to the king's "sulking egocentrism." Véri (vol. 1, p. 448) reports Louis XVI as saying about his principal minister, the most gifted official of the ancien régime, "*M. Turgot wants to be me, and I do not want him to be me.*" His inferiority complex was probably one of the many causes of his disastrous dismissal of Turgot in 1776.

Consider now rulers whose narcissism and megalomania *preceded* their rise to power by electoral means. Usually, these character features are an obstacle to gaining power. In the electoral campaign of 2015–16, commentators and rival candidates widely assumed, although with decreasing confidence, that in the case of Donald Trump they would make him ineligible. Instead, while Hillary Clinton turned out to be the "Velcro candidate," Trump surprised everybody by being the "Teflon candidate." Political psychologists still do not understand why—the sheer number of proposed explanations suggests that they are all wrong or incomplete. Be this as it may, the narcissistic megalomaniac did win the White House. Once there, he acted like the French kings whose narcissistic megalomania was structurally induced. The description of Louis XVI as "sulking" matches the common characterization of Trump as "petulant." On May 15, 2017, David Brooks wrote an op-ed piece in the *New York Times* titled "When the World Is Led by a Child." Although he does not mention the aspect of childishness that I cited from the French writers, his colleagues Glenn Thrush and Maggie Haberman (*New York Times*, May 17, 2017, p. A 16) nailed it down:

There is a fear among some of Mr. Trump's senior advisers about leaving him alone in meetings with foreign leaders

*out of concern he might speak out of turn. General
McMaster, in particular, has tried to insert caveats or
gentle corrections into conversations when he believes the
president is straying off topic or onto boggy diplomatic
ground. This has, at times, chafed the president,
according to two officials with knowledge of the situation.
Mr. Trump, who still openly laments having to dismiss
his first national security adviser, Michael T. Flynn,
has groused that General McMaster talks too much in
meetings, and the president has referred to him as "a
pain," according to one of the officials.*

Conjecturally, Trump's perception, which he expressed when James Comey was still director of the FBI, that Comey was "more famous" than him may have contributed to his decision to fire him.

Before discussing the rise of Louis Bonaparte, let me briefly note that he seems to have been only mildly afraid of competence when he did attain power. Although some of the passages I italicize in Tocqueville's portrait of him (reproduced in the Appendix) suggest that attitude, Louis Bonaparte chose many competent ministers and was, in some ways, quite competent himself.

III. THE THREE RESISTIBLE STEPS IN LOUIS BONAPARTE'S RISE TO POWER[1]

Louis Napoleon Bonaparte (1808–1873) was the nephew of Napoleon I. From an early age, he saw it as his life's mission to restore the dynasty. Since as a member of a former reigning family he was banned from living in France, he initiated several conspiracies from abroad: from Rome in 1830, from Switzerland in 1836, and from England in 1840. The first led to his expulsion; the second to banishment to the United States; and the third to imprisonment for life. He evaded prison in 1846 and settled in England. As Tocqueville observes in his portrait of Louis Bonaparte, he was an *adventurer*. Yet he had some solid intellectual achievements, notably a manual of artillery (written in prison) that was appreciated by military specialists and a life of Julius Caesar (written when he was emperor) that, while appreciated by historians, was essentially a quasi-Hegelian justification of himself as the instrument of progress.

One can distinguish four stages in his rise to power: his designation as a deputy in by-elections to the constituent assembly of 1848, his election as president on December 10, 1848, his seizure of dictatorial power on December 2, 1851 (his "18 Brumaire"), and the transformation of the republic into a hereditary empire in November 1852. Each move was "resistible" except the last, which for that reason I shall not discuss.

Election as deputy. The first elections to the constituent assembly took place on April 23–24, 1848. At the time, Napoleon was living in England. He was not a candidate for elective office, but nevertheless received 5,800 votes in one *département* and a few hundred in two others. As these votes were insufficient to elect him, the issue of his eligibility did not arise. When, following clever campaigning by his associates, three *départements* elected him in by-elections on

June 4, that issue immediately came up and divided the assembly. On June 12, the executive commission that had succeeded the provisional government applied a law from 1832 that banned members of the family of Napoleon I from entering France, and sent instructions to authorities in French ports to arrest Louis Napoleon were he to try to enter the country. On June 13, the assembly conducted a heated and confused debate over the issue. Although Louis Napoleon had no political followers or allies in the assembly, many speakers nevertheless defended his right to enter the country and serve as deputy. A recurrent argument was that denying him entry and eligibility would be *beneath the dignity* of the assembly and of the Republic. The most vocal exponent of this view was the *rapporteur* on the matter, the moderate Republican Jules Favre. He accused the commission of leaving the impression that "the people's state could be overthrown by a pygmy" and asserted that if "the citizen Louis Bonaparte should be mad enough, foolish enough to imagine today that he is [performing] a kind of parody of what he did in 1840, he would be covered by the contempt of his fellow citizens and of posterity." The socialist Louis Blanc was no less eloquent: "Let us not aggrandize the pretenders by removing them; we should see them close up better to take their measure." As he also said, "to give the appearance of shaking with fear for the fate of the Republic, is to insult it."

Some deputies argued against admitting Louis Bonaparte. The radical deputy Phillipe Buchez argued that only when the Republic was "perfectly founded and established" could the assembly "open its door to all"; for the time being, the risk of bloodshed was too great. The radical Alexandre Ledru-Rollin, a member of the executive commission, defended its decision in what seems like halfhearted terms, asserting that he might change his mind if Louis Bonaparte solemnly affirmed that he bowed before the Republic. At the end, a large majority voted to admit Louis Bonaparte as a deputy. According to Anceau (2012, p. 123), it was made up of "a coalition of [i] parliamentarians indignant for having been deceived, [ii] enemies of the government, [iii] republicans concerned with respecting the popular vote, [iv] legitimists[2] who were partisans of crisis maximisation (*la politique du pire*), and [v] *orléanists*[3] who hoped to create a precedent for their own princes." The list *does not include any supporters* of Louis Bonaparte.

On June 18, Louis Bonaparte resigned from the assembly. Fortuitously, this act served him well, as he did not have to take a position on either side of the insurrection of the workers of Paris on June 22–26, and appeared in the eyes of many as a potential savior. In new by-elections on September 17–18, he stood as a candidate in four *départements* and won the elections in all of them, as well as garnering thousands of votes in other *départements*. On September 24, the government bowed to popular opinion and authorized him to cross the Channel and take his place in the assembly. Yet public opinion did not amount to an organized movement that could have led to a civil war if Louis Bonaparte's eligibility had been denied. If the assembly had maintained the law of 1832 as well as the law that required hefty cautions for newspapers—whose abolition allowed Louis Bonaparte's campaign managers to create half a dozen newspapers targeting specific groups—there is no reason to believe that there would have been serious unrest.

Election as president. The second step in the rise of Louis Bonaparte was his election as president of the country on December 10, 1848. This step, too, was eminently resistible. To explain why, it is necessary to discuss the adoption of the first constitutional draft by the constitutional committee in the assembly and the plenary debates that followed the presentation of the committee's second draft. The committee did not include any supporters of Louis Bonaparte. In the assembly, there were perhaps half a dozen or a dozen deputies who "would form the core of the bonapartist troops" (Bastid 1945, vol. I, p. 191), but they were not yet organized, and in any case constituted a tiny minority of the nine hundred members of the assembly.

On the afternoon of May 27 and then again on June 14–15, the sixteen members of the constitutional committee discussed the mode of electing the president. On the first occasion, they voted to have the president elected by direct universal suffrage and a relative majority, with a minimum of two million votes being required. (The electorate was about 9.3 million.) On the second occasion, several members of the committee changed their minds, as a direct result of the success of Louis Bonaparte in the elections on June 4. The reversal of the only socialist member, Victor Considerant, is particularly striking. His only recorded contribution to the debate on May 27 was to oppose a proposal to have the president chosen by popular vote among five candidates nominated by the national assembly. According to the minutes, "M. Considerant said that this necessity for the people to limit its choice to certain men was a violation of the national sovereignty." On June 15, he "demanded that [the president] be elected by the national assembly. True principles, he said, would require him to be elected by the whole people. But the education of the people is not yet achieved; to let it exercise all its rights one must wait until it is more capable of appreciating them."

Tocqueville was a member of the constitutional committee. While his account of the debates in his *Recollections* is inaccurate and needs to be corrected by the minutes, his statements about his own views are presumably more trustworthy. Among his inaccurate statements is the claim that Armand Marrast, a fellow committee member, initially voted for election by the assembly because "he flattered himself that he would be the Assembly's choice" (Tocqueville 1987, p. 176). It is clear from the minutes that Marrast consistently advocated popular vote among five candidates nominated by the national assembly. Yet the idea is important, since it is arguable (see below) that the views of other leading politicians on the question of popular vote versus assembly election were shaped by their own electoral prospects under either scheme.

On May 27, Tocqueville went along with the rest of the committee. On June 15, he, too, changed his mind to counter the risk of Louis Bonaparte being elected. "It was the aftermath of the 4th June. Prince Louis Napoleon, who had been in nobody's thoughts a few days before, had just been elected to the assembly by Paris and three departments. It began to be feared that he would soon be placed at the head of the Republic if the choice of president was left to the people. The various pretenders and their friends got quite excited; the question was again out to the committee, and the majority voted as before" (Tocqueville 1987, p. 177). The last statement is true, in the sense that the committee did vote for popular election, but incomplete, since it does not mention the proposed changes in the electoral system. Inspired by the American system, which he knew well, Tocqueville proposed that the president would need an absolute rather than relative majority, and that the choice would go to the assembly if no candidate satisfied this requirement. This proposal was adopted and eventually made part of the constitution (Article 47). He also proposed the adoption of another feature of the American system, a two-tier popular election with electors chosen by universal suffrage. In the committee, the proposal received four votes (out of sixteen). When it was made again in the plenary assembly, Jean-Baptiste Payer effectively seems to have killed it by his remark that having the president chosen by an electoral college differed little from having him chosen by an elected assembly.

As noted, both Considerant and Tocqueville modified their positions in attempts to block Louis Bonaparte. As Tocqueville must have suspected that his proposal would fail, why did he not vote for election by the assembly? "The main reason that I gave [when later defending popular election in the constituent assembly] was that, having announced to the nation that this ardently desired right would be granted, it was no longer possible to refuse it" (Tocqueville 1987, p. 178). He had in fact asked the assembly on October 5, "Is it not true that the nation, the whole French people, has been nurtured by the idea that it would one day choose the head of the executive power?" As a matter of fact, his argument in the assembly was more complex, as he also made strong objections to the chaotic (he claimed) *régime d'assemblée*, similar to the revolutionary convention, that would be created if the president were to be elected by the assembly. These arguments do not ring true. I suspect Tocqueville was presenting the best case for a conclusion he had reached on other grounds. In the committee, he was probably influenced by the fact that defenders of election by the assembly were a small minority (three members supported it in their interventions, but only two voted for it). Rather than pursuing a lost cause, he preferred instead to improve the majority position in a direction less likely to lead to the election of Louis Bonaparte.

There remained the remedy that had failed in the first stage: adopting a constitutional clause banning members of former reigning families from being candidates. According to the minutes, on June 15, "M. [Jean-Pierre] Pagès demands the adoption of an article that excludes from the right to the presidency members of families that have ruled over France. There followed a long discussion of this proposal, which when put to the vote was rejected by nine votes to seven." I have not found any more details about this close and momentous vote than this tantalizingly brief narrative. Did Tocqueville and his close friend Gustave de

Beaumont vote for it? (Neither had spoken in the assembly when it debated the eligibility as deputy of Louis Bonaparte on June 13.) What were the *arguments* made in this "long discussion"? We are equally ignorant about the details of the next vote recorded in the minutes: "A member demanded the exclusion of army commanders. This proposal gathers only five votes." Was this proposal, too, made to exclude a specific person? We do not know.

After the committee presented its first draft (reproduced in Bastid 1945, vol. 1, pp. 293–98) on June 19, it was sent to be discussed in the fifteen bureaus of the assembly. Between July 24 and August 3, their delegates met with the constitutional committee, which presented its final draft (reproduced in Bastid 1945, vol. 2, pp. 317–24) to the assembly on August 30. A minority of the bureaus demanded election of the president by the assembly, and among those that accepted popular election a minority demanded the exclusion of members of foreign ruling families. In one bureau, a proposal that the president should be required to have been domiciled in France for ten years was rejected as "undignified." It does not seem that the deliberations in the bureaus affected the final discussions of the committee, except for a proposal by one bureau that in the first election the president should be chosen by the assembly, and only later by the nation. The committee had a "long debate" over this scheme, which was manifestly yet another device to exclude Louis Bonaparte. It decided to maintain its own proposal but only provisionally, until it could hear from the head of the executive branch.

The previous sentence may seem puzzling, since earlier I have referred to a *collective* executive (the commission). The explanation lies in the events of June 22–26, briefly mentioned above. The insurrection of the Paris workers was brutally crushed by troops led by General Louis-Eugène Cavaignac, who as a result gained immense popularity in the assembly, which elected him chief of the executive. Although these events caused numerous changes from the first to the second draft of the constitution, withdrawing popular clauses such as the right to work and progressive taxation, they did not affect the proposed design of the presidency. However, the fact that the proposal was only provisional and might be modified after hearing from Cavaignac suggests that the committee envisaged him as a candidate for election by the assembly. Yet when Cavaignac appeared before the committee on August 12, he explicitly supported the principle of popular election.

Cavaignac was ambitious: he wanted to be elected. If he had signaled a preference for election by the assembly, it seemed certain that the framers would have adopted this scheme and that he would then have been elected by the first legislative assembly. The path to power for Louis Bonaparte would have been barred. We do not know why he didn't send the signal. He may have been genuinely convinced that popular election was the best solution for the nation, perhaps, as Tocqueville said, because it would accept nothing else, even if it made *his* election more uncertain. Alternatively, he may have made a self-interested calculation that the certitude of being elected by the assembly to a weak presidency was less valuable than a probable if uncertain election to a presidency whose power would have been enhanced by its popular backing. If the second assumption is correct, his self-interest was undermined by an irrational political assessment. Even if the members of the assembly were grateful to him for crushing the workers of Paris, there was no reason why the French peasants, who made up 75 percent of the electorate, should reward him for this action.

Cavaignac was not the only politician who both sought to be elected and expressed a preference for the mode of election. The poet-politician Alphonse de Lamartine, a member of the executive commission and perhaps the most eloquent speaker in the assembly (by the standards of eloquence of the time), may have tipped the balance in favor of popular election by a speech he gave on October 6 in response to a proposal by Jules Grévy to have the president elected by the assembly. To justify his proposal, Grévy had asked the assembly:

> Are you certain that among the persons who will succeed each other every four years there will be only pure republicans eager to step down from office? Are you certain there will never be an ambitious person who might be tempted to perpetuate himself in office? And if this ambitious man is a man who knows how to make himself popular; if it is a victorious general wrapped in the prestige of military glory that the French can never resist; if it is an offspring of one of the families that have ruled over France, who has never explicitly

renounced what he calls his rights; *if trade is languishing, if the people is suffering, if it is in one of the moments of crisis where misery and disappointment deliver the people to those who hide under promises their plans against its freedom—can you vouch that this ambitious person might not overthrow the Republic?* (My italics)

In an extraordinary speech, Lamartine responded:

Even if the people should choose that [candidate] that my perhaps uninformed foresight fears it might choose, what does it matter? Alea jacta est. *Let God and the people speak! We must leave something for Providence. That will be the light for those, like ourselves, [who] cannot read in the darkness of the future. Let us appeal to Providence, pray that it will enlighten the people, and submit ourselves to its decree. Perhaps we ourselves shall perish at the task? No, No, and in fact it would be beautiful to perish in initiating the people to freedom!*

So what if the people errs, if it lets itself be blinded by the splendor of its own past glory; if it withdraws from its own sovereignty after the first step, as if frightened by the greatness of the edifice we have opened for it in the republic and by the difficulties of its institutions; if it wants to abdicate its safety, its dignity, its liberty into the hands of a reminiscence of Empire; if it says: bring me back to the chains of the old Monarchy (ramenez-moi aux carrières de la vieille Monarchie);

if it disavows us and disavows itself; oh well, so much the worse for the people (eh bien! tant pis pour le peuple)! *It will not be ourselves, but the people that shall have been lacking in perseverance and courage.*

The speech is consistent with the judgment by Tocqueville (1987, p. 108) that Lamartine "always seemed ready to turn the world upside down to distract himself" (translation modified). Yet according to Bastid (1945, vol. II, p. 111), the speech, which was met with prolonged applause, was "decisive." We do not know, of course, how many deputies actually changed their minds after listening to it. We also do not know whether Lamartine counted on being himself the people's choice. Berton (1897, p. 711) cites a member of the assembly as reporting that Lamartine had predicted that no candidate would get an absolute majority, that the assembly would choose among Louis Bonaparte, Ledru-Rollin, and himself as front-runners, and that his eloquence would "subjugate" the assembly and make it elect him, "perhaps unanimously." If correctly reported, this remark is consistent with another observation by Tocqueville (1987, p. 108), that Lamartine was an "ambitious egoist [. . .] untroubled by any thought of the public good."

Louis Bonaparte swept the elections on December 10, with 5.5 million votes out of 7.5 million cast. Cavaignac received 1.4 million votes, and Lamartine 18,000. The result "showed in a flagrant manner *the gap that existed between the French people and its governing elites*" (Anceau 2012, p. 142; my italics). The elites were in fact guilty of a *double mis-*

take, not only that of underestimating the popular appeal of Louis Bonaparte but also that of overestimating their ability to control him were he to be elected. He had deliberately kept a low profile, cultivating his "phlegm, apathy, and silence [. . .] to allay the distrust of his interlocutors" (ibid., p. 136). Adolphe Thiers, later the first president of the Third Republic, supported his candidacy and imagined that he would become his mentor and successor. As Tocqueville said in a passage included in the Appendix below, his supporters "thought he would be a tool for them to use at will and break any time they wanted." They had their eyes opened when Louis Bonaparte published an ambitious program on November 27 (ibid., pp. 138–39), but by then it was too late to stop him.

On November 4, the very last day of the debates, the framers nevertheless adopted a parchment barrier against a future coup d'état: "Any measure by which the president of the Republic dissolves the national Assembly, prorogues it, or creates an obstacle to the exercise of its mandate, constitutes high treason. By this very fact, the president is ousted from his office; the citizens are obliged to refuse to obey him; the executive power passes automatically to the national Assembly" (Article 68). In the words of Bastid (1945, vol. II, pp. 147–48), this last-minute change "testifies [. . .] to the fact that the Assembly was haunted by the fear of a coup d'État by the President directed against itself. One is astonished that *these precise and manifest worries led to nothing but tragically illusory precautions*" (my italics).

From president to dictator. Louis Bonaparte took the

third step on December 2, 1851, on what Marx called his "18 Brumaire." The day (November 9, 1799) on which his uncle had assumed power was vividly present in everybody's mind. Among the many references to the event, that of Lamartine (in his speech on October 6) stands out: "To arrive at an 18th Brumaire in the time we live, two things are required: long years of Terror behind us and Marengos, victories, ahead of us."[4] One can hardly imagine a more superficial use of a historical analogy. In fact, what is surprising is not the coup d'état, but that Louis Bonaparte waited so long before carrying it out. His advisors had urged him to do so on four occasions (Anceau 2012, pp. 154, 159, 160, 165), but he had consistently refused. When he finally took the step, it was triggered by the process of revising the constitution to make him eligible for a second term.

Article 45 of the 1848 constitution states, "The president of the republic is elected for four years, and not reeligible till after four years from the expiration of his term of office." Article 111 says, "Should the Assembly, at the close of its session, express a desire for a total or partial change in the Constitution, the revision shall be proceeded with in the following manner: The wish expressed by the Assembly cannot become law till after three successive debates, which must take place after the interval of one month between each, and can be carried only by three-fourths of the votes, those voting being not less than 500 in number." Although Louis Bonaparte "very subtly alternated measures designed to intimidate the deputies, to seduce them or to discredit them" (Anceau 2012, p. 176), the numbers did not add up.

As Marx (1963, pp. 95–96) noted, the republican opposition in the assembly commanded more than a quarter of the votes and thus could block any revision. The proposal to revise Article 45 to allow Louis Bonaparte a second term fell with 446 votes for and 278 against.

Yet we must ask why the republicans and other opponents of the revision did not see the writing on the wall. Did they really believe that Louis Bonaparte would step down peacefully if he could not be reelected? On May 27, 1848, Tocqueville had stated in the constitutional committee, "It is true [. . .] that if the president cannot be re-elected, one might create an enormous dissatisfaction in the mind of an eminent man who cannot stay in power to accomplish his great projects, leaving him only with ambition born of desperation and inspiring him to break the constitution." He went on to say, however, that he thought this eventuality a lesser evil than exposing society to the corrupting influence of a president using the force at his disposal to extend his power. As we have seen, at that date Louis Bonaparte was still an unknown entity. Tocqueville's fear of making the president re-eligible was an abstract one, and probably based on his views about the danger of the re-eligibility of the American president (see Tocqueville 2004, p. 154). Surprisingly, the minutes of the debates on June 15, when the candidacy of Louis Bonaparte had become a real possibility, do not indicate any discussion of the re-eligibility of the president. Nor do the minutes show any references to this issue in the summaries of the opinions of the bureaus. In the plenary debates in October, only the deputy Vincent de Kerdrel argued, in a confused intervention that clearly bored the assembly, for the president to be re-eligible (for one four-year period). This scheme, he claimed, would prevent both the dangers that Tocqueville cited, a coup d'état as well as corruption. Yet even if the issue of re-eligibility had little salience in 1848, by 1851 its importance should have been obvious.

If the assembly had seen the writing on the wall, a revision of the constitution was not its only option. It could also, more conjecturally, have signaled its acquiescence in an extra-constitutional but nonviolent prolongation of the presidency. This was the outcome that Marx (1964, p. 144) predicted in 1850, and also the solution that Tocqueville (1987, p. 291) recommended to Louis Bonaparte in a conversation with him on June 15, 1851. Recent French constitutional history shows an example of this strategy, when de Gaulle amended the constitution in 1962 by means of an unconstitutional referendum.

In its arm-wrestling with the president in November 1851, the assembly made two crucial mistakes (Anceau 2012, pp. 183–84; Bastid 1945, vol. II, pp. 300–311). First, by rejecting on November 13, 1851, the president's proposal to abrogate the law of May 31, 1850, which had abolished universal suffrage, it discredited itself in the public opinion and allowed Louis Bonaparte to pose as the champion of the people. Second, in a complicated imbroglio, the assembly abstained from using a tool that could have preempted the anticipated coup. On May 11, 1848, the assembly had adopted a decree that authorized the president of the assembly to call out troops to protect it, which could have allowed it to bypass the war ministry. On November 17, 1851, the proposal to invoke this decree was rejected in the assembly by 408 votes to 300, "thanks to a heterogeneous coalition of supporters of the Elysée [the residence of Louis Bonaparte], pusillanimous or resigned conservatives, and the majority of the *montagnards* [radicals]" (Anceau 2012, p. 184). On December 2, Louis Bonaparte carried out his bid for power in an impeccably efficient manner, in stark contrast to the bungled counterrevolutionary coup attempt by Louis XVI in the days leading up to July 14, 1789 (Caron 1906–7).

Summary and discussion. The national assembly *could have resisted each step* in Louis Bonaparte's rise to absolute power:

> *It could have banned him from returning to the country.*
>
> *It could have prevented him from serving as a deputy.*
>
> *It could have excluded him from the presidency.*
>
> *It could have assigned the election of the president to the national assembly, where he had no support.*
>
> *It could have agreed to revise the constitution to make him eligible for a second term, thus preventing the coup d'état.*
>
> *It could have signaled acceptance of an extra-constitutional, nonviolent prolongation of his term.*
>
> *It could have avoided giving him a pretext for the coup.*
>
> *It could have preempted it by a coup of its own.*

Why did it take none of these actions?

The utter ineptness of the deputies and their tendency toward wishful thinking must surely enter into the explanation. For reasons of space, I have cited only a few instances of their empty and sentimental rhetoric, notably their repeated claims that the "dignity" of the Republic prevented them from protecting it against a notorious political adventurer. They mostly acted and talked as if the introduction of universal (male) suffrage, after fifty years of disenfranchisement of the vast majority of the population, had magically created a strong democratic culture in one fell swoop. At the same time, puzzlingly, they applauded wildly Lamartine's proposal to gamble on democracy: if they lost the gamble, so much the worse for the people. It is perhaps revealing that the socialist Victor Considerant, who presumably knew the people better, was unwilling to take the gamble. Another effect of the sudden enthusiasm for democracy was more unpredictable. Under the July Monarchy, the government could control the press by censorship and by heavy cautions on newspapers. As noted, the abolition of this caution played into the hands of the campaign managers of Louis Bonaparte, at a time when he was still short of funds.

It is also possible, but remains conjectural, that the choice of popular election of the president was due to wishful thinking on the part of two rival contenders, Cavaignac and Lamartine. Less conjecturally, wishful thinking made the political elites believe that they could easily control and manipulate Louis Bonaparte were he to be elected. They were predisposed to take more account of his apparent passivity than of his past record as an adventurer and conspirator. Their underestimation of his electoral appeal may have been due to wishful overestimation of the grip of democratic norms on the voters.

IV. CONCLUSION: ANALOGIES AND HOMOLOGIES

As Khong (1992) showed in a pathbreaking book, *Analogies at War*, American politicians and generals constantly used historical analogies to justify their decisions in the Vietnam War. As I have argued elsewhere (Elster 2015, pp. 49–50, 172–73), their use amounted to lazy intellectual shortcuts and had disastrous effects. The analogies proposed by historians who compare the rise of Napoleon III to the rise of fascism are also useless or worse (Anceau 2012, pp. 18, 612). In the Trump era, journalists and even scholars have used analogies to illuminate his rise to power and, more occasionally, his behavior in office. I believe that these, too, are uniformly unhelpful. Analogies can provide a pleasing or comforting *mental click* that is easily confused with the click of explanation (Elster 2015, pp. 171–72), but it is not the real thing.

I believe, however, that *homologies* can be more valuable (see Wise and Bozarth 1987 for this distinction, illustrated on page 304).

Among the similarities between Bourbon kings and Donald Trump, which are analogies and which are ho-

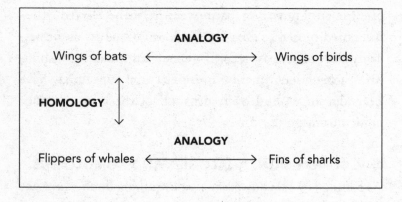

mologies? A reckless sex life (in the cases of Louis XIV and Louis XV) provides an analogy but has no further predictive power, any more than the fact that birds and bats both have wings allows us to predict a common reproductive system. By contrast, I believe that their shared narcissistic megalomania provides a homology. Despite the innumerable surface differences between Trump and the Bourbons, comparable to the differences between bats and whales, the deep similarity in psychological makeup allows us to predict that their efforts will fail, because success would have required listening to competent advisors who might then take the credit.

I shall not pursue these speculations here, but ask instead whether the rise to power of Louis Bonaparte and that of Donald Trump might be homologous. Is there a *common causal mechanism* that can explain how a political adventurer and a scandal-ridden hero of the tabloids could rise to the highest office in their countries? The mechanism, if there is one, cannot be found in their character, but in the weakness of their opponents. In Trump's case, I can see two weaknesses: wishful thinking and lack of coordination. When Trump's candidacy ceased to be a joke, as he was eliminating his rivals one by one, there may have been a moment when a *coordinated withdrawal* in favor of, say, John Kasich would have saved the country from the disaster that unfolded. If there was such a last-chance moment, why did the candidates not seize it?

Wishful thinking may have led some to believe that they could still beat Trump. Others may have counted on Trump not gathering the number of votes needed to win the nomination at the Republican Convention, or on the convention changing the rules of the game. Also, each of the other candidates may have thought that the others should withdraw in favor of *him*. It is in fact possible—although we shall never know—that even one of the more extreme candidates might have beaten Trump if the others had withdrawn in time. In that case, there would have been a classical coordination problem: the existence of several possible paths to beating Trump, *all of which* would have been preferred to his victory *by all his rivals* and *each of which* would have been the first choice of *one of them*. To this problem, we can add that of *distrust*: could other candidates really be trusted to carry out their promise to withdraw?

In the opposition to Louis Bonaparte, we can firmly identify the operation of wishful thinking. As we have seen, the wishful thinking took two distinct forms: underestimating the popular appeal of Louis Bonaparte and overestimating the ease of manipulating him were he nevertheless to be elected. I do not know whether Trump's rivals or the leadership of the Republican Party committed the second mistake, but they were certainly guilty of the first. When Trump made the first of his many outrageous statements, it was perhaps rational to believe that the voters would reject him, but once the primaries had demonstrated his Teflon quality, only irrational wishful thinking can explain the blindness of his rivals.

The standard political tactic of shaping the rules of the game to generate a desired outcome is not always feasible. The belief among some Republicans that Trump could be blocked by manipulating the voting rules at the Republican Convention was manifestly irrational. By contrast, the main rival of Louis Bonaparte, Cavaignac, had it in his power to make the constituent assembly write election of the president by the legislative assembly into the constitution. As noted, the choice would have fallen on him. However, for reasons we do not know, he chose not to use his power to shape the rules.

The constituent assembly of 1848 was composed of roughly 50 percent moderate republicans, 25 percent radicals, and 25 percent monarchists, split between the two dynastic factions. The last were perhaps the most important in facilitating the rise to power of Louis Bonaparte. The supporters of each of the two dynastic pretenders might prefer him over the other (Marx 1963, pp. 97–100). Also, as noted, admitting him to the country and to the assembly could set a precedent that favored their own candidate. Anceau (2012, p. 184), writes that "the left refused to support the proposal [to authorize the president of the assembly to call out troops], because it feared a coup by the monarchists even more than one by the president." I know too little about the political sociology of the Second Republic to assess the importance of this factor. What seems certain, however, is that the question of *coordinating the opposition* never arose. In this respect, the rise to power of Trump differed from that of Louis Bonaparte.

APPENDIX: TOCQUEVILLE'S PORTRAIT OF LOUIS BONAPARTE

(Tocqueville 1987, pp. 202–5; modified translation; my italics.)

He was a great deal better than the impression of him one might fairly have formed from his earlier career and mad enterprises. That was my first impression as I got to know him. In this he disappointed his adversaries, but perhaps he disappointed his friends even more, if one can give that name to the politicians who supported his candidature. For most of them had chosen him, not for his worth, but for his presumed mediocrity. *They thought he would be a tool for them to use at will and break any time they wanted.* In this they were mightily deceived.

As a private individual, Louis Napoleon had some attractive qualities: a kindly, easy-going temperament; a humane character; a soul that was gentle and even rather tender, but without delicacy; great confidence in his relations with people; a perfect simplicity; an element of personal modesty mixed with immense pride in his ancestry;

and a better memory for kindnesses than for resentment. He could feel affection, and arouse it in those who came near him. He spoke little and poorly; he had not the art of making others talk and establishing intimacy with them, and no facility in expressing himself; he had the habits of a scribbler and something of an author's amour-propre. *His power of dissimulation, which, as one would expect from a man who had spent his life in conspiracies, was profound,* and was peculiarly assisted by the immobility of his features and his want of expression; his eyes were lustreless and opaque like thick glass portholes that let light through but are not transparent. Careless of danger, his courage in moments of crisis was fine and cool, but at the same time, as is common enough, his plans were very vacillating. He was often noticed changing course, advancing, hesitating and drawing back, to his great damage. For the nation had chosen him to dare all and expected audacity, not prudence, from him. He was said to have been always much given to physical pleasures and not discriminating in his choice of them. This taste for vulgar enjoyments and comforts increased with the opportunities given by power. This was a daily drain on his energy, and it blunted and reduced his very ambition. His mind was incoherent and confused, being filled with great thoughts ill-clothed, some of them borrowed from Napoleon's example, some from socialist theories, and some from memories of England where he had lived for a time—those were very different and often contradictory sources. And they were the laborious result of solitary meditations far from men and affairs, for he was by nature a fantastic dreamer. But when forced to come down from these vast, vague regions and confine his attention within the limits of a definite matter, he could take a fair view of it, sometimes with subtlety and compass; but sure he never was, being always ready to put some fantastic idea beside a reasonable one. One could not be in intimate contact with him for long without noticing a little vein of madness running through his good sense, which constantly brought the escapades of his youth to mind and served to explain them.

But yet, in the actual circumstances, he owed his success and strength more to his madness than to his sense, for the world's stage is a strange place. Sometimes the worst plays are the ones that come off best there. If Louis Napoleon had been a wise man, or a genius if you like, he would never have been President of the Republic.

He trusted his star, firmly believing himself the instrument of destiny and the necessary man. I have always thought that he was really convinced of his right, and I do not think Charles X was more infatuated with his legitimacy than he was. He was also no more capable than he was of giving any reason for his faith, for while he had a sort of abstract adoration for the people, he had very little taste for liberty. In political matters, the basic characteristic of his mind was hate and contempt for assemblies. The rule of constitutional monarchy he found even more insupportable than that of the Republic. *The pride he derived from his name, which knew no limit, would willingly bow before the nation but revolted at the idea of submitting to the influence of a parliament.*

Before he came to power, he had had a long time in

which to *strengthen the taste that mediocre princes always have for lackeys,* by the habits of *twenty years spent in conspiracies with low-class adventurers,* ruined men or men of blemished reputations, and young debauchees, the only persons who all that time would consent to serve him as flatterers or accomplices. In him, too, for all his good manners, *traces of the adventurer and accidental prince showed through.* He continued to take pleasure in inferior company when he was no longer obliged to live in it. I think his difficulty in expressing his thoughts except in writing drew him to people who had long been familiar with his ideas and his dreams, and that his inferiority in discussion *made the company of men of parts uncomfortable to him.* Besides *he desired above all devotion to himself and his cause* (as if either he or his cause could inspire devotion); he felt *hampered by merit when it was combined with any touch of independence.* He wanted believers in his star and vulgar adorers of his fortune. So one could not reach him except through a group of intimate servants and personal friends, and I remember General Changarnier telling me at that time that they could all be described by two matching words: sharpers and knaves. To conclude, nothing was worse than his familiars except his family, who were mostly scoundrels and hussies.

REFERENCES
Anceau, E. *Napoléon III.* Paris: Tallandier, 2012.
Argenson, Marquis de. *Journal et Mémoires.* Paris, 1859–87.
Babelon, J.-P. *Henri IV.* Paris: Fayar, 1982.
Bastid, P. *Doctrines et institutions politiques de la Seconde République.* Paris: Hachette, 1945.

Berton, H. "La constitution de 1848." *Annales de l'école libre des sciences politiques* 12 (1897): 673–712.

Caron, P. "La tentative de contre-révolution de Juin-Juillet 1789." *Revue d'histoire moderne et contemporaine* 8 (1906–7): 5–34 and 649–78.

Chevallier, P. *Louis XIII.* Paris: Fayard, 1979.

Craveri, P., ed. *Genesi di une Costituzione.* Naples: Guida Editori, 1985. (Contains the complete minutes from the debates in the constitutional committee of the 1848 assembly.)

Elster, J. *Explaining Social Behavior.* Cambridge, UK: Cambridge University Press, 2015.

Faure, E. *La disgrâce de Turgot.* Paris: Gallimard, 1961.

Khong, Y. *Analogies at War.* Princeton, NJ: Princeton University Press, 1992.

Lavisse, E. *Louis XIV.* Paris: Robert Laffont, 1989.

Louis XIV. *Mémoires.* Paris: Garnery, 1806.

Marx, K. *The 18th Brumaire of Louis Bonaparte.* New York: International Publishers, 1963.

———. *The Class Struggles in France.* New York: International Publishers, 1964.

Petitfils, J.-C. *Louis XIII.* Paris: Perrin, 2008.

Saint-Simon, Duc de. *Mémoires,* ed. G. Truc. Paris: Gallimard (Bibliothèque de la Pléiade), 1953–61.

Tocqueville, A. de. *Recollections.* New Brunswick, NJ: Transaction Books, 1987.

———. *Democracy in America.* New York: Library of America, 2004.

Véri, Abbé de. *Journal.* Paris: Tallandier, 1928–30.

Veyne, P. *L'empire greco-romain.* Paris: Seuil, 2005.

Wise, J., translator. *The Resistible Rise of Arturo Ui.* London: Bloomsbury, 1972.

Wise, R., and M. Bozarth. "A Psychomotor Stimulant Theory of Addiction." *Psychological Review* 94 (1987): 469–92.

NOTES

1. Details about the life and career of Louis Napoleon are taken from the recent biography by Anceau (2012), which supersedes all previous studies. The best study of the politics of the Second Republic remains Bastid (1945). Extensive minutes of the discussions in the 1848 constitutional committee are found in

Craveri, ed. (1985). Verbatim reports of the plenary discussions in the constituent assembly are available and searchable online in books.google.com under "Histoire parlementaire de l'assemblée nationale" (several volumes). I shall cite from all these writings, often without referencing them.

2. The legitimists favored the restoration of the older branch of the Bourbon monarchy, which was overthrown in 1830.

3. The orléanists favored the restoration of the July monarchy (belonging to the younger branch of the Bourbon monarchy), which was overthrown in 1848.

4. Napoleon won the Battle of Marengo in Italy on June 14, 1800.

COULD MASS DETENTIONS WITHOUT PROCESS HAPPEN HERE?

MARTHA MINOW

Could it happen here? Mass detentions without process, targeting individuals based on their membership in a racial, ethnic, or religious group?

It already has happened here. The infamous Japanese-American internment followed removal of some 120,000 individuals of Japanese descent under Executive Order No. 9066. Most were United States citizens. Despite executive, judicial, and legislative repudiation, the precedent stands. Indeed, despite intense contemporaneous dissents and ongoing scholarly criticism, the Supreme Court has never overturned its decision, leaving the executive order unscathed by constitutional challenge. That decision, *Korematsu v. United States* (1944), may once have seemed outmoded and "no longer good law," yet citations to it recur. Just after the 2016 presidential election, a prominent supporter of candidate Donald Trump cited the precedent as a basis for the president-elect's proposed registry of immigrants from Muslim countries.[1]

I do not know whether we will see an actual official registry of Muslim immigrants, including those legally present in the United States, or if removals and detentions of Muslims may be coming. Even more worrisome, political processes and the court may stand by without creating a successful bar. The test will come. Consider the history of the Korematsu case, its legal and political legacies, and the noxious context facing not just the United States but the world in 2017.

I. BEHIND THE KOREMATSU CASE

Issued by President Franklin D. Roosevelt during World War II after Japan bombed Pearl Harbor, the order authorized military leaders to prescribe military areas from which any person could be excluded as protection against espionage and sabotage. Under that authority, General John L. DeWitt deemed the entire Pacific Coast, including all of California and parts of Oregon, Washington, and Arizona, such a region and directed relocation of all persons of Japanese ancestry living along the West Coast of the United States. The military directed the removal and incarceration of the individuals—some 70,000 American citizens, including families and children—to detention camps.

The asserted reason was national security. But investigations commissioned by the federal government and well known to President Roosevelt in 1941 and 1942 identified the intense loyalty of Japanese and Japanese-American residents to the United States and refuted assertions of disloyalty.[2] Housed in crude barracks or horse stalls, shipped to remote relocation centers that many prefer to call concentration camps guarded by military personnel, shorn of their personal and real property, and deprived of privacy, dignity, and opportunities to be heard promptly about objections based on their citizenship, their loyalty, or any other claim during the early 1940s, the affected individuals lost any semblance of the equal protection, liberty, and due process embedded in the United States Constitution.

Fred Korematsu resisted. A citizen of the United States with no evidence of disloyalty, he was twenty-three, worked as a welder, and refused to comply with the evaluation order, he sought to make enough money to move to the Midwest with his girlfriend.[3] Charged with violating a federal law criminalizing disobedience to a military relocation order, Korematsu worked with the American Civil Liberties Union to challenge both the evacuation and detention policies.[4] His family did not support his challenge and felt shamed by his conduct.[5] At trial, he testified that he had registered for the draft, had never been to Japan, and spoke little Japanese; the judge found Korematsu guilty and issued a sentence of five years' probation, to be served back at the detention camp. He and several others, convicted for violating either curfew or exclusion orders, challenged their convictions in the United States Supreme Court without success.

The Court granted, for the first time, that the Equal Protection guarantee required rigorous scrutiny of legal restrictions based on race alone. Nonetheless, the Court's majority treated the exclusion orders as justified by the real military danger.[6] The assertion of national security concerns with little to connect them with the classification by race, ethnicity, and national origin sufficed to overcome the doubts raised. Even the failure to separate loyal individuals from disloyal ones, or citizens from noncitizens, did not undermine the program's constitutionality.

Vigorous dissenting opinions challenged the inference of disloyalty simply from group membership. Justice Frank Murphy described the order as "one of the most sweeping and complete deprivations of constitutional rights in the history of this nation."[7] In subsequent cases, the Court rejected only detention of individuals whose loyalty was conceded by the government.[8] Justice Robert Jackson warned that judicial approval would make the problem last a long time.[9] Scholars and journalists objected as well to the Court's decision.

Although initially the mainstream media was neutral or approving of the Supreme Court's action, by the 1980s the media criticized the decision and covered efforts to question or overturn it.[10] Condemnation has mounted through the years, so much that the Korematsu decision itself is treated by many observers as part of the "anti-cannon," decisions to be abhorred and rejected.[11] The Japanese-American Citizens' League pressed for congressional action; Edison Uno, in turn, pushed the league to seek reparations and an official governmental apology, but others in the group resisted out of shame or fear. Congress enacted the Non-Detention Act in 1971, forbidding detention of individuals absent congressional action. Japanese-American reformers and other advocates pressed for further redress and persuaded Congress to create a commission to investigate the internment.

Senator Daniel Inouye argued for a congressional commission made up of a cross-section of Americans. Launched in 1981, the commission held hearings and received testimony from 750 witnesses. The Congressional Commission on Wartime Relocation and Internment of Civilians traced the internment orders to racial prejudice, war hysteria, and failed political leadership while documenting the humiliating conditions of the internment camps. Its 1983 report urged legislative reparations, and showed that evidence available at the time of the internment indicated there was no military necessity and yet the military knowingly concealed that evidence. That concealment misled the Supreme Court in Fred Korematsu's case. This report assisted an effort by some fifty volunteer lawyers to vacate the convictions of Korematsu and others who resisted the orders against Japanese-Americans during the war. Judge Marilyn Patel granted Korematsu's petition for a writ of *corum nobis*, erasing the conviction and providing public acknowledgment of the egregious violation of his constitutional rights.[12]

Five more years of legislative lobbying followed, and legislators themselves spoke out. California representative Norman Mineta read a letter written by his father, who described the forcible removal of the family. Congressman Mineta concluded, "We lost our homes, we lost our businesses, we lost our farms. But worst of all we lost our basic human rights."[13]

As a bill authorizing reparations gained steam, Senator Jesse Helms proposed an amendment to forbid any appropriations unless the Japanese government compensated the families of men and women killed at Pearl Harbor on December 7, 1941. Once again, a US government official confused the nation of Japan and individuals of Japanese ancestry—most of them US citizens—living in the United States. Congress tabled the Pearl Harbor amendment and enacted the Civil Liberties Act of 1988, providing an apology by the United States for the internment, and authorized a payment of $20,000 for each interned individual who survived.[14]

In 1988, President Clinton awarded Fred Korematsu the Presidential Medal of Freedom for his efforts to right the wrong and to educate the country.[15] Thus, a federal district court, Congress, and the president tried to atone for the internment and its judicial sanction.

Public recognition and education efforts followed. For example, in 1992 the Manzanar camp was designated a National Historic Site to "provide for the protection and interpretation of historic, cultural, and natural resources associated with the relocation of Japanese Americans during World War II."[16] The government similarly designated the site of the Minidoka War Relocation Center in Idaho as the Minidoka National Historic Site. In yet a further step, the US Solicitor General's office offered an unusual formal admission of error while admitting in 2011 that it had withheld reports showing the loyalty of Japanese-Americans when defending the internment in the Supreme Court.[17] The *Los Angeles Times* has called the decision one of the "worst equal protection rulings," "an abomination . . . a case in which the Supreme Court yielded to fear and pressure," and "infamous."[18] Law students who learn of all these steps may assume that the Supreme Court's decision in the Korematsu case has been eroded or eliminated as authoritative law.

Yet none of these steps by Congress, by the Executive, or by the district court undid the Supreme Court's own precedent, which the Court itself has not overturned and which remains available to advocates, judges, and government officials as legitimate authority.

II. THE PRECEDENT

Observers of the initial travel ban issued by President Trump against residents of Muslim countries point to the Supreme Court's decision in *Korematsu*. Georgetown law professor and national director of the ACLU David Cole observed: "It took four decades to acknowledge the error of that decision—through legislation that formally apologized and paid reparations to the survivors. If the Supreme Court has learned anything from the experience, it will think twice about the kind of blank check the Trump administration requests in the executive order cases."[19] Although one observer calls the decision "one of the court's darkest moments, along with the court's ruling in the Dred Scott case," denying citizens the chance to challenge enslavement of any "negro" whether enslaved or free,[20] the *Korematsu* decision was nonetheless cited by the Supreme Court many times.

Only some of the time is the decision cited with disapproval. Some of the Justices have cited *Korematsu* (and

often one of its dissents) as a warning about the deprivations of liberty or equality at risk in wartime, in deference
to military concerns.[21] Many of the federal courts of appeal
continue to point to *Korematsu* as dangerous, as erroneous,
as the result of hysteria; as lamentable, or worse.[22] One dissenting appellate judge calls it an example of "constitutional
casualties."[23] When cited in dissenting opinions, *Korematsu*
is noted in appellate courts as a warning to the courts and to
the nation and a path to avoid.[24]

Yet the Supreme Court has mainly cited the decision as
establishing that the Constitution requires rigid or "strict"
judicial scrutiny of rather than deference to any governmental classification drawn on racial grounds.[25] In so doing, it
treats the majority opinion and the case as an ordinary, accepted precedent rather than as an aberration or disturbing
failure. As the Court over time subjected affirmative action
initiatives meant to benefit members of minority groups to
the same stringent scrutiny as that applied to classifications
harming minority groups, it pointed to *Korematsu* for the
standard of review for use of a racial classification, regardless
of purpose.[26] Sometimes when citing *Korematsu*, the Court
acknowledges that even stringent review did not reject the
use of the racial classification in that case and seems to treat
this as a reason for vigilance in using strict scrutiny.[27] Justice Clarence Thomas in particular repeatedly points to *Korematsu* in opinions rejecting affirmative action measures.[28]

In a media interview, Justice Stephen Breyer specu-
lated that *Korematsu* is not likely to happen again because
"[t]his country has developed a stronger tradition of civil

liberties."[29] In comments during a visit to a law school, Justice Antonin Scalia without qualification treated the ruling as "wrong" and in that respect departed from some, like Judge Richard Posner, who have in recent years defended the decision.[30] But Justice Scalia also warned that a similar internment might be upheld in the future: "[Y]ou are kidding yourself if you think the same thing will not happen again. Because *Inter arma enim silent leges* . . . in times of war, the laws fall silent."[31] Professor Ilya Somin, who reported this exchange, found merit in the prediction and argued that "the error of *Korematsu* is less likely to be repeated if the Court clearly repudiates that ruling."[32]

The Supreme Court has not yet done so. Professor Noah Feldman argues that nonetheless, the decision should not be treated as precedential authority because it was wrong factually and legally when it was decided.[33] The district court decision to vacate Fred Korematsu's conviction rested on evidence that the Court was misled about the asserted national security risk.[34] Moreover, he argues, courts have greater skepticism now toward executive power exercised within the country.[35] And Congress has repudiated the decision with its apology and reparations authorization.[36] Ultimately, Feldman concludes, "relying on *Korematsu* would be bad constitutional law."[37] The problem is that such an assertion, even if widely shared by constitutional experts, neither prevents nor impedes a Court from doing so.

Some note that the Supreme Court has not had occasion to revisit the decision because federal and state governments have not since tried to intern an entire group defined by race or ethnicity.[38] President Trump's travel ban—even as amended—offers such a review opportunity.[39] Thus far, government lawyers have not relied on *Korematsu* in their arguments defending the travel ban, but this could change.[40]

III. IT COULD HAPPEN HERE

Despite the widespread condemnation of the *Korematsu* decision by appellate judges and constitutional scholars, it provides potential authority for federal or state officials who assert public necessity as a basis for detaining or confining a group of people based on race, religion, ethnicity, or national origin; as Justice Jackson noted in his dissent, *Korematsu* remains like a loaded weapon, ready to be used unless vigorously and repeatedly repudiated at the highest levels of government—and that has not yet happened: *Korematsu* is even more likely to supply justification for detention or confinement for a group of people identified as carrying a risk to public health, even if the fear and misunderstanding color assessments of the risk.

Challenges to such actions can be difficult to pursue. When the Centers for Disease Control issued guidelines about the danger of the Ebola virus, New Jersey detained a nurse who had been exposed to the virus, and a federal court dismissed complaints against the governor and other state officials on grounds of qualified immunity.[41] The District Court judge dismissing the complaints observed:

> *I sympathize with Hickox's plight, but I cannot find*
> *that her isolation violated any clearly established*

constitutional principle embodied in quarantine case law. Of course, even as to a dread [sic] disease, it is possible to overreact; as it was with cholera and yellow fever, so it is with Ebola today. A restriction can be so arbitrary or overbroad as to be impermissible. The parties cite no case striking down a quarantine order, however, that is even close to Hickox's faulty scenario, or that would have clearly indicated to any of those defendants that their actions violated established law.[42]

When it comes to detaining noncitizens, we do not need to speculate. The United States already has three detention centers for noncitizen migrant children and their mothers.[43] Since the administration of President George W. Bush, such individuals have faced detention for months or even more while ostensibly awaiting administration or judicial consideration of their immigration or refugee status.[44] Although the number of detention centers substantially diminished under the administration of President Obama, Judge Dolly Gee described the conditions as deplorable and ordered then-President Obama to release those detained, but the detentions continued.[45] Yes, noncitizens differ from citizens as a legal matter. But the public indifference to and judicial impotence in response to incarceration under deplorable conditions, maintained on our borders, is already well under way.

NOTES

1. Derek Hawkins, "Japanese American Internment Is 'Precedent' for National Muslim Registry, Prominent Trump Backer Says," *Washington Post*, November 17, 2016, https://www.washington

post.com/news/morning-mix/wp/2016/11/17/japanese
-internment-is-precedent-for-national-muslim-registry-prominent
-trump-backer-says/?utm_term=.4c284af3496a (describing
remarks of Carl Higbie, former spokesperson for a major Trump
Super PAC, on Megyn Kelly's Fox News show).

2. Michi Nishiura Weglyn, *Years of Infamy* (New York: William
Morrow & Company, 1976), 34 (discussing report of Curtis
Munson and work of Kenneth Ringle); Greg Robinson, *A Tragedy
of Democracy: Japanese Confinement in North America* (New York:
Columbia University Press, 2009), 55 (same).

3. Erick Trickey, "Fred Korematsu Fought Against Japanese
Internment in the Supreme Court . . . and Lost," *Smithsonian*,
January 30, 2017, 235, http://www.smithsonianmag.com/history
/fred-korematsu-fought-against-japanese-internment-supreme
-court-and-lost-1809619671/.

4. Ibid.

5. Ibid.

6. 323 US 214 (1944).

7. 323 US, at (Murphy, J., dissenting).

8. "A military order, however unconstitutional, is not apt to last
longer than the military emergency. Even during that period,
a succeeding commander may revoke it all. But once a judicial
opinion rationalizes such an order to show that it conforms to the
Constitution, or rather rationalizes the Constitution to show that
the Constitution sanctions such an order, the Court for all time
has validated the principle of racial discrimination in criminal
procedure and of transplanting American citizens. The principle
then lies about like a loaded weapon, ready for the hand of any
authority that can bring forward a plausible claim of an urgent
need. Every repetition imbeds that principle more deeply in our
law and thinking and expands it to new purposes." Id., at 323 US,
at (Jackson, J., dissenting).

9. See Ex parte Endo, 323 US 283 (1944), 246.

10. "Repudiated by Congress and decried by Americans generally,
the shabby treatment of Japanese residents on the West Coast
during World War II continues to prick the nation's conscience."
Leon Lindsay, "Three Who Resisted—Japanese Internment
Case Reopens," *Christian Science Monitor* (1908-Current file),

January 21, 1983, 15, ProQuest Historical Newspapers: The Christian Science Monitor, http://search.proquest.com.ezp-prod1 .hul.harvard.edu/docview/512332376?accountid=11311.

11. Matt Ford, "The Return of *Korematsu,*" *Atlantic,* November 19, 2015, https://www.theatlantic.com/politics/archive/2015/11/the -shadow-of-korematsu/416634/.

12. *Korematsu v. United States,* 584 F.Supp. 1406 (N.D. Cal. 1984). The pathbreaking 1983 book *Justice at War: The Story of the Japanese-American Internment Cases* by Peter Irons demonstrated the cover-up by the government of exonerating materials.

13. Quoted in Garrett Hongo, HR: 442: Redress, in Susan Richards Shreve and Porter Shreve, eds., *Outside the Law: Narratives on Justice in America* (Boston: Beacon Press, 1997), 89.

14. 38 U.S.C. section 4214 (1988).

15. Caitlin Rother, "Rebel with a Medal Talks to UCSC Students," *San Diego Union-Tribune,* February 5, 1998, B8.

16. Public Law 102–248.

17. "U.S. Official Cites Misconduct in Japanese American Internment Cases," *Los Angeles Times,* May 24, 2011; "Confession of Error: The Solicitor General's Mistakes During the Japanese-American Internment Cases," *The Justice Blog,* Department of Justice, archived from the original on February 19, 2013.

18. "worst equal protection rulings": David Savage, "Affirmative Action Case Splits Asian Americans," *Los Angeles Times,* March 30, 2003, A30, http://articles.latimes.com/2003/mar/30/nation /na-affirm30; "an abomination . . . a case in which the Supreme Court yielded to fear and pressure": Jonathan Turley, "Commentary: 60 Years On, Again Battling an Abomination of Power," *Los Angeles Times,* November 17, 2003, B11, http:// articles.latimes.com/2003/nov/17/opinion/oe-turley17; "infamous": Stephen Vladeck, "Opinion: The Lost Padilla Verdict," *Los Angeles Times,* August 17, 2007, A31. It was also called "one of the most infamous legal decisions in the history of our country" in John Inazu and Karen Tani, "Why the Korematsu Decision Matters," *Los Angeles Times,* December 18, 2015, A27. Inazu and Tani are both law professors and grandchildren of internees.

19. David Cole, "Trump's Travel Bans—Look Beyond the Text," *New*

York Review of Books, May 11, 2017, http://www.nybooks.com /articles/2017/05/11/trumps-travel-bans-look-beyond-the-text/.

20. Erick Trickey, supra note 3 (discussing *Dred Scott v. Sandford*, 60 US 393 (1857)).

21. *Hamdi v. Rumsfeld*, 542 US 507, 535 (2004) (plurality opinion, O'Connor, J.)(citing Justice Murphy's dissent in *Korematsu*); *Skinner v. Railway Labor Executives' Ass'n*, 488, US 602, 639, 371(1989) (Marshall, J., dissenting); *O'Lone v. Estate of Shabazz*, 482 US 342 (1987)(dissent, Brennan, J.)(citing Justice Jackson's dissent in *Korematsu*); *Goldman v. Weinberger*, 475 US 503 (1986)(Brennan, J., dissenting)(citing Justice Jackson's dissent in *Korematsu*).

22. E.g., *Patrolmen's Benevolent Ass'n of N.Y., Inc., v. City of New York*, 310 F.3dr 43, 54 (2d. Cir. 2002); *Faise v. Terhune*, 283 F.3rd. 506, 530 (3rd. Cir. 2002)(dissenting opinion); *Jaffee v. United States*, 663 F.2d, 1226, 1252 (3rd. Cir. 1081)(dissenting opinion); *United States v. Zapata-Ibarra*, 223 F.3rd 281, 282 (5th Cir. 2000) (dissenting opinion); *United States v. Smith*, 73 F.3d. 1414, 1422 (6th Cir. 1996); *United States v. Harvey*, 24 F.3rd 795, 799 (6th Cir. 1994)(dissenting opinion); *Boim v. Holy Land Found. For Relief & Dev.*, 549 F.3rd 685, 719 (7th Cir. 2008)(dissenting opinion); *United States v. Fern*, 484 F.2d 666, 670 (7th Cir. 1973) (dissenting opinion); *Phillips v. Perry*, 106 F.3rd 1420, 1439 (9th Cir. 1997)(dissenting opinion); *Bay Area Peace Navy v. United States*, 914 F.2d 1224, 1237 (9th Cir. 1990)(dissenting opinion); *Bridges v. United States*, 184 F.2d 881, 887 (9th Cir. 1950); *Soskin v. Reinertson*, 353 F.3rd 1242, 1265 (10th Cir. 2004)(dissenting opinion); *United States. v. Affleck*, 765 F.2d 944, 960 (10th Cir. 1985)(dissenting opinion); *Ali Hamza Ahmad Suliman Al Bahlul v. United States*, 840 F.3rd 757, 837 (D.C.Cir. 2016)(dissenting opinion citing Justice Jackson's dissent in *Korematsu*); *Jacobs v. Barr*, 959 F.2d 313, 373 (D.C.Cir. 1992).

23. *Hartness v. Bush*, 919 F.2d 170, 175 (D.C.Cir. 1990).

24. E.g., *Ali Hamza Ahmad Suliman Al Bahlul v. United States*, 840 F.3rd 757, 837 (D.C.Cir. 2016)(dissenting opinion citing Justice Jackson's dissent in *Korematsu*); *United States v. Burwell*, 690 F.3rd 500, 533 (D.C.Cir. 2012)(dissenting opinion citing Justice Jackson's dissent in *Korematsu*); *National Treasury Employees Union v. United States Custom Serv.*, 27 F.3rd 623, 630 (D.C.Cir. 1994)(dissenting opinion).

25. E.g., *McCleskey v. Kemp*, 481, US 279, 316 (1987); *Loving v. Virginia*, 388 US 1, 11 (1967); *Bolling v. Sharpe*, 347 US 497, 499 (1954). See also *Moore v. East Cleveland*, 431 US 495 (1977)(citing *Korematsu* as example of strict scrutiny in fundamental rights case).

26. *Regents of University of California v. Bakke*, 438 US 265, 387 (1978).

27. *Missouri v. Jenkins*, 515 US 70 (1995); *Fullilove v. Klutznick*, 448 US 448, 523 (1979)(Powell, J., concurring).

28. *Fisher v. University of Texas*, 133 S.Ct. 2411, 2432, n.10 (2013) (Thomas, J., concurring); *Parents Involved in Community Schools v. Seattle School District No. 1*, 551 US 701, 759 (2007) (Thomas, J., concurring); *Grutter v. Bollinger*, 539 US 306, 351 (2003)(Thomas, J., dissenting, joined in part by Scalia, J.). Professor Mark Kende argues that Justice Thomas supports a broad view of wartime executive power and approves of the Court's ruling in *Korematsu*. Mark Kende "Justice Clarence Thomas's *Korematsu* Problem," *Harvard Journal of Racial & Ethnic Justice* 30 (June 19, 2014): 201. Available at SSRN: https://ssrn.com/abstract=2456868.

29. "Breyer: *Korematsu* Could Not Happen Again. Scalia: Of Course It Could," *Josh Blackman Blog*, December 28, 2015, http://joshblackman.com/blog/2015/12/28/breyer-korematsu-could-not-happen-again-scalia-of-course-it-could/.

30. Ilya Somin, "Justice Scalia on *Kelo* and *Korematsu*," *Washington Post*, February 8, 2004, https://www.washingtonpost.com/news/volokh-conspiracy/wp/2014/02/08/justice-scalia-on-kelo-and-korematsu/?utm_term=.23ff04d36022.

31. Ibid. The phrase has been traced to Marcus Tullius Cicero.

32. Ibid.

33. Noah Feldman, "Why *Korematsu* Is Not a Precedent," *New York Times*, November 18, 2016, https://www.nytimes.com/2016/11/21/opinion/why-korematsu-is-not-a-precedent.html?_r=0.

34. *Korematsu v. US*, 584 F.Supp. 1406, 16 Fed. R. Evid. Serv. 1231 (N.D.Cal. Apr. 19, 1984) (noting the Army had destroyed documents in an effort to hide alterations that had been made to a report justifying the internment to reduce their racist content). The Department of Justice was represented at the time by Tom C. Clark, who wrote in the epilogue to a book on the internment: "The truth is—as this deplorable experience proves—that

constitutions and laws are not sufficient of themselves. . . . Despite the unequivocal language of the Constitution of the United States that the writ of habeas corpus shall not be suspended, and despite the Fifth Amendment's command that no person shall be deprived of life, liberty or property without due process of law, both of these constitutional safeguards were denied by military action under Executive Order 9066." Maisie Conrat, ed., *Executive Order 9066: The Internment of 110,000 Japanese Americans* (San Francisco: California Historical Society, 1972). See Peter Irons, *Justice Delayed: The Record of the Japanese American Internment Cases* (Middletown, CT: Wesleyan University Press, 1989), 175.

35. Feldman, supra note 33.
36. Id.
37. Id. Richard Primus describes the decision as "anti-canonical: Every student of constitutional law studies it as an object lesson in what courts should not do." See Richard Primus, "How Trump Gave the Supreme Court a Second Chance on Japanese Internment," *Politico*, May 30, 2017, http://www.politico.com/magazine/story/2017/05/30/donald-trump-korematsu-japanese-internment-supreme-court-215208.
38. Matt Ford, supra note 11.
39. See Richard Primus, supra note 37. As of October 2017, President Trump has issued three travel bans and each has been halted by temporary judicial orders, but final review awaits. Connor Finnegan, "A Timeline of Trump's Battle with the Courts to Keep His Travel Ban Alive," ABC News (October 19, 2017), http://abcnews.go.com/Politics/timeline-trumps-battle-courts-travel-ban-alive/story?id=50559798.
40. See id.
41. *Hickox v. Christie*, Civ. No. 15–7647 (D.N.J. Sept. 2, 2016).
42. Id., at 15.
43. J. Weston Phippen, "Is it an Immigration Detention Facility or a Child-Care Center?" *Atlantic*, May 6, 2016, https://www.theatlantic.com/national/archive/2016/05/immigration-childcare/481509/.
44. Wil S. Hylton, "The Shame of America's Family Detention Camps," *New York Times*, February 4, 2015, https://www.nytimes.com/2015/02/08/magazine/the-shame-of-americas-family-detention-camps.html.
45. Phippen, supra note 43.

THE COMMONSENSE PRESIDENCY

DUNCAN J. WATTS

Since the seventeenth century, politicians have invoked "common sense" as a source of authority when settling political disagreements. Rarely if ever, though, has a president brandished a commonsense approach to governing the way Donald Trump has. Whereas common sense is typically used as a rhetorical device to justify positions at which the speaker has arrived by other means, Trump appears to take the advertised virtues of common sense literally, preferring it over technical expertise and governing experience (Gessen 2017). Although this aggressive deployment of common sense appears to be popular among some percentage of the electorate, it has caused deep concern among policy experts, both liberal and conservative. Here I argue that a literal embrace of common sense as a basis for running a country is wrongheaded and dangerous, for two reasons. First, belying its name, common sense is intrinsically divisive, transforming differences in opinion into differences in identity. And second, common sense is intrinsically incapable of grappling with the complexities of large-scale social and economic problems. Such problems, I argue, require a scientific approach to decision-making, meaning one that starts from a position of epistemic modesty, seeks out competing explanations for observed phenomena, decides among these explanations on the basis of available evidence, and continually seeks to refine its understanding of the world. However, if scientific thinking is to gain legitimacy among a public persuaded of the virtues of common sense, the scientific community needs to better explain to the public how science works and why it should be trusted.

INTRODUCTION

Common sense, defined roughly as "knowledge, judgement, and taste which is more or less universal and which is held more or less without reflection or argument" (van Holthoon and Olson 1987), has long been regarded as an unalloyed virtue possessed by all sensible people. For example, any sensible person knows that dropped objects fall to the ground, that hot things will burn you, and that inanimate objects don't suddenly spring to life. One doesn't need to argue the case for any of these truths because they are self-evident, or at least they should be. In a similar vein, sensible people rely on common sense to guide their behavior in a wide range of everyday situations, from what they choose to wear (at work versus at the beach) to raising or lowering their voices according to the environment (a library versus a loud restaurant) to determining how close to stand next to one another (on a crowded subway car or elevator versus an empty one). When faced with any of these decisions, sensible people don't need to think too hard before knowing what to do, nor could they necessarily explain how they know what they know. Rather, the answer simply presents itself instinctively and with complete certainty. Failure to accept it is not grounds for questioning common sense but rather the reasonableness, potentially even the sanity, of the objector.

As I have argued elsewhere (Watts 2011), the speed and flexibility of commonsense reasoning makes it indispensable for navigating everyday life, but the universal admiration of common sense has propelled its use well beyond the domain of the everyday. In particular, as Sophia Rosenfeld documents in her fascinating book *Common Sense: A Political History* (Rosenfeld 2011), common sense has played an important role in American politics, starting with Thomas Paine's 1776 pamphlet of that name. Although not the first to extoll the virtues of common sense, Paine deployed it in an especially clever way, using this "basic, instinctive, immediate and irrefutable form of perception and judgment natural to all humans" (Rosenfeld 2011, p. 142) to rationalize what was actually a radical and novel proposal—namely that the American colonies form a unified, self-governed republic without either king or nobility. Rather than attempting to ground his argument for what was, in effect, a whole new system of government in philosophy or social science, Paine simply asserted that its desirability was self-evident; that, as Rosenfeld writes, "there was common sense in a form of government that began from common sense" (Rosenfeld 2011, p. 138). Although logically self-referential, Paine's overt appeal to the plain, simple reasoning of everyday people in preference to the superficially clever but presumably devious or muddleheaded thinking of experts and elites resonated deeply with the independence movement. In this way, Paine managed to pull off the remarkable feat of convincing his readers that his conclusions were correct without ever having to explain why. Rather, by relying on the reader's belief that common sense—whatever it is—is axiomatically *good*, Paine insisted that his conclusion required no further justification.

Rosenfeld argues that this combination of features—simultaneously desirable and devoid of specific content—has made common sense extremely popular among American politicians as a rhetorical device. In the modern era, for example, invocations of common sense are widespread and bipartisan. Ronald Reagan claimed that "preservation of our environment is not a liberal or conservative challenge, it's common sense." Both Hillary Clinton and Barack Obama have argued for "commonsense gun control" efforts such as legislation that would require universal background checks. Paul Ryan has called for "commonsense conservatism," including immigration reform and rolling back of FDA regulations. And Ted Cruz has referred to reductions in top marginal tax rates as commonsense tax reform. In all these cases, the speaker is appealing to what Rosenfeld (2011, p. 145) calls "the instinctive perceptions, unschooled logic, and simple style of . . . 'plain sensible men,' " often in contrast with so-called elites.[1] The irony, of course, is that those invoking common sense are almost always members of the political elite whose agendas may well be at odds with the interests of "plain sensible men." Nevertheless, by flattering the sensibilities of their perceived audience and, critically, by avoiding any specifics about what is and isn't common sense (other than, of course, the point being argued), the speaker can invoke common sense on behalf of almost any agenda at all.

But rarely if ever have we witnessed a prominent politician embrace common sense as wholeheartedly as Donald Trump has. Whereas other politicians frequently invoke common sense when selling their policies to the public—and may even rely on their own intuition when formulating their policies—the development process also typically involves experienced staffers and other experts. Common sense, in other words, is invoked mostly rhetorically, where the substance is often arrived at by other means. In contrast, Trump's reliance on "instinctive perceptions, unschooled logic, and simple style" is so complete that it leaves little room for the opinions of experts even within his own administration. He has publicly feuded with his own intelligence agencies, and actively sought to undermine the Congressional Budget Office. He has nominated far fewer presidential appointments than his predecessors, leaving his administration dangerously understaffed (Yourish and Aisch 2017). Several of his cabinet members are either uninterested in or actively hostile to the missions of their agencies.

He has announced or enacted major policy shifts—on immigration, climate change, health care, and trade—without informing himself of the issues involved. Above all, he has adopted the posture that the business of government cannot be that hard, that all difficulties are a result of the incompetence, weakness, or corruption of entrenched political elites, and that all problems can therefore be solved by plain speaking and blunt action.

Trump's posture clearly resonates with at least part of the electorate, who share his disregard for experts and suspicion of elites. At the same time, it has caused widespread alarm among expert communities, including scientists, economists, foreign policy experts, intelligence professionals, former government officials, and career civil servants. Are all these constituencies simply seeking to undermine Trump's disruptive influence to protect their selfish interests, as he and his supporters claim? Or is there something inherently flawed with the claims made on behalf of common sense? In this essay, I argue the latter. Specifically, there are two fundamental problems that work against common sense as a basis for governing. The first is that, contrary to its name, common sense is not "common" in any universal sense but rather is intrinsically specific to socially and culturally homogeneous groups. In any large, diverse society, therefore, appeals to common sense are almost certain to prove divisive and resilient to compromise, undermining consensus and impeding political progress. The second reason is that common sense, although extremely useful for navigating everyday situations, is intrinsically unsuited to reasoning about the kind of complex, large-scale issues that confront contemporary governments. Relying too much on one's common sense when devising policies is therefore likely to produce bad policies.

COMMON SENSE IS INTRINSICALLY DIVISIVE

As noted above, definitions of common sense are characteristically circular with respect to its actual content: common sense is what is commonly known to be true. An important consequence of this definitional circularity is that common sense makes no distinction between *objective* and *subjective* truths—i.e., between beliefs that are commonly held because they are true and beliefs that are held to be true because they are common. To illustrate, consider the following list of commonsense beliefs compiled by the eighteenth-century Scottish professor James Beattie (Rosenfeld 2011, p. 56): "I exist. I am the same being today that I was yesterday—or even twenty years ago. Things equal to one and the same thing are equal to one another. Ingratitude ought to be blamed and punished. The three angles of a triangle are equal to two right angles. A whole is greater than a part. Every effect has a cause. The senses can be believed. The ground on which I stand is hard, material, solid, and has real, separate, independent existence. The sun will rise tomorrow. I have a soul distinct from my body. Virtue and vice are different. So are heat and cold, red and white, an ox and an ass. Truth exists. There is a God."

From a scientific perspective, these statements could not be more different, ranging as they do from mathematical truths (e.g., "the three angles of a triangle are equal to two right angles"), definitional truths ("a whole is greater than a part," "every effect has a cause"), and undisputed empirical facts ("the sun will rise tomorrow") to claims that are disputable to varying degrees ("I am the same being today that I was yesterday—or even twenty years ago," "truth exists"), articles of faith ("there is a God"), and normative opinions ("ingratitude ought to be blamed and punished"). But from a commonsense perspective, they are indistinguishable.[2] To Beattie, it was no less self-evident that one's soul is distinct from one's body than it was that the sun would rise tomorrow: he was equally certain of each, and, critically, certain that any other sensible person would be certain about them also. Indeed, it is precisely the consensus of sensible people that conveys commonness, and hence legitimacy.

But who, then, are these sensible others? Definitions of common sense are frustratingly vague on this point also. Typically, the speaker asserts the existence of a body of like-minded individuals who are, presumably, equally possessed of common sense. But then "all reasonable people" is indistinguishable from "all people who agree with me." As I mentioned earlier, this definitional vagueness is a useful rhetorical weapon—because anyone who does not agree with me can be written off as unreasonable, obviating the need for me to justify my beliefs any further. But it also makes common sense a very bad way to resolve political disputes—because when two people disagree, their only recourse is to brand each other as unreasonable. It's therefore no surprise that arguments that invoke common sense quickly degenerate into ad hominem attacks and name-calling. In matters of common sense, every disagreement is personal as well as substantive.

For the same reason, what is common sense to one group of people in one time and place is not necessarily common to other groups. For example, while the impossibility of talking animals or inanimate objects coming to life may be self-evident to (most) adults, it isn't necessarily so to children, who may well believe such things. Going further, babies have such a poor understanding of commonsense notions like gravity, heat, and water that they must be prevented from burning themselves, drowning, or falling out of their cribs. What is common sense to adults is not common to babies and children, who must be taught. Typically, this learning process happens naturally, because children generally trust their parents, teachers, and other adult role models sufficiently to simply accept that what they are being told is true. But that doesn't mean it is unproblematic. Because most of us learn common sense from the adults around us when we are children, what we learn is generally specific to our region, culture, class, and era. By the time we start interacting with people who are very different from us we have already absorbed a lot of "self-evident" truths, many of which are not actually self-evident, or even necessarily true. Yet because the way we learn truths like "dropped objects will fall to the ground" or "hot things will burn you" is the same as how we learn truths like "God exists" and "ingratitude ought to be blamed and punished"—that is, by being told them repeatedly by people we trust—just like Beattie, we can't tell the difference.

The result is that disagreements over common sense are not only bitterly personal—in any large, diverse society, they are inevitable. Within any society, that is, members of different cultural backgrounds, races, geographic regions, socioeconomic statuses, education levels, and time periods will inevitable develop their own distinct collections of beliefs about the world. Taken literally, in other words, common sense—meaning a single body of knowledge that is shared by all sensible people—does not exist. Rather there exists a multitude of "common senses," possibly as many as there are people. Yet because these beliefs are internalized as self-evident truths rather than as subjective opinions, each person believes his or her own (possibly unique) version of common sense to be the universally correct one, shared by all sensible others. The sarcastic remark that "there is nothing common about common sense" is therefore right, but for the wrong reasons. Whereas the remark is usually intended as a lament on the stupidity of others, the reality is that there is no single body of knowledge that is self-evident to everyone.

NOT EVERYTHING THAT IS TRUE IS SELF-EVIDENT

The highly subjective and group-specific nature of common sense already makes it ill-suited for governing any group of people diverse enough to disagree about what counts as self-evident. But common sense has an even bigger problem when applied to government, which is that much of what

THE COMMONSENSE PRESIDENCY

is true is not self-evident to anyone. Science, for example, is filled with statements that are "true" in that they are supported by the preponderance of theory and evidence, but are not self-evident no matter how much personal experience one acquires. One way to think about science, in fact, is as a method for discovering truths about the world that can't be gleaned from ordinary, everyday experience. In certain domains of science, such as in physics, we are reasonably comfortable accepting the existence of truths that are non-obvious, or even mind-bending. For example, when a team of astronomers announces that they have detected a new planet orbiting a distant star, we have no way of seeing the planet ourselves, nor do we have detailed knowledge of the complicated theories and methods that the astronomers are using to infer its existence. Nevertheless, we accept that the astronomers, building on the work of hundreds of years of science, have established what they and their colleagues consider to be compelling evidence. Thus, we accept the existence of extra-solar planets as a truth about the universe even though nothing about it is self-evident.

In contrast, our treatment of social science is often less than deferential. Whether it is economists explaining how a nation's debt is different from a family's debt, or biostatisticians explaining how mammograms might actually cause more harm than good, or sociologists claiming that Harry Potter might just have been a fluke of history, when the conclusions of social scientists do not jibe with common sense, our reaction is not surprise and delight—like when astronomers claim to have detected earth-like planets orbiting a distant star or physicists claim to have slowed light to walking pace—but rather skepticism and even anger.[3] The difference, I would argue, is essentially one of familiarity. Because so much of physics deals with topics like subatomic particles and gravity waves that are very distant from everyday experience, it feels more like a complement to common sense than a challenge to it. In social science, however, almost *everything* overlaps to some extent with everyday experience. We are all members of social networks, we all engage in economic transactions, we all seek to persuade and influence others, and we all participate in politics. Unlike explanations about distant planets or subatomic particles, therefore, the explanations of social science bear on phenomena about which common sense also has a lot to say.

This is not to say that social science can't discover truths about the world that are not self-evident from our own experience. In a world of billions of people interacting with one another in countless ways to produce all manner of phenomena, from business cycles and financial crises to social norms and political revolutions to cultural fads and fashions, there are plenty of mysteries for science to explore. Yet because common sense has already staked out so much of this terrain for itself, social science seems less like a useful complement and more like an unwelcome interloper. Rather than explaining mysteries that we had never even thought about, let alone expected to understand, it seeks to explain familiar outcomes and objects that we thought we already understood. If the intuition we gain from personal experiences were a reliable guide for social and economic theory, then there would be no problem (and social science would be much easier); but it is not, for at least three reasons. First, intuition is a surprisingly poor predictor of individual behavior, especially when that behavior concerns people who are not like us or whose circumstances differ from ours. Second, individual actions aggregate in counterintuitive ways through networks of dependencies. And third, we learn less from history than we think we do.

THREE LIMITATIONS OF COMMONSENSE REASONING

The first problem with common sense as a means of reasoning about human behavior is that it is intrinsically rational. I don't mean rational in the sense of *homo economicus*—the toy model of human behavior advanced by neoclassical economics and easily debunked by everyday observation (McFadden 1999)—but rather the older and more general notion of rationality that comes from sociology (Weber 1968), in which human decision-making resides in our conscious minds: people *anticipate* the future, form *preferences* over the possible outcomes they might experience, and make *plans* to attain the outcomes they prefer. It follows from this framework that the choices people make necessarily reflect their preferences (Mayhew 1980). This notion of rationality is extremely plausible (commonsense even) and is highlighted in *Freakonomics*-style books that extol the power of incentives to guide and explain behavior. But as several decades of psychology and behavioral economics research has demonstrated (Ariely 2008; Gilovich, Griffin, and Kahneman 2002), it ignores what Daniel Kahneman calls "system 2" thinking (Kahneman 2011), which resides in our unconscious brains and can be influenced by, among other things, subtle details in the presentation of options (Thaler and Sunstein 2008)—e.g., default settings (Johnson and Goldstein 2003), cognitive loads imposed by background environmental stresses (Mullainathan and Shafir 2013), and implicit biases arising from cultural stereotypes and irrelevant personal experience (Banaji and Greenwald 2016). Complicating matters further is Marx's famous observation "Men make their own history, but . . . they do not make it under self-selected circumstances, but under circumstances . . . transmitted from the past." To cite a simple but profound example, 80 percent of the global variation in lifetime wealth can be accounted for by which country one is born in (Milanovic 2010), and most of the rest is accounted for by the wealth and education of one's parents—both "circumstances" that are clearly outside anyone's choosing.

The broad lesson is that choices are often governed by factors to which common sense is largely oblivious. From this perspective, it is no surprise that advocates of common sense react to "nudging" and related approaches with some combination of contempt and alarm. It simply isn't common sense that the placement of items in the cafeteria, or the format of an application form, or the default option for 401(k) deductions should make any difference to consequential decisions. It follows that interventions of this sort must either be useless or else some Machiavellian plot by social scientists to manipulate the masses; either way, they should be rejected out-of-hand. Likewise, evidence that circumstances can powerfully shape life-course trajectories is dismissed out-of-hand on the grounds that a single counterexample can be found. Indeed, the current secretary of Housing and Human Development, Ben Carson, has recently argued that poverty is a "state of mind," using as evidence his own experience growing up in Detroit and becoming a successful brain surgeon (Alcindor 2017). Although Carson's reaction was deservedly panned as naive, it is not that different from widely accepted meritocratic explanations of success and failure that place the bulk of responsibility on the choices of the individual, systematically discounting the pervasive influence of circumstances on outcomes (Frank 2016).

The second problem is that individual choices are often subject to social influence, or what economists call peer effects, meaning that the choice that is most desirable, or simply the most available, to one person depends on what others are doing. Individuals are bound together by complex networks, which can propagate beliefs and behavior in ways that are fundamentally at odds with common sense. In a seminal paper, Mark Granovetter (1978) showed how surprising the dynamics of networked systems can be. Granovetter imagined a hypothetical crowd of agitators on the brink of violence, where each member has some "threshold" for acting out that depends on how many others are. If one member has a threshold of zero, he will trigger without provocation. If a second actor has a threshold of one, the first actor will set him off. If another actor has a threshold of two, he will then trigger, and so on. The point is that in an environment where everyone is responding to what everyone else does, a single action can trigger a series of knock-on effects that unravel into total chaos. But Granovetter's analysis also showed that this unraveling is highly susceptible to small deviations in the underlying distributions of thresholds. For example, if there is no one with a threshold of one and two actors with a threshold of two—a tiny, probably undetectable difference in underlying preferences—the violence will stop with just the first actor; no unraveling will occur. To an observer, the two scenarios could not look more different—a single agitator jostling an otherwise orderly crowd versus a full-scale riot—yet ex ante there is essentially no difference (Watts 2011).

Effects like these show up everywhere. For example, markets can exhibit *network effects* (Economides 1996), meaning that small differences in market share can be amplified over time for reasons unrelated to intrinsic quality, possibly creating *lock-in* (Arthur 1989), whereupon dominant players can be near impossible to displace (e.g., Microsoft in PCs, Google in search, Facebook in social media). In a similar way, individuals can benefit from *cumulative advantage* (DiPrete and Eirich 2006; Rigney 2010) such that initially similar people can experience wildly different careers because of small early fluctuations. Collective social and economic behavior can also display both surprising sensitivity and robustness: over the course of little more than a decade, same-sex marriage transformed from a socially aberrant practice among an excluded minority to a fundamental civil right, while over the same period attitudes about religion, immigration, and taxation hardly budged. Finally, social systems can suffer from *collective action problems* (Olson 1965; Schelling 1973) in which the outcome that everyone would prefer (e.g., clean air, pristine wilderness, reliable infrastructure, safe neighborhoods) fails because no one individual has the ability or incentive to provide it—a situation that is sometimes called a *tragedy of the commons* (Hardin 1968).

Following Granovetter's logic, the gravest danger of Trump's recent decision to exit the Paris Climate Accord is not the direct impact that US noncompliance would have on global temperatures—although that could indeed be grave—but rather the second, third, and higher-order effects of the move. Just like in Granovetter's model, if other countries hold firm, the impact of the US withdrawal may be minimal. But if even a few other countries use the US withdrawal as an excuse to withdraw themselves, then Trump's action could trigger a cascade of defections leading to the complete unraveling of the pact. Likewise, the stability of the health insurance marketplaces under the Affordable Care Act (otherwise known as ACA or Obamacare) depends on essentially the same dynamics. If, say, Congress takes away subsidies and the individual mandate, the cost of health insurance will rise, leading healthier people to drop their insurance. The costs of covering the remaining, sicker, people will then also rise, causing some companies to raise prices or to drop out of the market, thereby reducing competition and raising prices even further. Costs then go up further, leading other consumers to drop coverage, and so on. Death spirals can result, destroying the whole market.

A commonsense leader like Trump is untroubled by such imponderables. He just makes a strong, simple, and clear decision and lets the chips fall where they may. But that's the point: common sense is not wired to think about second- and higher-order effects of policy interventions (Fisman and Golden 2017), and as a result decisions based only on the first-order effects continually elicit unintended consequences (Merton 1936; Scott 1998). Of course, by the time these consequences have arrived, lots of other things have happened, so there is plenty of scope for disavowing responsibility. If the climate accord unravels, Trump can claim it was a bad deal that was doomed to fail and the US was right to get out first. If the health insurance markets crater, he can say Obamacare was a disaster and their collapse just proves it. Ultimately, there's no way to prove him wrong: we can't go back in time and rerun history with a different decision to see if it would have worked out better. If no one understands the dynamics at play—because, after all, none of this is common sense—it's just one person's story about what happened versus another's.

This leads us to the third problem with common sense, which is that it systematically mishandles *counterfactuals*: what might have happened had things played out differently. Counterfactuals are central to scientific explanations, because explanations are fundamentally answers to causal questions—did X *cause* Y to happen? And the only way to show that X caused Y is to observe both the "factual" outcome (X happened) and also the "counterfactual" (X did not happen) and check the effect on Y. Only if Y is significantly more likely to happen in the presence of X than in its absence can we say that X caused Y. It is not an exaggeration to say that without considering counterfactuals (or, as they are sometimes called, *potential outcomes*), statements about causality, and hence scientifically valid explanations, are impossible (Morgan and Winship 2014). It is for this reason that experiments are so important to the scientific method, because in an experiment you can systematically vary X (the "treatment") and then directly observe the causal effect on Y. In much of social science, however, true experiments are impossible: the US can't invade half of Iraq and not the other half to see which approach works out better; the Federal Reserve can't set the interest rate at one level for a year and then rerun history with a different rate to measure the causal effect on inflation; and companies can't hire two CEOs who get to run different instances of the same company to see who is more successful. As a result, social scientists and statisticians have devoted a huge amount of effort to devising clever ways to "identify" causal effects in non-experimental data (Dunning 2012; Imbens and Rubin 2015; Morgan and Winship 2014).

Common sense, however, has no problem coming up with answers to causal questions without doing experiments or using any fancy statistics. We just focus on some particular Y, say Donald Trump's surprise victory in the 2016 presidential election, and some particular X, say James Comey's decision to reopen his investigation of Hillary Clinton's email usage, and *imagine* how Y might have been different had X been different. This process comes so naturally to us that you are probably now shaking your head and asking "what's wrong with that?" What's wrong is that the resulting explanations are not in fact explanations at all in the causal sense, but rather are "causal stories": plausible-sounding narratives that are dressed up to look like explanations (Mitchell 2004). Just like ordinary stories, causal stories are generally invoked to make sense of individual outcomes that we find interesting (the outcome of an election, the financial crisis), and just like stories, they can be told only after we know the outcome in question. Finally, like ordinary stories, the main point of causal stories is to make us feel better—by allowing us to feel that we have made sense of something, or simply by entertaining us. Unfortunately, because causal stories have the form of real explanations, they also mislead us into thinking that we have understood the mechanisms behind what we have observed when in fact all we have done is describe it (Watts 2014).

In summary, the combination of neglecting unconscious biases, background circumstances, and network dynamics makes common sense surprisingly bad at understanding—and, more important, predicting—human behavior, especially at scale and over time. Once the outcome is known, however, the ease with which we can imagine contrafactuals allows us to construct plausible causal stories out of mere associations. In this way, common sense constantly covers up its own mistakes, effortlessly inventing explanations that seem obvious regardless of the outcome. If we wish to actually understand how the world of human affairs works, therefore, we need to move beyond common sense and adopt the same kind of scientific approach that has worked in other areas of science.

A SCIENTIFIC APPROACH TO DECISION MAKING

Of course, one might point out that many experts who have sold themselves as advocates of science also have a lousy track record of predicting political outcomes (Tetlock 2005), designing economic development plans (Easterly 2006; Scott 1998), running hedge funds (Lowenstein 2000), and averting financial crises (Bookstaber 2017; Reinhart and Rogoff 2009). Even if common sense is a flawed basis for managing human affairs, what grounds do we have for believing that science can do any better? It is a reasonable question, but there is a big difference between "decisions made by experts" and "decisions made in a scientific manner." That is, while experts often characterize their decision-making process using the language of science, the reality is that a great deal of what is presented as "expert" judgment is very often still just one person's opinion about what should work (Scott 1998). That the person in question happens to have a PhD or some other qualification does not immunize him or her against cognitive biases (it may even exacerbate them; Camerer and Johnson 1997), nor does it improve the accuracy of the person's predictions (Tetlock 2005). The all-too-frequent failures of experts should therefore be interpreted not as arguments in favor of abandoning expertise in favor of common sense, but rather as an argument to emphasize systematic evidence and rigorous evaluation over individual intuition and anecdotal experience, regardless of whose intuition and experience is being relied upon (Watts 2011).

In other words, adopting a scientific approach to decision-making in government is not as simple as stacking your bench with "experts." Rather it is about finding people who can recognize the complexity of the problems they are facing and who are therefore suspicious of their own instincts about how a complex system will respond to some intervention. Rather than leaping to the "obvious" conclusion in a moment of gut consultation, a scientific thinker considers a range of competing explanations, demands evidence for all of them, and strives to avoid logical fallacies when evaluating the evidence. If the evidence is inconclusive, the scientific thinker demands that additional evidence be collected before proceeding—for example, by conducting experiments—or looks for ways to hedge risk by pursuing multiple strategies simultaneously. Rather than seeking to solve every problem de novo, a scientific thinker looks for existing solutions that have already been shown to work—possibly in other contexts—and seeks either to spread the relevant knowledge or adapt it to the context in question. Finally, when a risky decision must be made about a situation that has never existed before and about which no more evidence can be collected—the kind of big call that heads of state and corporations sometimes have to make—a scientific thinker exhibits epistemic modesty; that is, he or she doesn't conflate the necessity of a decision (which may be high) with his or her own certainty in making it. In other words, scientific decision-making in government looks for evidence-based solutions when they exist, and minimizes the possibility of catastrophic errors even when they do not.

Of course, this is easier said than done. Many of the outcomes that we care about—the future of the Paris accords, the future state of health care in the US—are so complex and involve so many interconnected decisions that they are, for all intents and purposes, impossible to predict, even with all the data and scientific knowledge in the world. Maybe one day we'll be able to do a better job of predicting them, but for the foreseeable future even the most prudent decision maker will occasionally blunder. For example, of all recent administrations Obama's placed a lot of weight on expert opinion, but that didn't stop them from staging a disastrous intervention in Libya, where toppling a ruthless dictator led to an even worse situation than existed before. And then, having presumably absorbed that lesson, they declined to intervene aggressively in Syria, only to watch helplessly as that ruthless dictator proceeded to unleash the world's worst humanitarian crisis since World War II—a crisis that is now fueling terrorist actions far beyond the region. Even in the matter of his signature domestic achievement—the Affordable Care Act (aka Obamacare)—Obama failed to anticipate the relentless hostility with which it would be greeted by conservatives, and which at the time of writing continues to threaten its survival.

Obama himself seems to have recognized the difficulty of his approach to problem solving, conceding in an interview (Lewis 2012), "Nothing comes to my desk that is perfectly solvable. Otherwise, someone else would have solved it. So you wind up dealing with probabilities. Any given decision you make you'll wind up with a 30 to 40 percent chance that it isn't going to work. You have to own that and feel comfortable with the way you made the decision. You can't be paralyzed by the fact that it might not work out. On top of all of this, after you have made your decision, you need to feign total certainty about it. People being led do not want to think probabilistically." Unfortunately, while Obama may have diagnosed his situation correctly, he was unable to persuade the American people that his solution was the right one. Common sense relies on narratives, and good narratives require conflict, drama, and, most of all, an end point at which the story can be wrapped up, a victor can be declared, and a message can be told. A probabilistic approach like Obama's, by contrast, seeks to improve performance on average, and over many decisions. It doesn't yield a good outcome every time, and emphasizes evidence and correctness over drama and resolution. Much like science, it is slow, complicated, and very often lacks any clear resolution. Unlike issuing commands, making stirring speeches, or dropping bombs on your enemies, probabilistic thinking comes across as bloodless, even spineless. If your efforts fail even once, you're a disaster, and even if you succeed, the fruits of your labor will likely not be realized until long after you're out of office. As dramatic as the shift from Obama to Trump has been, the direction is perhaps not surprising: from a PR standpoint, probabilistic thinking and epistemic modesty are no match for common sense.

THE PROBLEM OF LEGITIMACY

To summarize the argument so far, leaders wishing to avoid the lure of common sense face three serious challenges. First, centuries of paeans to common sense have persuaded a large part of the electorate that common sense is all that is required to solve the problems of government; that failures of government are not failures of common sense, but rather failures to use common sense. Second, although common sense is fundamentally unsuited to reasoning about the sort of large-scale social and economic phenomena that are the province of modern government, the nature of common sense makes its own shortcomings extremely difficult to perceive. Third, a scientific approach—which in theory at least has a better chance of generating good results—is extremely hard to sell, in part because social science is generally viewed as precisely the kind of fancily worded but ultimately muddleheaded thinking that common sense so proudly disdains. In other words, making the case for a scientific, as opposed to a commonsense, approach to government depends critically on the perceived legitimacy of science as a way of understanding, and ultimately intervening in, human affairs. If science has no better claim on the truth than common sense or any other way of generating explanations about the world, then rhetorical appeals to the "instinctive perceptions, unschooled logic, and simple style of . . . 'plain sensible men' " will remain politically preferable to scientifically informed, evidence-based approaches to policy.

Ultimately, therefore, the viability of a scientific approach to government turns on the question of trust in science more generally. In the end, an astronomer cannot *prove* to a nonspecialist that invisible planets are orbiting some distant star any more than a parent can prove to her child that fairies don't exist. At some point, the listener must simply trust that astronomers have spent centuries honing their theories and methods, and that if they have reached a consensus about some "fact," then they should be believed. The key point is that as different as scientific knowledge is from common sense *in theory*, in practice it attains its legitimacy in much the same way that common sense does—namely by trusting the consensus wisdom of some community. Scientific knowledge trumps commonsense knowledge only to the extent that scientific communities are trusted more than other communities. Without that trust, arguments between science and common sense are not really any different than arguments between different versions of common sense: scientists become just another constituency with a point of view, to be believed or derided depending on whether it coincides with one's own. If social scientists and other experts want their claims to be viewed as more legitimate than other claims on the truth, they must first persuade the public that their methods for reaching consensus are worthy of their trust.

To this end, scientists need to do a better job of explaining to the public how the scientific process works. As any working scientist can tell you, science is a painstaking and often adversarial process of persuading one's peers that your ideas, methods, and evidence are worth taking seriously. It is not unusual for a single contribution to take years to research, write, and publish, and even then it is likely to be ignored, contradicted, or otherwise overridden by someone else's. Building a broad consensus around a topic is therefore extremely challenging and typically takes decades—when it happens at all. After so much collective effort to establish something that can pass as scientific fact, it is not surprising that scientists assume that it will be treated with deference. Yet, as climate scientists have discovered, even the broadest and most carefully established consensus—say, around the claim that global warming is both real and caused by human activity—can be dismissed with surprising ease on the grounds that the whole thing is a fiction cooked up by the research community to increase its own funding. As anyone who has endured the indignity of peer review or applied for research grants or otherwise struggled to have their ideas taken seriously can attest, the idea that thousands of scientists could collude on anything at all is ridiculously implausible. That the public can so easily be persuaded of the manipulability of entire scientific communities suggests that they have little appreciation of how science works.

Part of the problem may be that the way science is portrayed in the media—with its focus on bold claims, exciting breakthroughs, and sudden flashes of genius—is quite unlike the frustratingly slow and incremental reality (contrary to every movie involving mathematicians, very little useful science is conducted while scribbling equations furiously on a blackboard or a window). But even when scientists themselves try to reach the public directly, the pressure to tell an easily digestible and engaging story invariably influences what they say and how they say it. Not every idea lends itself equally to a seventeen-minute TED talk. Not every argument can or should be made using cute analogies, seven-point lists, or personal anecdotes. And the grander and more sweeping a claim is, the less likely it is to be true. In other words, both for the journalists who cover science and for scientists themselves, communicating with the public presents an unavoidable conflict between engaging one's audience and accurately conveying the careful, systematic nature of science. If that element is left out of public portrayals on the grounds that it's boring and no one wants to hear about it, then it is not just that some poetic license has been taken for the sake of telling a good story; the whole essence of what makes science different from other ways of knowing, including common sense, has been omitted.

One possible solution is for scientists to work with journalists and the media to more accurately characterize the painstaking and deliberative nature of science. Another is for scientists themselves to pay more attention to the "science of science communication" (National Academies of Sciences and Medicine 2017), an emerging field in which research on persuasion and decision-making is being applied to questions about scientific messaging specifically. For example, research in science communication consistently finds that trust in science does not correlate strongly with knowledge; to the contrary, learning more about some topic (e.g., climate change, vaccines, GMOs, etc.) can even increase skepticism about scientific claims (Simis et al. 2016). Simply "presenting the facts," therefore, is not an effective means of communicating scientific findings—a result that flies in the face of traditional science training. Instead, scientists may have to rethink their relationship with the public. Rather than treating the public as a passive audience either to be informed or entertained, scientists may need to treat the public more as a partner, with an active interest in both the process of science and also its consequences. In this way, scientists may more persuasively convey the facts about which they are certain, as well as better understand the concerns that their work may raise.

Finally, if scientists want science to have the kind of legitimacy in the public eye that they believe it deserves, it is incumbent upon them to improve their own systems for aggregating reliable, replicable scientific knowledge (Collaboration 2015; Munafò et al. 2017). To be clear, the problem is usually not that scientists have been negligent or malfeasant—although fraud does occur in science, it appears to be relatively rare—so much as that the methods on which generations of social scientists have been trained turn out to be based on faulty assumptions (Gigerenzer 2004; Ioannidis 2005; Meehl 1990). Thus, even careful, well-intentioned scientists following what they believe to be the best practices of their field can end up producing work that is invalid (Gelman and Loken 2014; Simmons, Nelson, and Simonsohn 2011). And because the scientists reviewing their work for publication have all been trained the same way, peer review is ill equipped to catch these errors. Indeed, by favoring work that makes bold, original contributions over boring replications, peer review may even increase the prevalence of erroneous research (Smaldino and McElreath 2016). Given the difficulty that even professional scientists have when evaluating the validity of claims within their own areas of expertise, it is unreasonable to expect journalists and members of the public to do so either.

CONCLUSION

It is common these days to lament the lack of respect for truth in political debate, and for good reason: it is hard to think of a precedent for Trump's near-constant stream of misleading statements, falsehoods, and outright lies, including about relatively objective, verifiable facts like Barack Obama's birthplace, the size of his own inauguration crowds, the millions of illegal voters, and so on. Adding fuel to the fire, a shocking number of undeniably fake news stories circulated on social media during the election campaign, in some cases generating more reader eyeballs than competing "real" news. Whether any of this is worse than it has been in the past is difficult to establish, but it is certainly bad enough that a discussion of the place of truth in public debates—or at least a shared sense of reality—seems urgently needed.

It has been my contention in this essay that deference to common sense is detrimental to this goal. As useful as common sense may be in navigating ordinary, everyday circumstances, the fundamental assumption of common sense—that truth should be self-evident—is wrong for two important reasons. First, because common sense draws no distinction between objective and subjective "truths," what is self-evident to one person can be non-obvious, wrong, or even abhorrent to another. And second, much of what is true in a scientific sense is not self-evident in any meaningful sense to most people. If truth is to be the guiding principle of political debate, therefore, common sense must defer to science in matters of social and economic policy as it has in matters of physics and chemistry. If *that* is to happen, however, then science—and social science in particular—must do a much better job than it has of building public trust. In part that will require scientists to do a better job of persuading a skeptical public that their methods are better suited to establishing truth than other ways of knowing, including common sense. And in part it will require scientists to improve their methods, which currently do not work as well as advertised.

In closing, it is worth noting that science has dealt successfully with legitimacy problems before. In the late eighteenth and early nineteenth centuries, the scientific world was undergoing transformative changes, in no small part because new instruments and methods were allowing scientists to observe and quantify phenomena that had previously been ephemeral. As is the case today with "big data" transforming once-sleepy areas of social science, public interest in the sciences was extremely high—scientists like Humphry Davy, a celebrated chemist, inventor of the Davy safety lamp, and fierce advocate of the scientific method, occupied almost celebrity status—but so was public skepticism. In effect, science was claiming for itself areas of human knowledge—like the size of the universe and the nature of the elements—that had for hundreds of years been the province of religion and poetry. The traditional arbiters of truth found their status increasingly challenged by a new breed of experts who brought with them methods—and a level of self-assurance in their answers—that the old guard naturally found deeply threatening. No less a figure than Isaac Newton was castigated by John Keats, himself a giant figure in the culture of the time, who claimed that Newton's historic discovery of the color spectrum of white light had "destroyed all the poetry of the rainbow" (Holmes 2010). These days it is hard to imagine a poet directly criticizing the work of the world's preeminent physicist—if anything, physicists have coopted the language of poets to describe their work. But something similar *is* arguably happening in politics and business, where centuries of explanation based on intuition and narrative are being challenged by reams of data and statistical analyses. As with the Romantic-era poets, traditional sources of authority resent the intrusion and seek to undermine the challengers with appeals to common sense. And yet there is a glimmer of hope in this story: if the hard sciences also had to overcome public skepticism about their legitimacy, perhaps the social sciences can also.

REFERENCES

Alcindor, Yamiche. "Ben Carson Calls Poverty a 'State of Mind,' Igniting a Backlash." *New York Times*, May 25, 2017, https://www.nytimes.com/2017/05/25/us/politics/ben-carson-poverty-hud-state-of-mind.html.

Ariely, Dan. *Predictably Irrational.* New York: Harper, 2008.

Arthur, W. Brian. "Competing Technologies, Increasing Returns, and Lock-In by Historical Events." *The Economic Journal* 99, no. 394 (1989): 116–31.

Banaji, Mahzarin R., and Anthony G. Greenwald. *Blindspot: Hidden Biases and Good People.* New York: Bantam, 2016.

Bookstaber, Richard. *The End of Theory: Financial Crises, the Failure of Economics, and the Sweep of Human Interaction.* Princeton, NJ: Princeton University Press, 2017.

Camerer, Colin F., and Eric J. Johnson. "The Process-Performance Paradox in Expert Judgment: How Can Experts Know So Much and Predict So Badly?" *Research on Judgment and Decision Making: Currents, Connections, and Controversies* 342 (1997).

Collaboration, Open Science. "Estimating the Reproducibility of Psychological Science." *Science* 349, no. 6251 (2015): 10.1126/ science.aac4716.

DiPrete, Thomas A., and Gregory M. Eirich. "Cumulative Advantage as a Mechanism for Inequality: A Review of Theoretical and Empirical Developments." *Annual Review of Sociology* 32, no. 1 (2006): 271–97.

Dunning, Thad. *Natural Experiments in the Social Sciences: A Design-based Approach.* Cambridge, UK: Cambridge University Press, 2012.

Easterly, William. *The White Man's Burden: Why the West's Efforts to Aid the Rest Have Done So Much Ill and So Little Good.* New York: Penguin, 2006.

Economides, Nicholas. "The Economics of Networks." *International Journal of Industrial Organization* 14, no. 6 (1996): 673–99.

Fisman, Raymond, and Miriam Golden. "How to Fight Corruption." *Science* 356, no. 6340 (2017): 803–4.

Frank, Robert H. *Success and Luck: Good Fortune and the Myth of Meritocracy.* Princeton, NJ: Princeton University Press, 2016.

Gelman, Andrew, and Eric Loken. "The Statistical Crisis in Science Data-dependent Analysis—a 'Garden of Forking Paths'—Explains Why Many Statistically Significant Comparisons Don't Hold Up." *American Scientist* 102, no. 6 (2014): 460.

Gessen, Masha. "Trump's Incompetence Won't Save Our Democracy." *New York Times,* June 2, 2017, https://www.nytimes.com/2017/06/02 /opinion/sunday/trumps-incompetence-wont-save-our-democracy.html.

Gigerenzer, Gerd. "Mindless Statistics." *The Journal of Socio-Economics* 33, no. 5 (2004): 587–606.

Gilovich, Thomas, Dale Griffin, and Daniel Kahneman, eds. *Heuristics and Biases: The Psychology of Intuitive Judgment.* Cambridge, UK: Cambridge University Press, 2002.

Granovetter, M. S. "Threshold Models of Collective Behavior." *American Journal of Sociology* 83, no. 6 (1978): 1420–43.

Hardin, Garrett. "The Tragedy of the Commons." *Science* 162, no. 3859 (1968): 1243–48.

Holmes, Richard. *The Age of Wonder: How the Romantic Generation Discovered the Beauty and Terror of Science.* New York: Vintage Books USA, 2010.

Imbens, Guido W., and Donald B. Rubin. *Causal Inferences in Statistics, Social, and Biomedical Science.* Cambridge, UK: Cambridge University Press, 2015.

Ioannidis, John P. A. "Why Most Published Research Findings Are False." *PLoS Medicine* 2, no. 8 (2005): e124.

Johnson, Eric J., and Daniel Goldstein. "Do Defaults Save Lives?" *Science* 302, no. 5649 (2003): 1338–39.

Kahneman, Daniel. *Thinking, Fast and Slow.* New York: Macmillan, 2011.

Lewis, Michael. "Obama's Way." *Vanity Fair*, September 11, 2012, https://www.vanityfair.com/news/2012/10/michael-lewis-profile-barack-obama.

Lowenstein, Roger. *When Genius Failed: The Rise and Fall of Long-Term Capital Management.* New York: Random House, 2000.

Mayhew, Bruce H. "Structuralism versus Individualism: Part 1, Shadowboxing in the Dark." *Social Forces* 59, no. 2 (1980): 335–75.

McFadden, Daniel. "Rationality for Economists?" *Journal of Risk and Uncertainty* 19, no. 1–3 (1999): 73–105.

Meehl, Paul E. "Why Summaries of Research on Psychological Theories Are Often Uninterpretable." *Psychological Reports* 66, no. 1 (1990): 195–244.

Merton, Robert K. "The Unanticipated Consequences of Purposive Social Action." *American Sociological Review* 1, no. 6 (1936): 894–904.

Milanovic, Branko. *The Haves and the Have-Nots: A Brief and Idiosyncratic History of Global Inequality.* ReadHowYouWant.com, 2010.

Mitchell, Gregory. "Case Studies, Counterfactuals, and Causal

Explanations." *University of Pennsylvania Law Review* 152, no. 5 (2004): 1517–608.

Morgan, Stephen L., and Christopher Winship. *Counterfactuals and Causal Inference.* Cambridge, UK: Cambridge University Press, 2014.

Mullainathan, Sendhil, and Eldar Shafir. *Scarcity: Why Having Too Little Means So Much.* New York: Macmillan, 2013.

Munafò, Marcus R., Brian A. Nosek, Dorothy V. M. Bishop, Katherine S. Button, Christopher D. Chambers, Nathalie Percie du Sert, Uri Simonsohn, Eric-Jan Wagenmakers, Jennifer J. Ware, and John P. A. Ioannidis. "A Manifesto for Reproducible Science." *Nature Human Behaviour* 1 (2017): 0021.

National Academies of Sciences, Engineering, and Medicine. *Communicating Science Effectively: A Research Agenda.* Washington, DC: The National Academies Press, 2017.

Olson, Mancur. *The Logic of Collective Action: Public Goods and the Theory of Groups.* Cambridge, MA: Harvard University Press, 1965.

Reinhart, C. M., and K. Rogoff. *This Time It's Different: Eight Hundred Years of Financial Folly.* Princeton, NJ: Princeton University Press, 2009.

Rigney, Daniel. *The Matthew Effect: How Advantage Begets Further Advantage.* New York: Columbia University Press, 2010.

Rosenfeld, Sophia A. *Common Sense.* Cambridge, MA: Harvard University Press, 2011.

Schelling, Thomas C. "Hockey Helmets, Concealed Weapons, and Daylight Saving: A Study of Binary Choices with Externalities." *Journal of Conflict Resolution* 17, no. 3 (1973): 381–428.

Scott, James C. *Seeing Like a State: How Certain Schemes to Improve the Human Condition Have Failed.* New Haven, CT: Yale University Press, 1998.

Simis, Molly J., Haley Madden, Michael A. Cacciatore, and Sara K. Yeo. "The Lure of Rationality: Why Does the Deficit Model Persist in Science Communication?" *Public Understanding of Science* 25, no. 4 (2016): 400–414.

Simmons, Joseph P., Leif D. Nelson, and Uri Simonsohn. "False-Positive Psychology: Undisclosed Flexibility in Data Collection and Analysis Allows Presenting Anything as Significant." *Psychological Science* 22, no. 11 (2011): 1359–66.

Smaldino, Paul E., and Richard McElreath. "The Natural Selection of Bad Science." *Royal Society of Open Science* 3 (2016): 160384.

Tetlock, Philip. *Expert Political Judgment: How Good Is It? How Can We Know?* Princeton, NJ: Princeton University Press, 2005a.

Thaler, Richard H., and Cass R. Sunstein. *Nudge: Improving Decisions about Health, Wealth, and Happiness.* New Haven, CT: Yale University Press, 2008.

van Holthoon, F. L., and David R. Olson. *Common Sense: The Foundations for Social Science.* Lanham, MD: University Press of America, 1987.

Watts, Duncan J. *Everything Is Obvious:* Once You Know the Answer.* New York: Crown Business, 2011.

Watts, Duncan J. "Common Sense and Sociological Explanations." *American Journal of Sociology* 120, no. 2 (2014): 313–51.

Weber, M. *Economy and Society,* edited by Guenther Roth and Claus Wittich. New York: Bedminster, 1968.

Yourish, Karen, and Gregor Aisch. "The Top Jobs in Trump's Administration Are Mostly Vacant: Who's to Blame?" *New York Times,* July 20, 2017, https://www.nytimes.com/interactive/2017/07/17/us/politics/trump-appointments.html.

NOTES

1. Elsewhere, Rosenfeld (2011, p. 23) reinforces the point, noting that "common sense came also to mean . . . those plain, self-evident truths or conventional wisdom that one needed no sophistication to grasp and no proof to accept precisely because they accorded so well with basic (common sense) intellectual capacities and experiences of the whole social body."

2. A similar mixture of subjective and objective truths appears in an eighteenth-century English commentator's writing: "By a man of common sense . . . we mean one who knows, as say, white from black, and chalk from cheese; that two and two make four; and that a mountain is bigger than a molehill" (Rosenfeld 2011, p. 22).

3. Interestingly, when their conclusions *do* jibe with common sense, our reaction is often not positive either—rather we tend to wonder why such "obvious" research was necessary in the first place (Watts 2011). Common sense thus puts social science in something of double bind, wherein to be seen as useful it must seem nonobvious, and yet to be believed it must seem obvious.

LAW AND THE SLOW-MOTION EMERGENCY

DAVID A. STRAUSS

If it happens here, it won't happen all at once. A large, diverse society with democratic traditions and a strong civil society is unlikely to become an autocracy overnight. The more plausible scenario is a gradual erosion of liberal democratic norms. Each step might be objectionable but not, by itself, alarming. Even at the end of the line, a version of democratic institutions might remain: there will be elections, although they will have predictable outcomes; civil servants and judges will sometimes be independent, although not on important matters; and occasionally dissidents will be tolerated.[1] The institutions will have been hollowed out; much of what we value in a liberal democracy will be lost. But there will have been no single, cataclysmic point at which democratic institutions were demolished.

For the same reason, the steps toward authoritarianism will not always, or even usually, be obviously illegal.

Grossly illegal acts are unlikely to get very far; there are too many sources of resistance to them. Each individual step will stretch the law only a little. In fact, each step might conform to the letter of the law. But each step, legal in itself, might undermine liberal democracy a little bit more. This is a paradox, but it reflects an intrinsic feature of a liberal society: Well-functioning liberal institutions are inherently vulnerable to antiliberal actors. Opponents of democracy can win free elections. Intolerant sects can take advantage of religious toleration. Individuals determined to eradicate free expression can invoke laws protecting free expression and, ultimately, might get the power to demolish those protections. And the same thing can happen with government officials: they can exploit features of a liberal democracy to turn it in an illiberal direction.

They can do this because the legal system of a functioning democracy is not set up to deal with a systematic effort to undermine democratic institutions. In particular, on an everyday basis, a legal system has to give officials some leeway to use their judgment. Courts obviously can't redo every decision that every official makes; most of the time, courts have to uphold most decisions, provided they fall within a range of acceptability. They have to assume that officials usually act in good faith. Officials who set out to subvert liberal democratic norms—whether they do it by design or by instinct—will be able to take advantage of that assumption. Courts, following the law—which is designed for conscientious officials who are committed to liberal democracy—might give officials with authoritarian inclinations the benefit of the doubt, time after time, until liberal democratic institutions are fatally undermined.

When that seems to be happening, how should courts respond? Actions that take advantage of weaknesses in the law are still, at least in one sense, lawful. But if judges follow the law and allow those actions, they may be contributing to the erosion of democracy. What is the alternative, though: violating the law they are sworn to uphold?

Sometimes that is the choice: either break the law or contribute to the downfall of liberal democracy. But the dilemma need not be that stark. The better response is to treat a systematic effort to undermine liberal democratic norms as a kind of emergency, in the way that, say, a natural disaster or a terrorist attack is an emergency. There are two differences, though. An attack on liberal democratic norms is a slow-motion emergency, one that, as I've said, unfolds gradually, unlike the more familiar sudden emergency. And unlike the more familiar kind of emergency, which might require granting *more* power to government officials, a slow-motion slide toward authoritarianism requires the opposite: limiting the power of government officials.

But, fundamentally, the dilemma for a judge, or someone in a similar position, is the same in both kinds of emergencies. Following the law in the usual way might bring about a calamity; departing from the law is a gravely troubling step. There is a school of thought that holds that emergencies call for extralegal action,[2] and one can imagine extreme cases in which a threat to liberal democratic norms is so severe that courts, and other officials, should resist it by illegal action if need be. But apart from the most extreme cases, the right response to an emergency, sudden or slow-motion, is not to disregard the law but to shape it and adapt it. Rather than either acting in the way they would in normal circumstances or treating the law as irrelevant, judges, or others in a similar position, should push the limits of the law in a way that addresses the emergency conditions—that resists the slide into illiberality or authoritarianism.

In a deep way, that can be a lawful thing to do. The rule of law requires that courts apply established principles. But it also allows those principles to evolve in response to particular circumstances. In the past, some actions by courts that seemed to go too far in adapting principles to specific threats—that seemed to subvert the law in order to prevent a greater evil—turned out to be not just acceptable but celebrated examples of how the law should work. The civil rights era of the mid-twentieth century gives us several examples: actions that seemed legally questionable at the time but that we later came to see as examples of how the law can adapt itself to circumstances that threaten the foundations of our liberal democratic order. The response to the threat of authoritarianism can take the same form.

There are many questions buried here: Do we trust judges, or anyone else, to know when there is a slow-motion emergency? Isn't it common for people to think that policies they strongly oppose are the first step toward the collapse of the basic norms of democratic society? How far can judges go in "adapting" the law before their actions become simply unlawful? Can judges be trusted to find that limit? These questions are very hard to answer. But, as with sudden emergencies, there are risks in both directions: not just overreacting to the emergency but failing to react.

I

Early in its tenure, the Trump administration issued, and later revised, an executive order that temporarily restricted immigration from certain predominantly Muslim countries. The litigation about that executive order shows how courts might respond to a slow-motion emergency.

The basis for the executive orders was a federal statute that says the president may "suspend the entry of all aliens or any class of aliens" if the president "finds that" their entering the country "would be detrimental to the interests of the United States." The executive orders asserted that the restrictions were needed to protect against terrorists' entering the United States. Ordinarily courts would unhesitatingly uphold such an executive order. The phrasing of the statute suggests that the decision is the president's alone. The criterion that the president is to apply—whether entry into the country is "detrimental to the interests of the United States"—invites the exercise of discretion. And both national security and immigration are, traditionally, subjects on which the courts defer to the decisions of the executive branch.

The courts did not react that way to the Trump order, though. An early version of the executive order was enjoined, and the injunction was upheld on appeal. The administration then withdrew that version of the order and issued a second version that was designed to address the problems the courts had found in the initial version. But the second version, too, met a hostile reception in several courts. Some courts said there was evidence that the executive orders were the result of animosity toward Muslims and therefore violated constitutional protections of religious neutrality. Others said the president had not adequately explained why the restriction was needed to prevent harm to the United States. The courts also had to overcome some technical barriers before they could block the executive order; noncitizens living outside the United States are generally not protected by US law, so the suits against the executive orders were brought by people and institutions inside the country who claimed they were harmed by the restrictions on immigration. There was a question of whether their interests were the kind that could support a lawsuit.

Strictly as a legal matter, were those courts' decisions correct or not? The answer to that question is more complicated than it seems. Often legal rules are entirely clear; there is a right answer to a legal question and no room for reasonable disagreement. But sometimes—and commonly, in cases that wind up in litigation—there is a range of plausible answers. That is not to say they are all equally plausible. A judge who has to decide the case will identify the answer that, in her view, is better than the others. But even incorrect legal conclusions might be plausible.

Many important legal institutions are built on the idea that there can be a range of plausible answers to a legal question, even if one answer is better than the others. Lawyers have an ethical obligation not to make arguments that lack any legal basis, and they can be punished if they violate that duty. But they also have an obligation to make plausible arguments on behalf of their clients, even if they think those arguments are, in the end, not convincing. Government officials—police officers, for example—can be sued for violating an individual's constitutional rights, but they will not have to pay money damages even for a constitutional violation if a reasonable constitutional argument could have been made in support of what they did. In some circumstances, a court will overturn another court's decision if that decision was outside the bounds of reasonableness, but not if the decision was merely incorrect.

The decisions of the courts that rejected the Trump executive orders were not obviously correct, but they were within the bounds of plausibility. There is a well-established principle that the government may not deliberately favor some religions over others, and there was evidence that Trump intended to act with hostility toward Muslims. Trump's own statements were such evidence, and the first version of the executive order contained an explicit exemption that, in practice, would favor Christians. But it was not entirely clear that the evidence showed the kind of hostility that would impugn the revised version of the executive order. It is also not entirely clear how the principle of religious neutrality applies to noncitizens who were outside the country, and whether a claim based on that principle could be raised by the individuals and institutions inside the US who brought the suit.

The courts that said the administration did not show a

real risk of harm "to the interests of the United States" also had a point. While courts would ordinarily be very deferential to a presidential action dealing with national security and immigration, especially when that action was based on a broadly worded statute, there are still some limits to what even a president can do, even in those circumstances. The statute would not permit a presidential action that was completely arbitrary. The first version of the executive order seemed very ill-considered. It was so sloppily drafted that it was not even clear whether it applied to green-card holders: noncitizens who have a right to be in the United States but who might have been temporarily outside the country when the order was issued. The first version of the order was not reviewed by some of the government agencies that should have been involved in the process. The evidence that the restriction was needed was thin or nonexistent. The second version of the executive order was more carefully done, but there was reason to think that the problems were just papered over, not seriously addressed.

On the other hand, in an ordinary case, courts would not look too deeply into the internal workings of the executive branch. If the order was unclear or otherwise flawed, they might just correct the flaws, or even overlook them, rather than using them as a basis to declare the order invalid. And, ordinarily, not much evidence would be needed to support an executive order of this kind. So while there was a basis for striking down the orders, some solid legal arguments were also made in support of them.

So were the decisions correct? If there was a significant

risk that the administration's actions reflected a systematic undermining of liberal democratic values, then the courts were right to rule in a way that limited the president's power. That is how courts should respond to a slow-motion emergency. The evidence that there was such an emergency could come from both the executive order litigation itself and the larger context of the administration's actions. The internal executive-branch processes of information gathering and critical analysis are not always visible, but they are crucial ways in which an ill-considered or malign political agenda can be held in check; when those processes are systematically lacking or are subverted, courts are entitled to be wary. The executive orders, in the context of statements made by the president in particular, seemed to be part of an effort to stigmatize a vulnerable religious minority. That evidence of a slow-motion emergency combined with other indications of illiberal and undemocratic impulses—a lack of transparency and accountability, the vilification of political opponents, hostility to courts and other institutional checks, insensitivity to the risks of corruption and nepotism. The courts may have had reason to think there was the kind of threat to democratic institutions that justified them in choosing, among the legally plausible conclusions, the one that limited executive power, irrespective of whether that would otherwise have been the better view of the law.

II

It's hardly surprising that, quite apart from what the law might formally say, courts will sometimes push back against what they see as overreaching by the president.[3] But this is not just an empirical reality, and it is not something that has to be treated as extralegal, as a kind of judicial civil disobedience. Within limits, it is an example of how the law develops. Foundational principles—like the principle that courts should defer to the president's decisions about matters having to do with national security—should not be discarded or ignored. But sometimes they should be qualified, modified, or adapted to deal with exceptional circumstances.

It goes without saying that this is a fraught process. Part of the point of having principles is to resist the temptation to do something that seems expedient in the moment but is wrong. In the more familiar kinds of emergencies, like a war or a terror attack, the "adaptation" of fundamental principles can lead to gross abuses of human rights. The internment of Americans of Japanese descent during World War II is the most notorious example, but there are others. When the apparent emergency is a descent into authoritarianism, the analogous risk is that the courts' response will unnecessarily, and maybe dangerously, limit the government's power to serve the national interest. But we can't avoid this problem by just insisting on the immutability of certain principles. Courts, and others in positions of power, will, as a matter of fact, respond to what they see as exceptional circumstances; no amount of insisting on the inviolability of foundational principles will prevent that. The challenge is to try to identify when the courts should engage in this kind of adaptation and how they might do it so as to minimize the risks of abuses.

In US constitutional law, the civil rights era of the mid-twentieth century gives us some examples of this process—adapting legal principles in ways that are plausible but certainly questionable in response to exceptionally threatening circumstances. Discussions about whether "it could happen" in the United States sometimes overlook that it did happen in the United States. From roughly the late nineteenth century to the mid-twentieth century, parts of the United States were ruled by an undemocratic, illiberal, racist regime. African-Americans were denied the right to vote and were violently repressed both by the government and by private individuals acting with the tacit approval of the government.

When the courts began to respond to that regime, established legal rules seemed to be a barrier. For example, it is a long-standing principle, supported by the text of the Constitution, that, with few exceptions, constitutional rights are rights against the government only, not against private individuals. Civil rights laws enacted by the federal government in the 1960s allowed people to enforce comparable rights—rights against discrimination in housing, employment, and places like restaurants and hotels, for example—against private individuals. But before then, in states that did not have those laws, the only weapon against a racist regime was the Constitution, and it, among other limitations, did not reach private conduct. And private conduct, or ostensibly private conduct tacitly supported by the state, was one of the principal weapons that regime used.

The courts responded in the ways I have suggested are

appropriate for dealing with a threat to democracy. They stretched the law, not beyond the limits of plausibility but in ways that could be criticized—and were criticized, in good faith, by some analysts—as legally incorrect. One of the most famous examples, the case of *Shelley v. Kraemer*,[4] dealt with a racially restrictive housing covenant—a provision in a deed that obligated the buyer of a house not to sell it to a non-white person. These covenants were a way of making sure that blacks could not move into the same neighborhoods as whites; they were common, so the effect was essentially the same as a law that forbade blacks from buying homes in white areas. But the covenants were just agreements among private buyers and sellers, and because the Constitution is limited to actions by the government, they seemed to be beyond the reach of constitutional law. In *Shelley*, the Supreme Court got around that limit by saying that racially restrictive covenants could not be enforced in court. The theory was that the courts are part of the government, to which the Constitution applies. The effect was that a homeowner who was supposedly bound by a racially restrictive covenant could sell the property to a black person with impunity. So even private efforts to maintain all-white communities were defeated.

The decision in *Shelley* was not flagrantly outside the bounds of legal respectability—the courts are, after all, part of the government—but to this day no one is quite sure how to justify it. Courts routinely enforce all kinds of contracts; to say that the government is complicit in discrimination whenever the courts enforce a contract motivated by private prejudice seems to collapse the Constitution's distinction between government and private action. Or, in the terms of a familiar law-school hypothetical example, if the police are called to eject an uninvited guest from a private home, do they first have to check to see if the guest was uninvited because of race, sex, religion, or sexual orientation, on the theory that otherwise they will be engaging in discrimination, just like the courts that enforced the discriminatory housing covenant?

Another example, from the same period, dealt with the lengths to which politicians went to keep blacks from voting. Elections themselves, of course, are run by the government, and the Fifteenth Amendment explicitly forbids racial discrimination by states in voting. But the states that practiced racial apartheid were, like many autocracies, one-party states—for the most part, only Democrats were ever elected to state or local office. So the authorities could effectively disenfranchise African-Americans by keeping them from voting in the Democratic Party primaries that selected the Democratic Party nominee. But the courts held that excluding African-Americans from the primaries was unconstitutional because the party primaries used state election facilities, and the state placed the winners of the primaries on the election ballot.

Democrats in Texas tried a different tactic to evade the Constitution: they set up something they called the Jaybird Club. It was a private organization—but a private organization whose members were all the white members of the Democratic Party in Texas. The Jaybird Club had elections to decide which candidate to support in the Democratic Party primary, and that candidate routinely won the primary and the election. In *Terry v. Adams*,[5] the Supreme Court ruled that this arrangement was unconstitutional. The Justices could not agree on a rationale among themselves, and, as is true of *Shelley*, there is even today no generally agreed-upon justification for the decision. The Constitution does not prevent private clubs from discriminating; it obviously does not prevent private clubs from voting on which candidate to support in an election; and it does not forbid people from voting for their club's choice.

Both *Shelley* and *Terry* were criticized at the time as legally unsound. Some of the critics were people whose moral opposition to racist practices was unquestioned.[6] Those decisions, the critics said, were unprincipled; they were prompted by an admirable opposition to racism but could not be reconciled with established constitutional law. The same kind of criticism was, in fact, leveled against *Brown v. Board of Education*,[7] the now iconic decision declaring state-supported segregation unconstitutional. But today few people would say that *Shelley* or *Terry* (or certainly *Brown*) was wrong. They were important steps in helping to abolish a racist regime.

The courts that decided these cases were responding to an ongoing assault on liberal democratic values. The people waging that assault took advantage of the established legal principle that the Constitution applies only to government action by interweaving public and private action in a way designed to subvert constitutional norms. The Supreme

Court did not jettison the principle; perhaps the evil it was fighting was great enough that it would have been justified in doing so. But the Court also was not deterred by the entirely mainstream objections that its decisions were inconsistent with existing law. Instead the Court tried to stay within the bounds of plausible legality by stretching the definition of unconstitutional government action to cover the enforcement of racial covenants and the Jaybird Club. That is a model for how a court might respond to threats to liberal democracy more generally.

III

The civil rights era was an extraordinary period, and you have to be careful in drawing lessons from it. Still, we may be living through an extraordinary period now, and there are lessons to be drawn from the civil rights–era cases. The first is that courts have to decide how bad the problem is—how severe the threat to democratic institutions. Racial apartheid was more than a threat; it was an actually existing authoritarian system within the United States. That justified the Court's extraordinary actions. Something is an emergency only if there is a risk of serious damage to democratic institutions.

The second lesson, which may be less obvious, is that the courts have to assess how much harm they might cause when they stretch legal principles to address the threat. When the response to an emergency might allow human rights to be violated on a large scale, that is, of course, a reason not to choose that response. When the response might keep government authorities from protecting national security or otherwise dealing with a serious problem, that is also a reason to hesitate. In the civil rights cases, the possible harm was to allow the federal government, rather than the states, to determine what kinds of private actions would be lawful; it is fair to count that as a harm, but it is not on the same scale as ratifying the internment of people of Japanese ancestry. In the Trump executive order cases, the administration had acted in ways that suggested it was not really responding to a national security threat. So the courts had reason to think the potential harm from their intervention was not so great.

A related point, implicit in the idea that the courts are adapting rather than ignoring or revising the law, is that courts are most justified in taking the kinds of actions I have described when the government seems to be exploiting loopholes—acting in ways that are arguably consistent with the letter of the law but inconsistent with its purposes. In the Jaybird case, it was obvious that the white Democratic Party was doing exactly that. The core of the challenge to the Trump executive order is that it, too, was using claims about national security as a pretext. Pretextual action by the government is not always wrong; sometimes a government has to deal with an unanticipated problem by using legal tools that were designed for a different purpose. But courts are at least justified in viewing pretextual action suspiciously, and preventing such action is less likely to damage the government's legitimate interests.

The third lesson is that when courts respond to emergencies by adapting the law, they can be, and should be, tentative and experimental. Because they stay within the framework of the law, they, or future judges, can decide whether the law should continue to evolve in the same direction or should retreat. If the civil rights–era cases had allowed the federal government to interfere with truly private relationships that should have been sacrosanct, those cases could have been limited or rolled back. By demanding that the Trump administration show that its executive order really did have a basis in national security concerns, and that it was not an expression of animosity toward Muslims, the courts left open the option of backing off if those showings could be made.

All of this seems to suggest that the courts are themselves unmoved by the kinds of overreactions and biases they are supposedly correcting: that courts will be able to identify slow-motion emergencies and react accordingly. Of course that is very unrealistic. There are obvious and important risks in saying that courts can shape the law in response to what they think are slow-motion emergencies. In fact, the risks have been realized. Three examples come to mind.

First, many opponents of President Franklin Roosevelt's New Deal thought they were facing a threat of authoritarianism. They did not think the threat was developing in slow motion; they thought it was imminent.[8] The Supreme Court, to some degree, responded in the way I have suggested: not by stepping wholly outside the law but by pushing the law in a direction that would limit the president and, more generally, the federal government. The Court held that the president's power to dismiss executive-branch officials could be narrowed by Congress, and it struck down some of the laws that were, at least initially, centerpieces of the president's program on the ground that they exceeded the federal government's constitutional powers. Many of those decisions, although not all, have since been repudiated by the Court.

The second example is *Bush v. Gore*,[9] the case that effectively decided the presidential election of 2000. The decision was, in my view, legally indefensible. The Court did not just extend the law to its limits but instead went well beyond them. But it seems reasonably clear that the Court thought it was confronted with an emergency: either electoral chaos, because there might be no clear decision about who was president; or what some of the justices apparently saw as a partisan coup by state court judges, who, had the Supreme Court not intervened, would have effectively controlled the crucial electoral votes.

The third example was the Supreme Court's treatment of the Affordable Care Act in *NFIB v. Sebelius*.[10] The Affordable Care Act, and particularly the "individual mandate"—a provision that requires everyone to have health insurance—were attacked as a gross infringement on liberty. The attacks were unwarranted; the central features of the ACA were supported by a bipartisan consensus until the Act became identified with President Obama. But some members of the Supreme Court reacted as if they were confronted with a slow-motion emergency. The Court ruled, by a 5–4 vote, that Congress did not have the power to enact the individual mandate under the Interstate Commerce Clause of the Constitution, the clause that is the basis of much federal regulation of the economy. (The Court did say the individual mandate could be justified on a different basis, but four justices rejected both justifications.) The ACA also required states to extend Medicaid to a new class of recipients as a condition of continued funding for existing Medicaid programs; the Court held that the requirement unconstitutionally coerced the states, so states could refuse to expand Medicaid without further cost. Both of these rulings were, at the very least, questionable under existing law.

In each of these cases, in my view, the Supreme Court's action was unwarranted. There was no risk of incipient authoritarianism or electoral chaos. But the lesson is not, I think, that the kind of response to a perceived emergency I am defending—for the courts to adapt the law in a direction that mitigates the problem—should be condemned. The lesson is rather that the courts will engage in this kind of action when they think it is warranted. We are better off acknowledging that this is part of our system: courts will modify and shape principles in new ways in response to particular circumstances, and they will do so especially aggressively in response to what they see as an emergency, sudden or slow-motion.

Rather than saying this kind of behavior by the courts is wrong, we should instead say that judges ought to be self-consciously aware that they are doing it—that they are pushing the limits of existing principles in response to extraordinary circumstances—and that they should be prepared to justify their actions, at least to themselves and their colleagues. (Whether they have to explain everything in their published opinions is another matter; opinions are public documents that serve other purposes besides revealing the author's thought processes.) They should be prepared, at least introspectively, to say what the extraordinary circumstances are, why they think those circumstances exist, why their response still observes the outer limits of what is legally permissible, and why it is worth incurring the risks that come with reshaping established principles to push those limits. If we instead try to maintain the notion that it is improper for judges to adapt the law to deal with exceptional circumstances, judges, in response, will convince themselves they are not pushing the limits of the law when they are in fact doing so. If we acknowledge that this is a legitimate thing for judges to do, it will also encourage them to approach the response to emergencies, sudden or slow-motion, in an experimental vein, as I suggested: to be prepared to back off or go further when they see how matters play out.

There is one final danger we can avoid if we recognize that judges not only do but properly can respond in the ways I have described. Some judges, we know, will respond this way in any event. They are likely to be judges who are most ideologically motivated or who have the most exalted view of their role. Those judges should not have the field to themselves. It will be better if judges who are more restrained by temperament or self-conception understand that they can responsibly respond to emergencies, including slow-motion emergencies, by a carefully thought-through decision to adapt the law to the extraordinary circumstances they are confronting.

NOTES

1. For a discussion of such regimes, see, for example, Steven Levitsky and Lucan A. Way, *Competitive Authoritarianism: Hybrid Regimes After the Cold War* (Cambridge, UK: Cambridge University Press, 2010).

2. This idea is generally associated with Carl Schmitt, *Political Theology: Four Chapters on the Concept of Sovereignty*, George Schwab, trans. (Chicago: University of Chicago Press, 2010). See the discussion in Eric A. Posner and Adrian Vermeule, *The Executive Unbound: After the Madisonian Republic* (New York: Oxford University Press, 2010), 90–91.

3. See, for example, Jack Goldsmith [tweetstorm] June 5, 2017, https://twitter.com/jacklgoldsmith/status/871779981986287616; Eric Posner, "Judges v. Trump: Be Careful What You Wish For," *New York Times*, February 16, 2017, A27, https://www.nytimes.com/2017/02/15/opinion/judges-v-trump-be-careful-what-you-wish-for.html.

4. 334 US 1 (1948).

5. 345 US 461 (1953).

6. See, for example, Herbert Wechsler, "Toward Neutral Principles of Constitutional Law," in *Principles, Politics, and Fundamental Law*, (Cambridge, MA: Harvard University Press, 1961), 36–43; Archibald Cox, *The Warren Court*, (Cambridge, MA: Harvard University Press, 1968), 33–34.

7. 347 US 483 (1954). See Wechsler, supra note 6, at 43–47.

8. For an account, see Jeff Shesol, *Supreme Power* (New York: W. W. Norton & Co., 2010).

9. 531 US 98 (2000).

10. 567 US 519 (2012).

HOW DEMOCRACIES PERISH
STEPHEN HOLMES

They say "America First," but they mean "America Next!"
—Woody Guthrie

The populist venom being directed these days at politically vulnerable universities speaks against pejorative resort to the word *academic*.[1] Yet the currently beleaguered state of liberal democracy is definitely not an academic subject, or at least not only an academic subject. It is also an existential one, involving some of the most dismaying and unnerving trends of our time, with potentially ominous consequences for our personal and collective lives.

During the Cold War, many Western thinkers were tormented by the thought that liberal-democratic societies could succumb to totalitarian temptation. Jean-François Revel's 1980s bestselling *How Democracies Perish* was typical of the genre.[2] Then, in the hinge year of 1989, these dark clouds dissipated virtually overnight. From staggering helplessly at death's door, it seemed, Western-style democracy not only recovered its health but became joyously triumphant and even, according to one celebrated pundit, ideologically uncontestable. But the rebound was less enduring than had been hoped. After the Iraq War, the financial crisis of 2008, the derailing of the Arab Spring, economic dynamism in China where pro-democracy protesters are routinely charged with subversion, electoral victories of xenophobic authoritarians in East Central Europe, increasing support for anti-immigrant and anti-EU movements in Western Europe, the senseless Brexit referendum, the fraying of the Atlantic alliance, and the upset political victory of the forty-fifth president of the United States, the prospects for liberal democracy are once again in doubt. The unthinkable is not yet probable, but neither can it be casually ruled out. Wherever we are headed, we need to look seriously again at the conditions under which democratic government, hollowed out from within, might gradually sicken and suddenly die.

To broach the manifold infirmities and potential transience of democratic self-government, I begin with a revealing anecdote and a derivative generalization. During an electoral campaign in Brazil, Albert Hirschman once sighted a billboard that announced: "We are tired of austerity, we want promises." [3] The facetiousness of the slogan should not distract from its far-reaching implications. In reality, much of modern politics is about promising, disappointing, and managing the negative consequences of bitter disappointments. All governments promise and disappoint. One of the signal virtues of liberal democracy is its uncommon facility at mitigating the fallout of political discontent. Mitigation means, most importantly, preventing civic frustrations in the face of unpopular policies and deteriorating conditions from engendering violent confrontations between lethally armed and ideologically polarized citizens or between infuriated citizens and the forces of public order. This is a crucial task, because blood-splattered streets can be a breeding ground for that justly feared authoritarian temptation, precipitating the ruinous breakdown of democracy.

A multiparty representative system, where challengers have a reasonable chance of removing and replacing incumbents, may or may not align the preferences of politicians with the preferences of voters. It may or may not produce good governance and economic prosperity. And it may or may not be at peace with its neighbors.

But periodic elections in a pluralistic democracy ideally fulfill another function that they often perform quite well and that helps account for much of democracy's indisputable political appeal. They ensure domestic tranquillity despite the frequency of buyer's remorse or the all-too-common disappointment of citizens in the performance of their own popularly elected rulers. The very possibility of *l'alternance*, the expectation that a shadow government or rival governing team has a good chance of ousting the incumbents in an upcoming election, subsidizes patience with the deficiencies of the current administration. The mere possibility that the Outs may replace the Ins can dispel the nightmare of having to stare into the faces of an unchanging leadership tiresomely addressing citizens with dubious honesty for the indeterminate future. This is true even if, as is likely, the new incumbents turn out, after their proverbial honeymoon, to be just as disappointing as their predecessors. Well-organized democracies, in other words, systematically channel public disgruntlement *inside* the system rather than allowing it to fester unaddressed and eventually erupt onto the public squares, where minor clashes can accidentally escalate into uncontrollable violence. One of the principal functions of representative government, according to Max Weber, is to "break the irregular rule of the street."[4] Rather than burning Dumpsters at intersections, discontented citizens can be lured into organizing for the next elections, expending the fuel of political grievance and letdown on party-political competition, so long as the system is not blatantly rigged against them and they have a reasonable chance of prevailing in the future.

Political elites presumably found this system acceptable for analogous reasons. In early monarchies, when one political dynasty replaced another, the winners often felt compelled to murder all significant members of the ousted family grouping.[5] Multiparty democracy, whatever its other failings, is not so cruel to electoral losers in the struggle for power. However much they disagree ideologically, competing political factions today normally concur on the mutual benefits of soft-landing sites for the electorally defeated. In a stable liberal democracy, losers will not be stripped of their wealth and imprisoned together with their families. The last thing a candidate who respected liberal-democratic norms would say about his partisan opponent, in other words, is "lock her up!"

Incumbents as well as challengers willingly submit themselves to electoral competitions that they may conceivably lose for another reason too. Holding office pro tempore is more appealing than holding office for life, because the former is less likely than the latter to excite impatient rivals into committing desperate acts. After all, life tenure implies that the only way to remove an incumbent from office is to remove him or her from life. Holding out to one's restless competitors the possibility of a peaceful transfer of power in the not-too-distant future is an obviously attractive strategy for reducing enticements to political assassination.

These safety-valve rationales for democratic competition are plausible and important. They nevertheless remain excessively negative, placing sole focus on the avoidance of violence. They therefore wrongly neglect the positive effects of the "bias for hope" built into a political system where rival governing teams alternate in power. Even if such a system does not guarantee good governance or allow citizens to control politicians, it can nevertheless diffuse a sense of buoyant expectancy or social energy throughout the community, vividly illustrating the possibility of a fresh start and exciting a creative fertility and spirit of innovation in science, art, industry, and other spheres of activity in civil society, an outpouring of extra-political élan very unlikely to develop under a dead-hand government that cannot be challenged or peacefully changed.

But let us stick for the moment with the first—and, for our purposes, more essential—point that liberal democracy is a time-tested system for managing political disappointment. This perspective on how democracy works contains an implicit warning about the gravity and urgency of our current predicament. A properly functioning democracy helps diminish the level of political violence in a society by funneling discontent into legal channels rather than letting it rage unaddressed on the outside, where it can incubate extra-parliamentary attacks on the constitutional order. Our central problem today is the seemingly global discontent with liberal democracy itself.[6]

Many polls suggest that young people are especially likely to feel disenchanted or simply uninterested in electoral competition. In Italy, where popularly elected leaders seem paralyzed in the face of economic stagnation and unstanched migrant flows from the failed state of Libya, one shocking poll reports that 83 percent of voters between the ages of eighteen and twenty-nine prefer a strong leader to a democracy.[7] However methodologically sound, admittedly, such surveys provide scant evidence that elections are about to be canceled in any advanced Western democracy, much less that democracy in general is on the cusp of dying "to thunderous applause," to cite the renowned Senator Padmé Amidala. On the other hand, a general softening of public and elite commitment to the democratic legitimacy formula can, under especially stressful circumstances, prove disastrous.

In a severe crisis, disenchantment with democracy can

undermine the willingness of ordinary citizens and political elites to fight tenaciously for the survival of their embattled political system. Democracy depends for its endurance not on fair-weather democrats but on *loyalty in adversity*.[8] Those who have the capacity to defend a besieged democracy must also have the incentive and the disposition to do so. True, the numerous survey results suggesting a diminishing appreciation for democracy across social classes in the West do not necessarily imply that democracy is dying.[9] But optimism is no more justified than pessimism in this regard. Human beings have a roughly equal tendency to overestimate and to underestimate threats. As a result, the unjustified complacency echoed in best-case scenarios poses just as great a danger to the survival of crisis-stricken liberal democracies as the unjustified hysteria expressed in worst-case scenarios.[10] The Soviet Union collapsed because, among other reasons, those in a position to fight for its survival had ceased to believe that it was worth saving. Could the same fate be awaiting the liberal-democratic West?

Social scientists can track changes in public attitudes with greater or lesser accuracy. But social science can be defined as "history with the events left out." Democracies perish, when they do, because of events. Attitudinal changes are consequential or insignificant depending on cascades of unforeseen occurrences with which citizens and their rulers are forced to contend. For example, a relentless series of high-level political assassinations can create an atmosphere of panic and instability that will put intolerable pressure on any democracy that enjoys only anemic legitimacy in the eyes of organized interests and public officials.[11] A 9/11-style mass-casualty terrorist attack on, say, Washington, DC, would have similar consequences. And as mentioned, when street-level violence persists over time, lukewarm democrats will be tempted to throw themselves into the arms of an authoritarian demagogue who promises to secure public order. Democracy's survival therefore depends essentially on the readiness of the main social forces to combat populist demagoguery and other corrosive trends to maintain the norms, procedures, and values of democracy. The danger we face is great or small depending on the strength or weakness of our psychological and organizational defenses against it.

If allegiance to democracy becomes sufficiently uncertain, then, in a dizzying crisis, all bets are off. The failure of one of America's two great political parties to resist the rise of a candidate who announced in advance his refusal to accept the electoral victory of his opponent—that is, who publicly repudiated the basic norm of democracy—illustrates why we need to take seriously the multiple reasons for a general atrophy of public support for democratic government. But, to repeat, an attitudinal shift is not necessarily dangerous in itself. It is a serious problem only if an unspoken contempt for democracy, first, induces a political party's leadership and voters to support a candidate for the presidency who is manifestly indifferent to the constitutional order, and, second, if it presages an unwillingness by others to defend our highly complex system of government when push comes to shove.

Some of the most commonly discussed reasons for disappointment with democracy are country-specific. In the United States, for example, critics of the current system focus on the rivers of money corrupting the electoral process, permitting capture of the legislative process by corporate donors,[12] as well as on the gerrymandering that has reduced turnout by making the vast majority of House of Representatives races noncompetitive.[13] These difficulties and dysfunctions are not the principal reasons for democratic discontent elsewhere in the world, however. By contrast, the popularization abroad of American-style "primaries" that allow the most polarized swaths of the electorate to select the candidates who will face each other in the general election is a more widely shared pathology. The same can be said about the tendency for voters in the television age to select candidates whose skills at campaigning are prodigious but whose talents for governing are modest. For the sake of generality and to draw some illuminating parallels from abroad to the American case, I will be focusing in this chapter on such shared developments. I will look sequentially at a miscellany of factors that have cumulatively undermined public and elite confidence in the genius of democratic politics across many advanced democracies, including the United States.

First, one currently salient cause for widespread doubt about democracy is illustrated by the Brexit referendum and, once again, the election of Donald Trump. If a decisive vote is held two months earlier or later, the outcome can be completely different. This raises the question: what exactly do electoral tallies measure? Snapshot elections and referenda presumably register the preferences of the voters who go to the polls on a specific date. But the preferences of a majority of the motivated electorate are often highly volatile and unstable. In majoritarian referenda and the American Electoral College, moreover, the *lex majoris partis* creates a situation where a slight favorite for an evanescent moment can become the winner who takes all. As Joseph Schumpeter remarked, you cannot fool all of the people all of the time, but you can fool enough of the people for long enough to do irreversible damage.[14] On an individual level, potentially self-destructive decisions are sometimes structured to include waiting periods as a way to sidestep the conclusiveness of momentary whims.[15] Two-round voting, by informing the electorate about how other voters are likely to vote in the decisive election, roughly simulates a cooling-off period at the collective level. But Brexit-style referenda and American presidential elections benefit from no such bridle on capricious decision-making on the basis of ephemeral predilections. Supermajority requirements would have an analogously steadying effect but are incompatible with the salience of 50 percent–plus as the most easily agreed-upon measure of community will.[16] This vulnerability of liberal democracy to the volatility of public preferences makes its citizens into hostages to fortune, a condition highly unlikely to engender die-hard loyalty to the system. It was much easier for the author of this chapter, for example, to express unqualified adherence to American democracy before American democracy injudiciously raised the current incumbent to the White House.

Second, democracy creates a strong incentive for rival

parties to engage in *competitive overpromising*. When promises that awaken excessive and unrealistic expectations go unfulfilled, as is likely, the dashed hopes can fuel a degree of indignation too deep to be assuaged democratically. Today almost all candidates promise that, if elected, they will create jobs. Under conditions of jobless growth, unfortunately, this turns out to be a promissory note that cannot be cashed. In any single electoral cycle, such broken promises will alienate the electorate only from the party or coalition that failed to deliver on its pledges, triggering a shift of swing voters to the rival party or coalition. But the alternation in power of rival governing teams will cease to sustain the allegiance of the electorate to the democratic order if, over a series of elections, none of the parties competing for power end up creating the jobs or performing the other economic miracles they solemnly pledged to effect.

This brings us to our third factor. Although holding out the promise that the next election will unhorse the current crop of rascals and bring into office a more effective governing team, democracy is not always sufficient, on its own, to introduce a bias for hope into society. Politically generated energy and optimism can be stifled if underlying economic trends baffle the expectation that improvement across generations is to be expected. In 1970, it turns out, less than 10 percent of Americans were earning less than their parents at a similar age. By 2010, 50 percent were earning less.[17] The perception that each generation would be better off than their parents has arguably been "at the heart of Western civilization for the past 150 years or more."[18] It is no longer believable or believed. The expectation that living standards will worsen over time is an immensely consequential change in the social underpinnings of political life. It strikes at the heart of the politically stabilizing function of democracy as detailed above. The realistic prospect of upward social mobility for one's children may have provided an essential psychological support, at least since World War II, for the hope-galvanizing effect of multiparty democratic competition. If so, an essential economic underpinning of optimistic political engagement has now been ripped away. As a result, angry distrust of all major social institutions, including democratically elected governments, has soared. Is this a mere coincidence? It seems more plausible to assume that democracy was previously able to process public frustrations inside the system thanks at least in part to being buoyed up by historically specific and unusually encouraging economic conditions.

Fourth, popular and elite allegiance to liberal-democratic values and procedures has been curtailed by the amnesia that inevitably accompanies the passage of time. The end of history is an exotic myth, but the fading of historical memory is an everyday reality. According to Tony Judt, an important factor explaining the Reagan-Thatcher attack on transfer payments was memory loss at the collective level. Only a public that had largely forgotten the harrowing experience of the Great Depression could lend such cheerful support to the weakening of the welfare state.[19] An implication of this claim is that the concrete lived experiences of a generational cohort exert a greater influence on shared beliefs about the limits of acceptable behavior than abstract norms of justice. The same lesson applies to the crisis of liberal democracy. Only historical amnesia can explain the cavalier resuscitation of fascist-era slogans such as "America First" and "rootless cosmopolitan." The abominations of Nazism evidently lie too far in the past to reinforce shaken confidence in liberal democracy by reminding people of the dark sides of authoritarian and xenophobic alternatives.

Fifth, the Cold War between the liberal-democratic West and the illiberal and nondemocratic USSR is also fading from memory. It has in any case been replaced as the central obsession of US national-security policy by the War on Terror. This swivel of the cannon implies a downgrading of liberal-democratic procedures and norms. Rather than deploring the way communist societies deprived dissidents of their rights, democratic politicians now rally public support by parading their willingness to deprive terrorist suspects of their rights. Brazen violations of due process apparently communicate the tough-guy message that "there is nothing we will not do," a wild promise apparently reassuring to a spooked electorate with little capacity to gauge the real level of the risk they face. Moreover, the War on Terror has been accompanied by a concomitant shrinkage of social privacy and expansion of government secrecy. This displacement of the privacy/secrecy boundary means that the government is increasingly spying on its citizens while the citizens are increasingly unable to examine and evaluate the government's actions. An opaque state presiding over a transparent society is difficult to reconcile with the idea that government works for the people.[20] By swelling the budgets and influence of a largely unaccountable "Deep State" operating "on the dark side" where monitoring is weak and sporadic, in other words, the War on Terror is adding to public doubts about the virtues—not to mention the capacities—of electoral democracy.

This brings us to a sixth factor. Media pluralism is an essential condition of liberal democracy. Citizens cannot rely solely on their government to provide them with the information they need to decide if their elected officials are acting intelligently and in the public interest. This is why authoritarian rulers who nevertheless feel obliged to hold (and rig) elections invariably shut down independent media and monopolize the television broadcasts on which the majority of voters rely for political news. But the extraordinary proliferation of media platforms today has produced a distorted caricature of media pluralism, fragmenting political space into mutually sealed-off ideological fortresses between which no serious communication is possible.[21] In the 2016 presidential contest, moreover, the major American news outlets, profiting from public fascination with Trump's buffoonery, functioned less as a check on power than as a conveyer and magnifier of slander, disinformation, conspiracy theories, and politically calculated lies, again weakening public confidence in an essential pillar of democracy. As a final expression of post-truth populism, the current inhabitant of the White House has apparently decided that transferring power to "the people" means waging war on the First

Amendment, which, as he sees it, is unfairly protecting the people's greatest enemy, the independent press.[22]

Seventh, reliable polls report that a large majority of European voters distrust their elected parliaments and governments.[23] One reason is that, after the electorate votes, markets vote or banks vote or Brussels votes. The second series of votes are the ones that count. Decision-making by Central Bankers and EU technocrats, however rational economically, ignores the primacy of vanity over self-interest in human motivation. It underestimates the citizens' need to be consulted about alternatives rather than passively receiving "the best" policies crafted in their interests behind their backs. The Brazilian electoral slogan "We are tired of austerity" meant in part that voters were tired of being told by technocratic experts that austerity is "the only option." In fact, the opportunity to present genuine policy alternatives in a respected public forum makes it more likely that citizens will eventually go along with decisions they do not much like. Technocratic policymakers, however competent, ignore at their peril this proven democratic method for mobilizing public consent.

Similarly, the puppet-masters of global finance, who are often portrayed as initiating the economic policies justified in the jargon of technocrats, cannot be voted out of office. Their employment contracts do nothing to inspire in them "an habitual recollection of their dependence on the people."[24] The public patience subsidized by the prospect of ousting political incumbents does not apply to Goldman

Sachs. As a result, voters incensed by the failure of elections to jeopardize the veiled authority of behind-the-scenes decision makers will be tempted to indulge in middle-finger voting aimed at expressing their "politicophobiac" contempt for the entire ruling class, or even, if conditions are ripe (as they were in 2016), at dynamiting the constitutional order itself. In such cases, Western systems begin eerily to resemble those *protest-vote democracies* of Eastern Europe characterized, according to Ivan Krastev, by "high electoral volatility in which governments are never reelected but economic policies are rarely changed."[25] Voting against incumbents without any hope for improvement under a government formed by their challengers does not necessarily prefigure the imminent breakdown of democracy, but it does represent the incapacity of the electoral system to fulfill one of democracy's central functions.

An effortless alternative to protest voting is simply refusing to vote. Indeed, electoral abstentionism and electoral extremism are mutually reinforcing. Tocqueville, whose thinking has inspired much of my analysis so far, helps explain why. In a modern nation such as France, he argued, public opinion will make itself felt in one way or another. If public opinion cannot express itself through political associations, newspapers, and electoral politics, it will be channeled into mob violence. Ballots replace bullets only when elections allow frustrated citizens to vent their anger by tossing out one set of leaders and electing another.

Universal suffrage must be seen in this light. The most dangerous political figures are those who claim to speak for the majority. Pretending to act for the nation as a whole, the Jacobins of 1793–94 were able to perpetrate unthinkable atrocities. To avert this danger, according to Tocqueville, it is imperative to construct political institutions that manifestly deflate the pretension of populist demagogues to be incarnations of the popular majority. The only institution that can do this effectively is universal suffrage.

> *Of all the causes that help to moderate the violence of political associations in the United States, the most powerful, perhaps, is universal suffrage. In countries where universal suffrage is allowed, the majority is never in doubt, because no party can reasonably portray itself as the representative of those who did not vote. Associations therefore know that they do not represent the majority, and everyone else knows it too.*[26]

Where the franchise is severely restricted, extremist politicians and their followers tend to become conspiratorial, aggressive, and swollen with a sense of their own holy mission. Universal suffrage changes all this, Tocqueville argues. When most citizens can vote, revolutionary firebrands "forfeit the sacred character that attaches to the struggle of the oppressed against their oppressor."[27] That is how universal suffrage cuts the craziest politicians down to size, diminishing their prestige in the public eye and reducing their capacity to unleash violence on the streets.

What makes this intriguing analysis alarming today is its patent inapplicability to a political system where the suffrage is formally universal but where turnout is persistently low due to a variety of factors, including a widely shared belief that voting does not have any discernable impact on policy. The consequences of low turnout are similar to those of a restricted suffrage. In low-turnout democracies, such as the American, populist leaders can claim with superficial plausibility to be the sole legitimate representatives of the one authentic nation.[28] They can even boast about transferring power from Washington, DC, and giving it back to the people, even though they will obviously do nothing of the sort. Such self-inflating bluster may strike readers of this volume as preposterous, but when democracy fails to bring voters to the polls, such boasts are not that easy to refute.

Eighth, voters who are prevented from voting their interests will be tempted to vote their passions. Political scientists who stew endlessly about the irrationality of the very act of voting should not presume, as they often do, that the voters who end up going to the polls will vote with exquisite rationality. In our time, one of the principal aims of emotional and irrational voting is the desire to freeze demography or even reverse its secular drift, an obvious impossibility. Demographic anxiety may be the best available explanation not only for the successes of antiliberal movements and parties in Europe but also for the raging hostility toward President Obama among the Trump electorate. The essential message of the Obama presidency was that America can be a mixed-race nation and remain America in every important sense. This admirable attempt to reconcile democracy with demography was acutely unwelcome in white-nationalist circles. Since America is already a mixed-race nation, rejecting Obama's implicit message was tantamount to endorsing violence, casting another dark shadow over the prospects of American democracy today.

Ninth, the weakening of traditional parties in both Europe and the United States and the accompanying shift of public support to anti-system parties or to the leaders of movements (as opposed to parties) also bodes ill for democracy's future. After all, "Democracy is a system in which parties lose elections."[29] The weakening of the party system, dramatically revealed in the French presidential election of 2017, puts the effective functioning of *l'alternance* into question. Earlier, if the Républicains disappointed the French electorate, the Parti socialiste could be elected in its place, and vice versa. But what will happen if Emmanuel Macron, the leader of a middle-of-the-road movement, forced by parliamentary elections to improvise something that resembles a centrist party, ends up deluding the country after his five-year term? The record-low turnout in the June 18 parliamentary election means that large swaths of the French electorate will have minimal or no representation in the new legislature, giving some credence to radicals on the left and right who claim that *they* represent the true majority. Anger in France continues to mount against both imperious, know-it-all EU bureaucracy and poor (especially Muslim) immigrants. If this discontent is not voiced inside the system, the Macron government will be faced with violent and paralyzing protests on the streets. However welcome, his unexpected accession to power reflects a long-term weakening of France's democratic system for processing voter dissatisfaction through a system of rival parties alternating in power. If the political opposition under Macron's presidency consists largely of underrepresented extremist groupings, the next election could potentially bring a virulently antiliberal, anti-immigrant, pro-Putin, and anti-EU candidate to power.

Tenth, the ease with which certain democratically elected governments have used their constitutional authority to bulldoze democratic institutions has further tarnished the idea of accountability to the voters. The most obvious cases are Hungary and Poland, to be discussed below. Blocked by the American melting pot from echoing Hungarian and Polish appeals to the ethnic homogeneity of the nation, Trump nevertheless seems hell-bent on emulating East Central European attacks on democracy's core norms and institutions. Thus, democracy is being debased in America, just as it has been sabotaged in Hungary and Poland, by increasing returns to power.[30] Once elected, even by a slim margin, governments can take advantage of simmering discontent with democracy to slander and harass independent media, to turn important television channels into propaganda arms of the government, to deploy government agencies against inner enemies, to use the "loaded gun" of the law selectively to attack opposition politicians and decrease the funding for opposition parties, to populate the judiciary with ideological extremists or political flunkies, to enrich loyalists via the procurement process, and to pass voter suppression laws to make it difficult to challenge the ruling party electorally. Populist politicians also resort opportunistically to threat inflation, knowing that hostility to foreigners and yearnings for authoritarian rule both skyrocket when the public thinks existential dangers are on the horizon.[31] A final paradox here is that the failure of such a government to produce economic growth, alongside its defunding of transfer programs, can actually tighten its grip on power, since economic desperation is likely to foment an even more toxic style of attack politics, not to mention unleashing the rabid search for scapegoats typical of highly polarized societies.

Eleventh, the distinct American and European projects for exporting democracy to countries that had never before been governed democratically have proved so counterproductive and even self-defeating that they have further tarnished the already sullied name of democracy itself. Little thought was given to what would happen in Iraq after Saddam Hussein was toppled. The hope seems to have been that once the tyrant was deposed, democracy would pop up spontaneously, like toast out of a toaster. The facile optimism that a political culture could be changed by a six-week military campaign was based on a failure to distinguish between the absence of obstacles to democracy and the presence of preconditions for democracy. Democracy is a tiny spot in human history, and therefore obviously has complicated preconditions, many of which were almost certain to be lacking in Iraq. In the badly bungled occupation of the country, an ideological—and that means historically illiterate—commitment to democracy played a highly pernicious role, leading Americans to refuse to negotiate with nonelected leaders, including tribal sheikhs and religious authorities who, in line with the historical norms, were considered "legitimate" locally and could command the obedience of a considerable following despite having come to power nondemocratically. A dogmatic adherence to the democratic legitimacy formula, in other words, postponed for two terrifying years the decision by occupation forces to start negotiating with the local leaders who could have helped restore order to the country. The entire experience has not only discredited the idea of spreading democracy at the point of a gun[32] but also exposed the provincial blindness caused by a dogmatic commitment to the democratic ideal without regard to the social conditions that make democracy sustainable.

The twelfth cause of alienation from democratic government follows hard on the eleventh. The emergence of populist and xenophobic authoritarianism in East Central Europe has discredited the idea of spreading democracy by EU expansion, just as the Iraq War discredited the idea of spreading democracy at the point of a gun. So what explains this disheartening turn of events? The Fidesz Party in Hungary and the Law and Justice Party in Poland both came to power through elections. Once in power, as mentioned above, their leaders proceeded to dismantle virtually all checks on their power, neutering the courts, for instance, and undermining freedom of the press. Viktor Orbán and Jarosław Kaczyński excite their bases by railing against the technocratic EU, insalubrious migrants, thieving Roma, foreign-funded NGOs, the sex-obsessed Internet colonized by American corporations, the nose-in-air elite, the self-perpetuating establishment, meritocracy for a few, open-demography globalization, a high-stakes gamblers' capitalism that revealed its callous disregard for ordinary people in 2008, atheist consumerism, gays whose refusal to breed contributes to an embarrassing decline of national natality, and a multiculturalism that robs citizens of their national identity.

The contemporary populists of East Central Europe do not attack the US-led international system as a liberal global order, it should be said. Much like Trump, they see it not as an order but as a disorder, as a system that undermines or overrides the one true ordering principle, namely nationality. Liberal cosmopolitanism, Kaczyński claims, is devoted to destroying the kind of bounded communities to which people want to belong simply because mankind's emotional-moral conductivity, or ability to sympathize with the suffering of others, is limited.[33] According to Orbán too, "Europe is under invasion" by "a flood of people pouring out of the countries of the Middle East and . . . the depth of Africa."[34] The real Hungary and the real Poland are being attacked by the hyper-liberal EU, which is arrogantly pushing culturally inassimilable Muslim immigrants into these countries. The proof that liberals are enemies of the nation is that they refuse to admit that there are any downsides to immigration. That should sound familiar. True, there are virtually no immigrants in either Poland or Hungary. But verifiable facts seem less weighty than imaginary fears. Brussels' halfhearted effort to develop a quota system for distributing Syrian refugees across the EU has anti-cosmopolitan nativists screaming about a denial of the sovereign right of every nation to decide on its own absorption capacity. The abstract validity of the principle is undermined by its total irrelevance to the reality on the ground.

In any case, such acrimonious antiliberalism cannot be discounted as an expression of the peripheral location of Hungary and Poland at the eastern edge of the West, since the current president of the non-peripheral United States, after accidentally effecting a hostile takeover of the American constitutional system, also claims to be defending the country against migrants storming its shores and international institutions conspiring against its national interests. "This does not feel like my country anymore" has proved to be an electorally exploitable sentiment in core Western countries as well as on the postcommunist eastern fringe. The reassertion of a parochial and exclusive identity as an allergic response to the imperatives of liberal cosmopolitanism and internationalism has now appeared in Britain's Tory Party platform too. A citizen of the world is a citizen from nowhere, as the prime minister has explained, identifying today's most important political cleavage as the one between globalists and nativists, or between cosmopolitan classes who travel easily everywhere and whose "achieved" identities are based on education and local populations whose "ascribed" identities are rooted in the place where they are born, live, and die.[35] In the wake of the violent overthrow by electorally accountable democratic governments in the

West of the non-elected rulers of Iraq and Libya, migrant flows have surged dramatically, including into Europe, and anti-globalist our-boat-is-full parties with positive attitudes toward authoritarian leaders have become ubiquitous. It is nevertheless especially striking that the "open society" that Central and Eastern Europeans celebrated a quarter-century ago as a pathway to freedom is now widely decried by these same peoples as an invasion route for imaginary barbarian hordes. Universal human rights, formerly embraced as a defense against Soviet tyranny, are now scorned as an elitist plot to smuggle foreign refugees into the country at the expense of native Hungarians or Poles. The very language of rights seems insensitive to the emotional experience of national humiliation, fueling the indignation of parochial inhabitants at the lifestyles of liberal globalists who dismiss as irrational tribalism the kind of identity politics that offers some degree of dignity to the losers of global competition. Krastev has provided a succinct and lucid explanation of the way such resentment-fueled illiberal nationalism and right-wing populism, favoring a politics of exclusion over a politics of inclusion, has undermined the democratic idea in Western as well as East Central Europe:

> The new populist majorities perceive elections not as an opportunity to choose between policy options but as a revolt against privileged minorities—in the case of Europe, elites and a key collective "other," the migrants. In the rhetoric of populist parties, elites and migrants are twins who thrive off of one

another: neither is like "us," both steal and rob from the honest majority, neither pays the taxes that it should pay, and both are indifferent or hostile to local traditions.[36]

This diagnosis too is disturbingly applicable to the American case. For populists, the very act of voting has been emptied of rational content. Elections are not about policy choices but about highlighting the differences between "them" and "us." Populist voters, feeling ignored and victimized, go to the polls to avenge themselves symbolically against out-of-touch elites and under-the-radar immigrants. Collective solutions to shared problems are not on their agenda. That the swamping of democratic "voice" by such infantile emotionalism has done nothing to resurrect a withering faith in democracy is the least that might be said.

Keeping these parallels in mind, we can ask: What forces have brought about a worldwide antiliberal counterrevolution against the very idea of an open democratic society? To answer this question, a good place to start is again East Central Europe. The key to explaining the appeal of authoritarian xenophobia in Hungary, Poland, and elsewhere in the region lies in the aftermath of 1989. The end of the Cold War was experienced there as the beginning of the Age of Imitation.[37] This is why we can trace the roots of the current crisis of liberal democracy to the communist collapse. Francis Fukuyama's central thesis was that, after the Soviet Union dissolved, Western-style liberal democracy had no serious competitors. This thesis, put into practice, turned out to have exceptionally perverse consequences.[38] Because Western liberal democracy was unrivaled and uncontested, it allegedly offered the one and only political and economic model worthy of emulation. After 1989, refusing to imitate Western norms and institutions was no longer an option.

But the claim that emulating Western political and economic institutions and norms was now obligatory and unavoidable had unwelcome consequences for both the imitating and the imitated nations. In the West, it encouraged an unjustified complacency about the virtues of liberal democracy as well as a loss of interest in how other countries actually worked. In the East, it produced an anticolonial revolt.

After 1989, social sciences in the West became more moralistic than they had been during the Cold War. Western observers began to classify countries around the world, and not only those exiting from communism, along a single spectrum ranging from not-like-us to almost-like-us. Countries undergoing traumatic political changes were ranked according to simplistic metrics purporting to establish the point at which they had arrived in the single-track transition to democracy, transparency, anticorruption, human rights, and the rule of law. Naturally, after a few years, inhabitants of these countries began to resent being treated as botched or second-rate imitations of the West. A natural reaction to ham-fisted democracy promotion and human-rights monitoring was an aggressive reassertion of national sovereignty, accompanied by the claim that Westernizers were incapable of appreciating the true virtues of the cultures they aimed to replace with their own. An airbrushed image of the West sold to countries being encouraged to democratize also proved easy to satirize and discredit as neocolonial propaganda. It was not long before non-Americans subjected to the imitation imperative began to point out the unreasonable double standards and insufferable hypocrisy involved, reinforcing the growing cultural drift toward skepticism about democracy itself.

Democratic norms and procedures can be imported but not exported. The good intentions behind Western democracy-promotion efforts only exacerbated local resentment against the imperious requirement to imitate Western political and economic institutions. The unfortunate consequence has been that Hungary and Poland (among other countries) have thrown out the democratic baby along with the neocolonial bathwater. But this is far from being the last word on the subject.

To delve into the deeper causes of a widespread public disenchantment with democracy, we should focus not on inequality or the growing gap between rich and poor in liberal-democratic societies, but rather on economic *insecurity*, in the sense of fear of downward social mobility, and the mutual *ghettoization* of social classes, a disconnect that makes ordinary citizens feel that they have lost all leverage over their national elites. The Cold War gave economic elites in the West a strong motive to make capitalism seem legitimate in the eyes of ordinary people.[39] This became much less true after the Cold War ended. What followed was not simply a widening gap between rich and poor but also, and more important, a shredding of the connective tissue between rich and poor. This is the development that has done most to weaken faith in democracy throughout the West.

Democracy naturally forfeited much of its appeal once voters themselves lost the social sway derived from their simultaneous occupation of several other influential roles. The deterioration in question can be fruitfully described as the dis-embedding of voters from the parallel social statuses that gave them some degree of leverage over political elites. Citizen-voters were now deprived of the support once provided by their parallel lives as citizen-soldiers and citizen-workers. In republican theory and practice since ancient times, the influence of citizen-voters over their rulers was intimately connected to their leverage as citizen-soldiers. Depending on citizen-soldiers to safeguard their own power and wealth, political elites had a strong incentive to heed if not always to obey the voices of ordinary citizens. Now that mass armies have been replaced by lean volunteer forces equipped with high-tech, push-button weaponry, the existential dependency of the social elite on ordinary citizens has considerably diminished. Citizens are quick to realize that political rulers who do not depend on them cannot be trusted to act in their interest. The price of elite self-sufficiency is popular distrust. By decreasing the government's need for voluntary cooperation from its citizens, the possibility of warfare without mass conscription has contributed importantly to the sensation that voters have lost control over their rulers, indirectly undermining the idea that periodic elections are democratic in any substantial sense.

The citizen-voter has also been deprived by economic change of a sustaining partnership with the citizen-worker. In societies where wealth depends on labor and police powers are limited, some elite interest in the health and literacy of the workforce is highly likely. By contrast, the residual leverage of workers over employers is bound to dissipate whenever jobs are either fulfilled by robots who never strike for higher wages or cheaply offshored to low-wage countries where taxes are negligible by Western standards and workers are regularly bastinadoed by the army or police. In the US, vague hopes to counteract these trends probably rest on a low-probability revival of the labor movement.[40]

Whatever the chances for that, once the citizen-voter loses the leverage he or she once possessed as a citizen-soldier and a citizen-worker, the vote itself loses much of its appeal, since going dutifully to the polls does little to extract concessions from dominant economic and political elites. Some commentators say that politicians have ceased to pay attention to the poor, or even to visit their neighborhoods, because the poor have stopped voting. But the causality runs more powerfully in the other direction. The poor have stopped voting because they do not possess enough extra-electoral leverage over their rulers to make voting feel worthwhile. An extreme case of this disempowering of the citizen-voter can be found in Russia, where the citizen-consumer too attracts little attention from ruling groups, since the country's hydrocarbon princes sell their gas and oil to foreign buyers and therefore, rightfully unimpressed by sham elections, display zero interest in ordinary citizens' having money to buy products that are domestically produced. That is one reason, among many, why Russia's periodic elections have no effect at all on the way the country is governed.[41]

This analysis implies that faith in democracy, including in America, has been gravely undermined by a worldwide movement for the liberation of the rich, a freeing of social elites from dependency on ordinary men and women. It isn't simply a matter of technocrats making rational decisions without popular consultation. The threat to liberal democracy has deeper social roots. Hovercraft elites who inhabit gated communities, send their children to private schools, and rely on private doctors and private security forces are not powerfully motivated to take an interest in the fate of less privileged members of their community. Voting does little to change their calculations, especially when turnout is low and voter preferences are easily manipulated by political marketing gurus who apply commercial advertising techniques to electoral campaigns. Typically anglophone and living near airports, this hovercraft elite, inhabiting bubbles of prosperity in normal times, can easily escape the country in case of emergency. Such weakly rooted globalists are naturally resented by the locally grounded public. Indeed, they are frequently vilified as a fifth column flaunting foreign manners and favoring foreign interests—that is to say, as potential traitors to the homeland. The emphasis that right-wing populists place on loyalty to the nation is less a reassertion of historical tradition, therefore, than a new way for those without college degrees and who have never left the country to voice their scalding resentment against fellow citizens who seem too well-educated and too well-traveled to be genuinely patriotic.

We can now return to our opening question of how democracies perish. In a democratic system, the lack of communication between, on the one hand, average immobile citizens struggling for survival in a difficult economy and, on the other hand, a privileged, frequently airborne elite culturally committed to individual self-expression creates a golden opportunity for morally uninhibited political entrepreneurs. In societies split between globalists and localists, self-styled anti-establishment politicians can drum up considerable political support by slandering the vertically unintegrated but globally networked elite. Such an opportunistically populist *counter-elite*, thriving on attack politics, will often consist of kleptocrats such as Trump or Orbán, who promiscuously blur business interests with affairs of state. An important question is therefore: How do clientelism, nepotism, and cronyism permit them to win "thunderous applause" in soccer stadiums from a populace they are brazenly fleecing?

They do so by the arts of distraction—that is, by manipulating the focus of public attention. By clamoring against inner enemies, in particular, they can channel voters' frustration and resentment away from themselves and toward two eminently targetable social groups: those who endorse liberal-humanitarian values as a matter of principle and those who benefit personally and concretely from a liberal *Willkommenskultur*.[42] They discredit the liberal idea of toleration toward strangers, for example, by characterizing it as either an ideological cover used by employers seeking cheap labor or as an expression of political correctness. In East Central Europe, authoritarian populists such as Orbán attack foreign-funded liberals in particular. He accuses them not only of looking down their noses at ordinary Hungarians and betraying the national idea but also, interestingly, of supporting "meritocracy." This may seem odd at first, but it is actually quite logical from the populist perspective. Meritocracy is seen in Orbán's Hungary as a system based on a Western value-hierarchy that ignores the meritorious qualities of non-Westernized Hungarians, dismissing them as losers who conspicuously lack the talents (or have not made the effort) required to succeed. The latter naturally resent such a system and claim that those who profit from it have either benefited from a leg up or have simply had the dumb luck to be in the right place at the right time. Nothing is more infuriating than the braggadocio of those who succeed largely by luck but claim to have succeeded by merit alone.[43] This ordinary and understandable passion goes a long way toward explaining the success of elite-bashing populists, from Orbán and Kaczyński to Donald Trump, who deliberately seek electoral support among ill-informed and poorly educated voters.[44]

It is sometimes said that the class-based identities of rich versus poor or business versus labor are relatively easy to process inside the political system, while the identities at war in struggling democracies today—nativist versus globalist, rural versus urban, uneducated versus educated, and religious versus secular—make mutual adjustments and negotiated compromises much harder. This is far from obvious. It would be more accurate to say that the new populist counter-elites have a strong incentive to poison the public mind with scandalous untruths aimed at hyperbolizing such ordinary polarities into irreconcilable opposites. Polarization and divisiveness are perhaps the most effective tactics used by self-described representatives of "the true people" to stigmatize liberal pluralism and, if possible, to win periodic reauthorizations for populist rulers from a confused, angry, and frightened voting public.

When a politically adroit counter-elite has gained sufficient power to control the country's media, neutralize the courts, and undermine the capacity of the opposition to contest the next election, as it has in Hungary and Poland, liberal democracy will need some kind of miracle to help it back to life. If a populist ruler has not yet achieved this kind of monopoly on power, by contrast, and when his fraudulent claim to represent the majority of the nation is about to be tested in a national election, as in the US, one of two survival strategies is likely to be adopted.

Fixed-calendar elections mean that a duly elected populist toying irresponsibly with authoritarianism and xenophobia will soon be "compelled to anticipate the moment when their power is to cease, when their exercise of it is to be reviewed, and when they must descend to the level from which they were raised."[45] To this potential source of panic in the White House bunker we can add the two other constitutionally legitimate paths of removal (Art. 2, Sec. 4, Impeachment for Treason, Bribery, or other high Crimes and Misdemeanors, or 25th Amendment removal for inability to discharge the powers and duties of his office).

Reacting to the threat of being deposed, a populist president will, first of all, ramp up the rancorousness of his denunciations of clandestine foreign intruders and their liberal enablers as enemies of the people. He will invoke the idea of community to shred national solidarity, pitting citizen against citizen, channeling public resentments not toward electoral competition but toward physical aggression against vulnerable scapegoats. In a society where a loaded firearm is just another household appliance, the possibility of violence spiraling out of control, encouraged by the overheated rhetoric of an over-his-head attention-seeker clothed in presidential authority, cannot be excluded, with consequences about which one shudders to think.

An alternative scenario, just as likely in the United States, involves foreign adventurism. Hearing rumblings of impeachment or finding himself and his family to be a target of multiple criminal investigations, a populist president will presumably have the interest, the capacity, and the disposition to plunge the country into an international crisis. Vice President Dick Cheney showed clearly that the American system of checks and balances cannot prevent a single man from dragging the country into war. Sending US troops to defend the country on a distant battlefield inevitably triggers a rally-round-the-flag effect in the short term, and may therefore be irresistibly attractive to a besieged and mentally isolated president whose popularity is fatally sinking. Since wars are inherently unpredictable and can drag the belligerents into a sequence of unintended escalations, here we have another catastrophe waiting in the wings.

So what should we do to minimize the chance that "it can happen here"? How should we behave to prevent a mentally unstable president from unleashing violence for no good reason except to keep himself in power? Given the many reasons for disenchantment with democracy catalogued above, who will rally in democracy's name to stop an incumbent who is sorely tempted to burn down our common house to save his own skin?

The first thing to note is that "democracy in America," in the wider sense, is doing relatively well. Incorporating much more than election-day visits to the polls, democracy includes an incessant questioning and examination of the government by its citizens *between* elections. In Trump's America, contrary to Rousseau's jibe about English-style representative government,[46] the press, NGOs, the court, and the opposition have not behaved like slaves once the election results were in. On the contrary, they have demonstrated the will and the capacity to protest, monitor, investigate, and complain every single day. The administration's constant whining about this democratic effervescence[47] shows that the country's relentless political vigilance is far from impotent.

Second, populist leaders almost always prefer a personally loyal to a professionally competent staff. This makes it somewhat less likely that a cornered populist president will be able to design and implement a truly shrewd and effective survival strategy, although it does not of course rule out a lawless unleashing of chaos.

Third, an incumbent's efforts to insulate himself from an electoral reckoning will necessarily be destabilizing and most probably self-defeating, assuming he cannot conjure up a police state overnight. In a relatively free society, eliminating the democratic safety valve provided by the hope of removing the current officeholder by ballot will swell public pressure to the bursting point. The more the regular mechanisms for alternation in power are deliberately sabotaged and prevented from functioning normally, the more public opposition out of doors will be brought to a boil. This is the point at which elite and citizen commitment to democracy will meet its most important test. Will anti-incumbent sentiment flow into constitutional channels, or will it explode onto the streets?

This depends to some extent on how the incumbent himself behaves. Yet the opposition too has choices to make. Assuming a rogue president will not be removed by his own cabinet or his own party, ordinary citizens will wisely concentrate on reducing his legislative majority in the midterms and throwing him out of office in a general election. But, given the serious doubts about democracy canvassed in this chapter, can the uncertain promises of electioneering mobilize public support as a reasonable pathway to removing right-wing populism from power? This question is impossible to answer in the abstract. But the cavalier contempt with which our current populist president has treated long-standing constitutional norms may conceivably bring a previously blasé and politically alienated electorate to a renewed appreciation of democracy's political virtues. Perhaps President Trump's brutal assault on democracy's core norms and institutions will turn out to be a "blessing in disguise."[48] That depends entirely on what happens next. As mentioned at the outset, levels of commitment to democratic norms and institutions among politically active forces will be sufficient or insufficient depending on ensuing events. But whatever twists of fate await us, loyalty in adversity remains essential. Those of us who would defend democracy against its drunkenly reckless enemies must keep firmly in mind democracy's singular virtues even as we contemplate realistically all the reasons, surveyed in this chapter, why faith in democracy has been declining around the world, including most notably in the United States. That, after all, is why we have ended up where we are. The better we understand what we are up against, the greater are our chances not only to avoid the very worst but also to preserve the magic of our democratic system, namely its ability periodically to replenish society's sense of future possibility, arguably its rarest and most precious bequest.

NOTES

1.   Michael Ignatieff, "Academic Freedom, Under Threat in Europe," *New York Times*, April 2, 2017.

2.   Jean-François Revel, *How Democracies Perish* (New York: HarperCollins, 1985).

3.   Personal communication.

4.   Max Weber, "National Character and the Junkers," in *From Max Weber: Essays in Sociology* (New York: Oxford University Press, 1958), 395.

5. Moshe Halbertal and Stephen Holmes, *The Beginning of Politics: Power in the Biblical Book of Samuel* (Princeton, NJ: Princeton University Press, 2017).

6. Roberto Stefan Foa and Yascha Mounk, "The Danger of Deconsolidation: The Democratic Disconnect," *Journal of Democracy* 27, no. 3 (July 2016); Yascha Mounk and Roberto Stefan Foa, "Yes, People Really Are Turning Away from Democracy," *Washington Post*, December 8, 2016.

7. http://www.demos.it/a01344.php.

8. Stephen Holmes, "Loyalty in Adversity," in David Johnston, Nadia Urbinati, and Camila Vergara, eds., *Machiavelli on Liberty and Conflict* (Chicago: University of Chicago Press, 2017), 186–205.

9. Thomas Carothers and Richard Youngs, "Democracy Is Not Dying," *Foreign Affairs*, April 11, 2017.

10. Cass R. Sunstein, *Worst-Case Scenarios* (Cambridge, MA: Harvard University Press, 2009).

11. Eric D. Weitz, *Weimar Germany: Promise and Tragedy* (Princeton, NJ: Princeton University Press, 2013), 82.

12. Lawrence Lessig, *Republic, Lost: Version 2.0* (New York: Twelve, 2015).

13. Michael Wines, "Key Question for Supreme Court: Will It Let Gerrymanders Stand?," *New York Times*, April 21, 2017.

14. Joseph A. Schumpeter, *Capitalism, Socialism and Democracy* (New York: Harper & Row, 1950), 264.

15. Nicholas Bakalar, "Some Gun Laws Tied to Lower Suicide Rates," *New York Times*, March 15, 2017.

16. Thomas Schelling, *The Strategy of Conflict* (Cambridge, MA: Harvard University Press, 1960), 91.

17. David Leonhardt, "The American Dream, Quantified at Last," *New York Times*, December 8, 2016.

18. Larry Elliott, "Each Generation Should Be Better Off Than Their Parents? Think Again," *The Guardian*, February 14, 2016.

19. Tony Judt, "What Is Living and What Is Dead in Social Democracy?," *New York Review of Books*, December 17, 2009.

20. Geoffrey R. Stone, *Top Secret: When Our Government Keeps Us in the Dark* (Lanham, MD: Rowman and Littlefield, 2007); and "Secrecy and Self-Governance," *New York Law School Law Review* 56, no. 1 (2011–12):81.

21. Cass Sunstein, *#Republic: Divided Democracy in the Age of Social Media* (Princeton, NJ: Princeton University Press, 2017).

22. David Remnick, "Donald Trump and the Enemies of the American People," *New Yorker*, February 18, 2017.

23. "Public Opinion in the European Union," *Eurobarometer 2016*, 14.

24. *Federalist Papers*, No. 57.

25. Ivan Krastev, *Democracy Disrupted: The Politics of Global Protest* (Philadelphia: University of Pennsylvania Press, 2014), 22.

26. Alexis de Tocqueville, *Democracy in America*, Arthur Goldhammer, trans. (New York: Library of America, 2004), 221.

27. Ibid., 222.

28. Jan-Werner Müller, *What Is Populism?* (Philadelphia: University of Pennsylvania Press, 2016).

29. Adam Przeworski, *Democracy and the Market: Political and Economic Reforms in Eastern Europe and Latin America* (Cambridge, UK: Cambridge University Press, 1991), 10.

30. Adam Przeworski, *Sustainable Democracy* (Cambridge, UK: Cambridge University Press, 1995), 40–41.

31. Jonathan Haidt, "When and Why Nationalism Beats Globalism," *The American Interest* 12, no. 1 (July 10, 2016).

32. David Rieff, *At the Point of a Gun: Democratic Dreams and Armed Intervention* (New York: Simon & Schuster, 2005).

33. Jarosław Kaczyński, "Debate on Immigration, Refugees in Polish Parliament." September 17, 2015, https://www.youtube.com /watch?v=6NlRstWinSU.

34. Viktor Orbán, Speech at the Opening of the World Science Forum, November 7, 2015, http://2010–2015.miniszterelnok.hu/in _english_article/viktor_orban_s_speech_at_the_opening_of_the _world_science_forum.

35. David Goodhart, *The Road to Somewhere: The Populist Revolt and the Future of Politics* (London: Hurst, 2017).

36. Ivan Krastev, *After Europe* (Philadelphia: University of Pennsylvania Press, 2017).

37. This thesis is developed more fully in Ivan Krastev and Stephen Holmes, *The End of Victory: The Untold Story of the Unraveling of the Post-1989 Order* (forthcoming).

38. Francis Fukuyama, "The End of History?" *The National Interest* (Summer 1989).

39. Mary L. Dudziak, *Cold War Civil Rights: Race and the Image of American Democracy* (Princeton, NJ: Princeton University Press, 2011).

40. Thomas Geoghegan, *Only One Thing Can Save Us: Why America Needs a New Kind of Labor Movement* (New York: New Press, 2014).

41. Stephen Holmes, "Imitating Democracy, Feigning Capacity," in Adam Przeworski, ed., *Democracy in a Russian Mirror* (Cambridge, UK: Cambridge University Press, 2015), 30–57.

42. After the leader "names the inner enemy," his most zealous private followers can take matters into their own hands, sending death threats to outspoken critics and stabbing unloved minorities on the street.

43. Robert Frank, *Success and Luck: Good Fortune and the Myth of Meritocracy* (Princeton, NJ: Princeton University Press, 2016).

44. Elizabeth Williamson, "A Big Win for Donald Trump in Nevada," *New York Times*, February 24, 2016.

45. *Federalist Papers*, No. 57.

46. "The people of England regards itself as free; but it is grossly mistaken; it is free only during the election of members of parliament. As soon as they are elected, slavery overtakes it, and it is nothing." Jean-Jacques Rousseau, *The Social Contract*, bk. 3, ch. 15.

47. Michael M. Grynbaum, "Trump Strategist Stephen Bannon Says Media Should 'Keep Its Mouth Shut,' " *New York Times*, January 26, 2017.

48. Albert O. Hirschman, *A Bias for Hope: Essays on Development in Latin America* (New Haven, CT: Yale University Press, 1971), 318–27.

"IT CAN'T HAPPEN HERE": THE LESSONS OF HISTORY

GEOFFREY R. STONE

Any effort to impose authoritarian rule inevitably involves the suppression of criticism of those in positions of authority.[1] Put simply, authoritarianism and civil liberties do not go hand in hand. Americans tend to assume that because of our long-standing commitment to civil liberties we are reasonably safe from the dangers of authoritarian rule. Such an assumption is dangerously wrong. In fact, throughout our history, in times of real or perceived crisis, we have repeatedly collapsed in our commitment to individual freedom, often aggressively stifling dissent and endangering the central precepts of our democracy.

In order to cast aside our naive assumption that "it can't happen here" and to understand our vulnerability both to the suppression of freedom of speech and the danger of authoritarianism, it is necessary to recall several critical moments in our nation's history. To explore this history, I will briefly review our experience in 1798, the Civil War, World War I, World War II, the Cold War, and the Vietnam War. I will then offer some concluding observations.

IN 1798, MANY OF THE IDEAS GENERATED BY THE FRENCH REVOLUTION aroused fear and hostility in segments of the American population. A bitter political and philosophical debate raged between the Federalists, then in power, and the Republicans. The Federalists feared that the sympathy of the Republicans for the French Revolution indicated a willingness to plunge the United States into a similar period of violence and upheaval. The Republicans feared that the Federalist sympathy for England denoted a desire to restore aristocratic forms and class distinctions in America.

As the international situation deteriorated, President Adams sent John Marshall to Paris to negotiate a treaty that would guarantee the immunity of American shipping from attacks by French corsairs. When this effort failed because the French demanded "tribute" to help finance their war with England, the Adams administration initiated a series of defense measures that carried the United States into a state of undeclared war with France.

The Republicans fiercely criticized these measures, leading President Adams to declare that the Republicans "would sink the glory of our country and prostrate her liberties at the feet of France."[2] The Federalists attempted to discredit the Republicans by attacking their loyalty, their ideology, and their morality.

Against this backdrop, the Federalists enacted the Alien

and Sedition Acts of 1798.[3] The Alien Act empowered the president to deport any noncitizen he judged dangerous to the peace and safety of the United States. The Act accorded the noncitizen no right to a hearing, or even to present evidence on his behalf. Although the Alien Act was never enforced, it had a powerfully intimidating effect.

The Sedition Act prohibited the publication of "false, scandalous, and malicious writings against the government of the United States, the Congress, or the President, with intent to bring them into contempt or disrepute." Unlike the Alien Act, the Sedition Act was vigorously enforced, but only against supporters of the Republican Party. Prosecutions were brought against the leading Republican newspapers and the most vocal critics of the Adams administration. The Act proved an effective weapon for the suppression of dissent.

Consider, for example, the plight of Matthew Lyon, a Republican congressman from Vermont. During his reelection campaign, Lyon published an article in which he asserted that under President Adams "every consideration of the public welfare was swallowed up in a continual grasp for power and an unbounded thirst for ridiculous pomp, foolish adulation, and selfish avarice."[4] Because this statement clearly brought the president into "disrepute," Lyon was convicted and sentenced to prison. The Federalist press rejoiced, but Lyon became an instant martyr and was reelected to Congress while in jail.

The Supreme Court did not have occasion to rule on the constitutionality of the Sedition Act at the time, and the Act expired by its own terms on the last day of Adams's term of office. President Jefferson thereafter pardoned all those who had been convicted under the Act, and Congress repaid the fines. The Supreme Court has never missed an opportunity in the years since to remind us that the Sedition Act of 1798 has been judged unconstitutional in the "court of history."[5]

DURING THE CIVIL WAR, THE NATION FACED PERHAPS ITS MOST SEvere challenge. As in most civil wars, there were sharply divided loyalties, fluid military and political boundaries, and easy opportunities for espionage and sabotage. Moreover, the nation had to cope with the stresses of slavery, emancipation, conscription, and staggering casualty lists, all of which triggered deep division and even violent protest.

Faced with these tensions, President Lincoln had to balance the conflicting interests of military security and individual liberty. At the core of this conflict was the writ of habeas corpus, which has historically guaranteed a detained individual the right to a prompt judicial determination of whether his detention by government is lawful.

The issue first arose shortly after Fort Sumter, in April 1861, when anti-Union rioting in Baltimore effectively isolated the nation's capital from the rest of the Union. To restore order and assure the movement of Union troops through Maryland, Lincoln suspended the writ of habeas corpus and imposed martial law. There was no clear precedent for this action, and Lincoln's private secretaries later disclosed that his anxiety over this decision threw him into a state of severe "nervous tension."[6]

Given the perilous state of the Union in April 1861, it is perhaps not surprising that there was no significant public or congressional opposition to Lincoln's suspension of the writ in Maryland. During the course of the war, Lincoln went on to suspend the writ of habeas corpus on eight separate occasions. The most extreme of these suspensions, which was applicable throughout the entire nation, declared that "all persons . . . guilty of any disloyal practice . . . shall be subject to court martial."[7] Estimates of the number of civilians imprisoned by military authorities under these orders range from 13,000 to 38,000. Most of the arrests were premised on charges of draft evasion, desertion, sabotage, and aiding the enemy.

In some instances, civilians were taken into military custody for criticizing the war. The most prominent example of this was former Ohio congressman Clement Vallandigham, who was arrested by military authorities and later exiled by Lincoln because of a speech he delivered in 1863 in which he described the war as "wicked, cruel and unnecessary" and as a "war for the freedom of blacks and the enslavement of whites."[8] During the course of the war, as many as three hundred opposition newspapers were suspended because of their alleged "disloyalty" to the Union cause.

In 1866, a year after the war ended, the Supreme Court held in *Ex parte Milligan*[9] that Lincoln had exceeded his constitutional authority as commander in chief. The Court ruled that the president was not constitutionally empowered to suspend the writ of habeas corpus, even in time of war, if the ordinary civil courts were open and functioning.

THE STORY OF CIVIL LIBERTIES DURING WORLD WAR I IS, IN MANY ways, an even more disturbing chapter in our nation's history. When the United States entered the war in April 1917, there was strong opposition to both the war and the draft. Many citizens believed that our goal was not to "make the world safe for democracy," but to protect the investments of the wealthy. War opponents were sharply critical of the Wilson administration.

President Wilson had little patience for such dissent. After the sinking of the *Lusitania*, he warned that disloyalty "must be crushed out" of existence,[10] and in calling for federal legislation against disloyal expression he insisted that disloyalty "was . . . not a subject on which there was room for . . . debate."[11]

Shortly after the United States entered the war, Congress enacted the Espionage Act of 1917. Although the Act dealt primarily with espionage and sabotage, several provisions had serious consequences for the freedom of speech. Specifically, the Act made it a crime for any person willfully to "cause or attempt to cause insubordination, disloyalty, or refusal of duty in the military forces of the United States" or to willfully "obstruct the recruiting or enlistment service of the United States."[12]

Although the congressional debate makes clear that the 1917 Act was not intended to suppress dissent generally, but to address very specific concerns relating directly to the operation of the military, aggressive federal prosecutors and compliant federal judges soon transformed the Act into a full-scale prohibition of seditious utterance. The administration's intent in this regard was made evident in November 1917 when Attorney General Charles Gregory, referring to war dissenters, declared: "May God have mercy on them, for they need expect none from an outraged people and an avenging government." [13]

In fact, the federal government worked strenuously to create an "outraged people." Because there had been no direct attack on the United States and no direct threat to our national security, the administration found it necessary to generate a sense of urgency and a mood of anger in order to exhort Americans to enlist, to contribute money, and to make the many sacrifices that war demands.

To this end, President Wilson established the Committee on Public Information, under the direction of George Creel, whose charge was to promote support for the war. The CPI produced a flood of inflammatory and often misleading pamphlets, news releases, speeches, editorials, and motion pictures, all designed to instill a hatred of all things German and of all persons whose loyalty was open to doubt.

In the first month of the war, Attorney General Gregory asked "every loyal American to act as a 'voluntary detective,' suggesting that 'citizens should bring their suspicions to the Department of Justice.' " [14] As a result, literally thousands of accusations of disloyalty poured into the Department each day.

The general tenor of the legal profession in this era was to be severely patriotic, and lawyers who criticized the war—or even defended war critics—were subjected to ostracism and occasionally even formal discipline. In this environment, it was unlikely that many judges would stand up to the pressures for suppression. The Department of Justice prosecuted more than two thousand individuals for allegedly disloyal or seditious expression in this era, and in an atmosphere of fear, hysteria, and clamor, most judges were quick to mete out severe punishment to those deemed disloyal. As Harvard professor Zechariah Chafee observed at the time, under the prevailing interpretation of the Espionage Act, "all genuine discussion of the justice and wisdom of continuing the war becomes perilous." [15]

But even this was not enough. Angered by the rulings of a few courageous judges who interpreted the Espionage Act narrowly, Congress enacted the Sedition Act of 1918, [16] which expressly prohibited any person to utter any disloyal, scurrilous, or abusive language about the form of government, the Constitution, the flag, or the military forces of the United States.

Even the signing of the Armistice did not bring this era to a close. The Russian Revolution had generated deep anxiety in the United States, and a series of violent strikes and spectacular bombings triggered the period of intense public paranoia that became known as the "Red Scare" of 1919–1920. Attorney General A. Mitchell Palmer announced that the bombings were an "attempt on the part of radical elements to rule the country," and the *New York Times* proclaimed: "Red Peril Here!" [17]

Palmer established the General Intelligence Division within the Bureau of Investigation and appointed J. Edgar

Hoover to gather and coordinate information about radical activities. The GID unleashed a horde of undercover agents and confidential informants to infiltrate radical organizations.

From November 1919 to January 1920, the GID conducted a series of stunning raids in thirty-three cities. More than five thousand people were arrested on suspicion of radicalism. The general procedure was to make wholesale arrests of people in places believed to be radical hangouts. The *Washington Post* proclaimed that "there is no time to waste on hairsplitting over any supposed infringements of liberty."[18] More than a thousand individuals were summarily deported.

And where was the Supreme Court in all this? In a series of decisions in 1919 and 1920—*Schenck, Frohwerk, Debs, Abrams, Schaefer, Pierce,* and *Gilbert*—the Supreme Court consistently upheld the convictions of individuals who had agitated against the war and the draft—individuals as obscure as Jacob Abrams and Mollie Steimer, Russian-Jewish émigrés who had distributed antiwar leaflets in Yiddish on the lower East Side of New York, and as prominent as Eugene V. Debs, who had received almost a million votes as the Socialist Party candidate for president in 1916.[19]

Although Justices Holmes and Brandeis eventually separated themselves from their brethren and launched what became a critical underground tradition within the Court's First Amendment jurisprudence, the Court as a whole showed no interest in the rights of dissenters. As the University of Chicago First Amendment scholar Harry Kalven once observed, the Court's performance in these cases was "simply wretched."[20]

In December 1920, after all the dust had settled, Congress quietly repealed the Sedition Act of 1918. In 1924, Attorney General and future Supreme Court Justice Harlan Fiske Stone ordered an end to the Bureau of Investigation's surveillance of political radicals. "A secret police," he explained, is "a menace to free government and free institutions."[21] Between 1919 and 1923, the federal government released from prison every individual who had been convicted under the Espionage and Sedition Acts. A decade later, President Roosevelt granted amnesty to all these individuals, restoring their full political and civil rights.

Over the next half century, the Supreme Court of the United States overruled every one of its World War I decisions, holding in effect that every one of the individuals who had been imprisoned or deported in this era for his or her dissent had been punished for speech that should have been protected by the First Amendment.[22]

ON DECEMBER 7, 1941, JAPAN ATTACKED PEARL HARBOR. THE NEXT day, the United States declared war against Japan, Germany, and Italy. Two months later, on February 19, 1942, President Roosevelt signed Executive Order 9066, which authorized the US Army to "designate military areas" from which "any persons may be excluded."[23] Although the words *Japanese* or *Japanese-American* never appeared in the Order, it was understood to apply only to persons of Japanese ancestry.

Over the next eight months, more than 110,000 individuals of Japanese descent were forced to leave their homes in California, Washington, Oregon, and Arizona. Two-thirds of these individuals were American citizens, representing almost 90 percent of all Japanese-Americans. No charges were brought against these individuals; there were no hearings; they did not know where they were going, how long they would be detained, what conditions they would face, or what fate would await them. They were told to bring only what they could carry. Many families lost everything.

On the orders of military police, these individuals were assigned to temporary "detention camps," which had been set up in converted racetracks and fairgrounds. Many families lived in crowded horse stalls, often in unsanitary conditions. Barbed-wire fences and armed guard towers surrounded the compounds. From there, the internees were transported to permanent internment camps, which were located in isolated areas in windswept deserts or vast swamplands. There they remained for some three years.

Why did this happen? Certainly, the days following Pearl Harbor were dark days for the American spirit. Fear of possible Japanese sabotage and espionage was rampant, and an outraged public felt an understandable instinct to lash out at those who had attacked us. But this act was also very much an extension of more than a century of poisonous racial prejudice against the "yellow peril." Racist statements and sentiments permeated the debate from December 1941 to February 1942 about how to deal with these individuals.

Agitation for a mass evacuation of all persons of Japanese

ancestry—rather than a more targeted program focused only on enemy aliens found to be dangerous—was inflamed by a series of false reports of Japanese espionage, sabotage, and infiltration. California's attorney general, Earl Warren, argued that, unlike the situation with respect to Germans and Italians, it was simply too difficult to determine which Americans of Japanese ancestry were loyal and which were not.

On the other side of the debate, the Department of Justice argued that a mass evacuation of Japanese-Americans was both unnecessary and unconstitutional. FBI director J. Edgar Hoover reported to Attorney General Biddle that the demand for mass evacuation was based on "public hysteria," and he assured Biddle that the FBI had already identified suspected Japanese agents and taken them into custody.

Nonetheless, President Roosevelt signed Executive Order 9066. The decision to intern all men, women, and children of Japanese ancestry was made by the president, as commander in chief. The issue was never discussed in the Cabinet, and it was opposed by both the attorney general and the secretary of war. Although FDR explained the Order in terms of military necessity, there is little doubt that domestic politics played at least a role in his thinking.

In *Korematsu v. United States*,[24] decided in 1944, the Supreme Court, in a six-to-three decision, upheld the president's action. The Court justified its action by observing that "hardships are part of war, and war is an aggregation of hardships." In such circumstances, and deferring to the judgment of the Executive, the Court insisted that it could not "say that these actions were unjustified."[25]

In 1980, a congressional commission concluded that the implementation of Executive Order 9066 had violated the rights of Japanese Americans. Eight years later, President Ronald Reagan signed the Civil Liberties Act of 1988, which offered an official presidential apology and reparations to each of the Japanese-American internees who had suffered discrimination, loss of liberty, loss of property, and personal humiliation because of the actions of the United States government. The Court's decision in *Korematsu* has come to be seen as a black mark on the Court's jurisprudence.

AS WORLD WAR II DREW TO A CLOSE, THE NATION MOVED ALMOST seamlessly into what came to be known as the Cold War. When Harry Truman became president in 1945, the federal and state statute books were already bristling with anticommunist legislation. As the glow of our wartime alliance with the Soviet Union evaporated, Truman came under increasing attack from a coalition of Southern Democrats and anti–New Deal Republicans who sought to exploit fears of Communist aggression.

Thereafter, the issue of loyalty became a shuttlecock of party politics. By 1948, Truman was boasting on the stump that he had imposed on the federal civil service the most extreme loyalty program in the "Free World." Leaving no doubt of the matter, he proclaimed: "I want you to get this straight. I hate Communism."[26]

There were limits, however, to Truman's anticommunism. In 1950, Truman vetoed the McCarran Act, which required the registration of all Communists. Truman explained that the Act was the product of "public hysteria" and would lead inevitably to "witch hunts."[27] Congress passed the Act over Truman's veto.

Then, in 1954, Congress enacted the Communist Control Act, which stripped the Communist Party of "all rights, privileges, and immunities."[28] Only one senator, Estes Kefauver, dared to vote against it. Hysteria over the Red Menace now swept the nation and produced a wide range of federal and state restrictions on free expression and free association. These included not only the McCarran and Communist Control Acts but also extensive loyalty programs for federal, state, and local employees; emergency detention plans for alleged "subversives"; extensive and often abusive legislative investigations; and direct prosecution of the leaders and members of the Communist Party of the United States.

The key Supreme Court decision in this era was *Dennis v. United States*,[29] in 1951, which involved the direct prosecution under the Smith Act of the leaders of the American Communist Party. The indictment charged the defendants with advocating the violent overthrow of the government. In a six-to-two decision, the Court held that this conviction did not violate the First Amendment. In a highly prescient dissenting opinion, Justice Hugo Black observed that "public opinion being what it now is, few will protest the conviction of these" Communists. "There is hope, however, that in calmer times, when present pressures, passions and fears subside, this . . . Court will restore the First Amendment liberties to the . . . place where they belong in a free society."[30]

Over the next several years, in a series of decisions premised on *Dennis*, the Court upheld the Subversive Activities Control Act, far-reaching legislative investigations of "subversive" organizations and individuals, and the exclusion of members of the Communist Party from the bar, the ballot, and public employment.[31] In so doing, the Court clearly put its stamp of approval on an array of actions we today look back on as models of McCarthyism.

IN THE VIETNAM WAR, AS IN THE CIVIL WAR AND WORLD WAR I, THERE was substantial opposition both to the war and to the draft. After President Nixon announced the American "incursion" into Cambodia, student strikes closed a hundred campuses. Governor Ronald Reagan, asked about campus militants, replied, "If it takes a bloodbath, let's get it over with."[32]

On May 4, 1970, National Guardsmen at Kent State University responded to taunts and rocks by firing their M-1 rifles into a crowd of students, killing four and wounding nine others. Protests and strikes exploded at more than 1,200 of the nation's colleges and universities. Thirty ROTC buildings were burned or bombed in the first week of May. The National Guard was mobilized in sixteen states. As Henry Kissinger put it later, "The very fabric of government was falling apart."[33]

Despite all this, there was no systematic effort during the Vietnam War to prosecute individuals for their opposition to the war. There are many reasons for this, including, of course, the compelling fact that most of the dissenters in this era were the sons and daughters of the middle class, and thus could not so easily be targeted as the "other." But the courts, and especially the Supreme Court, played a key role in this period. In 1969, the Court, in *Brandenburg v. Ohio*,[34] overruled *Dennis* and held that even advocacy of unlawful conduct cannot be punished unless it is likely to incite "imminent lawless action." The Court had come a long way in the fifty years since World War I.[35]

But the government found other ways to impede dissent. The most significant of these was the FBI's extensive effort in this era to infiltrate and to "expose, disrupt and otherwise neutralize" allegedly "subversive" organizations, ranging from civil rights groups to the various factions of the antiwar movement. In this COINTELPRO operation, the FBI compiled political dossiers on more than a half million Americans.

WHAT CAN WE LEARN FROM THIS HISTORY? I WOULD LIKE TO OFFER three concluding observations.

First, we have a long and unfortunate history of overreacting to perceived dangers to our nation. Time after time, we have allowed our fears to get the better of us. Although each of these episodes presented markedly different challenges, in each we went too far in restricting individual liberties. Moreover, in each of these situations our national leaders abused their authority and misled the American people about their rights and responsibilities.

Second, one of the central safeguards of our democracy is a free, robust, and courageous marketplace of ideas. A critical function of free expression is to help us make wise decisions about whether our leaders are leading well. The freedom of speech is not merely a right of the individual but a fundamental national interest that is essential to the very existence of democratic decision-making.

My third and final observation brings me to the present. Today, in the era of Trump—a president who understands nothing of our history or of the necessary preconditions of our democracy—we face a truly serious threat to the rule of law, to our democracy, and to our constitutional freedoms. It is, of course, much easier to look back on past crises and find our predecessors wanting than it is to make wise judgments when we ourselves are in the eye of the storm. But that challenge now falls to us. As Justice Brandeis once observed, "those who won our independence" knew that "courage is the secret of liberty."[36] That, I think, is the most fundamental insight for us to bear in mind.

To strike the right balance in our time, we need political leaders who know right from wrong; federal judges who will stand fast against the furies of the age; members of the bar and the academy who will help us see ourselves clearly; members of the media who will fulfill their fundamental responsibility to keep our leaders honest; an informed public who will value not only their own liberties but also the liberties of others; and, perhaps most of all, elected officials with the wisdom to know excess when they see it and the courage to preserve liberty when it is imperiled. We shall see. It would be a grave mistake to think that "it can't happen here."

NOTES

1. Much of this essay is drawn from Geoffrey R. Stone, *Perilous Times: Free Speech in Wartime from the Sedition Act of 1798 to the War on Terrorism* (New York: W. W. Norton, 2004).

2. Letter from John Adams to the Inhabitants of Arlington and Bandgate, Vermont, June 25, 1798, in Charles Francis Adams, ed., *The Works of John Adams*, vol. 9 (Boston: Little, Brown, 1854), 202.

3. An Act Concerning Aliens, 5th Cong., 2d Sess., in *The Public Statutes at Large of the United States of America*, vol. 1 (Boston: Little, Brown, 1845), 570–72; An Act for the Punishment of Certain Crimes against the United States, 5th Cong., 2d Sess., in Ibid., 596–97.

4. Francis Wharton, *State Trials of the United States During the Administrations of Washington and Adams* (Philadelphia: Carey and Hart, 1849), 333.

5. *New York Times v. Sullivan*, 376 US 254, 276 (1964).

6. Mark E. Neely, *The Fate of Liberty: Abraham Lincoln and Civil Liberties* (New York: Oxford University Press, 1992), 5–7.

7. Roy P. Basler, ed., *The Collected Works of Abraham Lincoln*, vol. 5 (New Brunswick, NJ: Rutgers University Press, 1956), 436–37.

8. See Michael Kent Curtis, *Free Speech, "The People's Darling Privilege": Struggles for Freedom of Expression in American History* (Durham, NC: Duke University Press, 2000), 310.

9. 4 Wall. (71 US) 2 (1866).

10. Woodrow Wilson, "Third Annual Message to Congress," quoted in David M. Kennedy, *Over Here: The First World War and American Society* (New York: Oxford University Press, 1980), 24.

11. Quoted in Paul L. Murphy, *World War I and the Origin of Civil Liberties in the United States* (New York: W. W. Norton, 1979), 53.

12. Act of June 15, 1917, ch. 30, tit. I, § 3, 40 Stat. 219.

13. *New York Times*, November 21, 1917, 3.

14. Quoted in Murphy, *World War I*, 94–95.

15. Zechariah Chafee, *Freedom of Speech* (Cambridge, MA: Harvard University Press, 1941), 52.

16. Act of May 16, 1918, ch. 75, § 1, 40 Stat. 553.

17. Quoted in Robert K. Murray, *Red Scare: A Study in National*

Hysteria, 1919–1920 (New York: McGraw-Hill, 1955), 9; *New York Times*, March 11, 1919.

18. *Washington Post*, January 4, 1920, 4.

19. *Schenck v. United States*, 249 US 47 (1919); *Frohwerk v. United States*, 249 U.S. 204 (1919); *Debs v. United States*, 249 US 211 (1919); *Abrams v. United States*, 250 US 616 (1919); *Schaefer v. United States*, 251 US 466 (1920); *Pierce v. United States*, 252 US 239 (1920); *Gilbert v. Minnesota*, 254 US 325 (1920).

20. Harry Kalven Jr., *A Worthy Tradition: Freedom of Speech in America* (New York: Harper & Row, 1988), 147.

21. Quoted in Max Lowenthal, *The Federal Bureau of Investigation* (New York: Sloane, 1950), 298.

22. See *Brandenburg v. Ohio*, 395 US 444 (1969).

23. Executive Order No. 9066, 7 Fed. Reg. 1407 (1942).

24. 323 US 214 (1944). See also *Hirabayashi v. United States*, 320 US 81 (1943) (upholding the constitutionality of the curfew order); *Yasui v. United States*, 320 US 114 (1943) (same).

25. Id., 219–20, 223–24.

26. Quoted in David Caute, *The Great Fear: The Anti-Communist Purge under Truman and Eisenhower* (New York: Simon & Schuster, 1978), 33.

27. *New York Times*, September 21, 1950.

28. 68 Stat. 775, 50 USC § 841.

29. 341 US 494 (1951).

30. Id., 581 (Black, J., dissenting).

31. See, e.g, *Communist Party v. Subversive Activities Control Board*, 367 US 1 (1961) (upholding the Subversive Activities Control Act's requirement that Communist and Communist-front organizations register with the government); *Adler v. Board of Education*, 342 US 485 (1952) (upholding a New York law providing that no person who knowingly becomes a member of any organization that advocates the violent overthrow of government may be appointed to any position in a public school); *Barenblatt v. United States*, 360 US 109 (1949) (upholding the power of the House Committee on Un-American Activities to require an instructor at Vassar College to answer questions about his past and present membership in the Communist Party).

32. *San Francisco Chronicle*, April 8, 1970, 1.

33. Henry Kissinger, *White House Years* (New York: Little, Brown, 1979), 513.
34. 395 US 444 (1969).
35. See Frank Strong, *Fifty Years of "Clear and Present Danger": From Schenck to Brandenburg—And Beyond,* 1969 Sup. Ct. Rev. 41.
36. *Whitney v. California,* 274 US 357, 375 (1927) (Brandeis, J., concurring).

ACKNOWLEDGMENTS

It is a pleasure to thank three amazing people who have been especially helpful with this challenging project.

Thanks go first to the brilliant and generous Julia Cheiffetz, who was a wise and sharp-eyed adviser throughout. Sean Newcott did an extraordinary and indeed heroic job of shepherding the unruly chapters—unruly, at least, at an earlier stage—to their final form. Ashley Nahlen, my assistant, has superb organizational skills, and she served as a coeditor here.

I am also grateful to Harvard Law School and to two deans—Martha Minow and John Manning—for providing a superb working environment.

CONTRIBUTOR BIOGRAPHIES

Bruce Ackerman is Sterling Professor of Law and Political Science at Yale and the author of eighteen books that have had a broad influence in political philosophy, constitutional law, and public policy. His major works include *Social Justice in the Liberal State* and his multivolume constitutional history, *We the People*. His most recent books are *We the People: The Civil Rights Revolution* (2014), *The Decline and Fall of the American Republic* (2010), *Before the Next Attack* (2006), and *The Failure of the Founding Fathers* (2005). His book *The Stakeholder Society* (with Anne Alstott) served as a basis for Tony Blair's introduction of child investment accounts in the United Kingdom, and his book *Deliberation Day* (with James Fishkin) served as a basis for "PBS Deliberation Day," a national series of citizen deliberations produced by McNeill-Lehrer on national television for the 2004 elections. He also writes for the general public, contributing frequently to the *New York Times*, the *Washington Post*, and the *Los Angeles Times*, and has served, without charge, as a lawyer on matters of public importance. He was a lead witness for President Clinton before the House Judiciary Committee's impeachment hearings and a principal spokesman for Al Gore before the Florida legislature during the election crisis of 2000. Professor Ackerman is a member of the American Law Institute and the American Academy of Arts and Sciences. He is a Commander of the French Order of Merit and the recipient of the American Philosophical Society's Henry Phillips Prize for Lifetime Achievement in Jurisprudence.

Jack M. Balkin is Knight Professor of Constitutional Law and the First Amendment at Yale Law School. He is the founder and director of Yale's Information Society Project, an interdisciplinary center that studies law and new information technologies. He also directs the Abrams Institute for Freedom of Expression and the Knight Law and Media Program at Yale. Balkin is a member of the American Academy of Arts and Sciences and the author of over a hundred articles in different fields, including constitutional theory, Internet law, freedom of speech, reproductive rights, jurisprudence, and the theory of ideology. He founded and edits the group blog *Balkinization* and has written widely on legal issues for such publications as the *New York Times*, the *New England Journal of Medicine*, the *American Prospect*, the *Atlantic Online*, *Washington Monthly*, the *New Republic Online*, and *Slate*. His books include *Living Originalism; Constitutional Redemption: Political Faith in an Unjust World; The Constitution in 2020* (with Reva Siegel); *Processes of Constitutional Decisionmaking* (5th ed., with Brest, Levinson, Amar, and Siegel); *Cultural Software: A Theory of Ideology; The Laws of Change: I Ching and the Philosophy of Life; What Brown v. Board of Education Should Have Said*; and *What Roe v. Wade Should Have Said.*

Tyler Cowen is an economics professor at George Mason University, where he holds the Holbert C. Harris chair in the economics department. He hosts the economics blog *Marginal Revolution* together with coauthor Alex Tabarrok. Cowen and Tabarrok also maintain the website Marginal Revolution University, a venture in online education. Cowen wrote the "Economic Scene" column for the *New York Times*, and since July 2016 has been a regular opinion columnist at *Bloomberg View*. He serves as faculty director of George Mason's Mercatus Center, a university research center that focuses on the market economy. His latest book, *The Complacent Class*, appeared in 2017.

Jon Elster is Robert K. Merton Professor of the Social Sciences at Columbia University. His publications include *Ulysses and the Sirens* (1979), *Sour Grapes* (1983), *Making Sense of Marx* (1985), *The Cement of Society* (1989), *Solomonic Judgements* (1989), *Local Justice* (1992), *Political Psychology* (1993), *Alchemies of the Mind* (1999), *Ulysses Unbound* (2000), *Closing the Books* (2004), *Le désintéressement* (2009), *L'irrationalité* (2010), *Securities Against Misrule* (2013), and *Explaining Social Behavior* (2015). In 2016, he was awarded the 22nd Johan Skytte Prize in Political Science for his contributions to the discipline. He is currently preparing a comparative study of the Federal Convention and the French constituent assembly of 1789–91.

Noah Feldman is Felix Frankfurter Professor of Law at Harvard Law School. Feldman is also a Senior Fellow of the Society of Fellows at Harvard. In 2003 he served as senior constitutional advisor to the Coalition Provisional Authority in Iraq, and subsequently advised members of the Iraqi Governing Council on the drafting of the Transitional Administrative Law, or interim constitution. He received his AB summa cum laude in Near Eastern Languages and Civilizations from Harvard University in 1992. Selected as a Rhodes Scholar, he earned a DPhil in Oriental Studies from Oxford University in 1994. From 1999 to 2002, he was a Junior Fellow of the Society of Fellows at Harvard. Before that he served as a law clerk to Justice David H. Souter of the US Supreme Court (1998 to 1999) and to Chief Judge Harry T. Edwards of the US Court of Appeals for the DC Circuit (1997 to 1998). He received his JD from Yale Law School in 1997, serving as Book Reviews Editor of the *Yale Law Journal*. He is the author of seven books: *Cool War: The Future of Global Competition* (Random House, 2013); *Scorpions: The Battles and Triumphs of FDR's Great Supreme Court Justices* (Twelve, 2010); *The Fall and Rise of the Islamic State* (Princeton University Press, 2008); *Divided by God: America's Church-State Problem and What We Should Do About It* (Farrar, Straus & Giroux, 2005); *What We Owe Iraq: War and the Ethics of Nation Building* (Princeton University Press,

2004); and *After Jihad: America and the Struggle for Islamic Democracy* (Farrar, Straus & Giroux, 2003). He most recently coauthored *Constitutional Law, Eighteenth Edition* (Foundation Press, 2013) with Kathleen Sullivan.

Tom Ginsburg is Leo Spitz Professor of International Law, Ludwig and Hilde Wolf Research Scholar at the University of Chicago. Ginsburg focuses on comparative and international law from an interdisciplinary perspective. He holds BA, JD, and PhD degrees from the University of California at Berkeley. His books include *Judicial Review in New Democracies* (2003), which won the C. Herman Pritchett Award from the American Political Science Association; *The Endurance of National Constitutions* (2009), which also won a best book prize from APSA; *Constitutions in Authoritarian Regimes* (2014); and *Law and Development in Middle-Income Countries* (2014). He currently codirects the Comparative Constitutions Project, an effort funded by the National Science Foundation to gather and analyze the constitutions of all independent nation-states since 1789. Before entering law teaching, he served as a legal adviser at the Iran-US Claims Tribunal, The Hague, Netherlands, and he continues to work with numerous international development agencies and foreign governments on legal and constitutional reform. He is a member of the American Academy of Arts and Sciences.

Jack Goldsmith is Henry L. Shattuck Professor at Harvard Law School, a Senior Fellow at the Hoover Institution, and cofounder of *Lawfare*. He teaches and writes about national security law, presidential power, cybersecurity, international law, internet law, foreign relations law, and conflict of laws. Before coming to Harvard, Professor Goldsmith served as Assistant Attorney General, Office of Legal Counsel from 2003 to 2004, and Special Counsel to the Department of Defense from 2002 to 2003. He was a professor at the University of Chicago Law School from 1997 to 2002, and at the University of Virginia School of Law from 1994 to 1997. Before entering the academy, professor Goldsmith was an associate at Covington & Burling in Washington, DC. He clerked for Supreme Court Justice Anthony M. Kennedy from 1990 to 1991, for Court of Appeals Judge J. Harvie Wilkinson from 1989 to 1990, and for Judge George Aldrich on the Iran-US Claims Tribunal from 1991 to 1993. He is the author of *Power and Constraint* (2012), *The Terror Presidency* (2007), *The Limits of International Law* (2006), and *Who Controls the Internet* (2006).

Jonathan Haidt is Thomas Cooley Professor of Ethical Leadership at New York University's Stern School of Business. He is a social psychologist who studies the psychology of morality and its relationship with political activity. Haidt is the author of two books: *The Happiness Hypothesis: Finding Modern Truth in Ancient Wisdom* (2006) and *The Righteous Mind: Why Good People are Divided by Politics and Religion* (2012), which became a *New York Times* bestseller. He is the director of HeterodoxAcademy.org.

Stephen Holmes is Walter E. Meyer Professor of Law at New York University School of Law. He previously taught at Harvard, Princeton, and the University of Chicago. His fields of specialization include the history of liberalism, the disappointments of democratization after communism, and the difficulty of combating terrorism within the limits of liberal constitutionalism. He is the author of *Benjamin Constant and the Making of Modern Liberalism* (1984), *The Anatomy of Antiliberalism* (1993), *Passions and Constraint: On the Theory of Liberal Democracy* (1995), and *The Matador's Cape: America's Reckless Response to Terror* (2007). He is coauthor (with Cass Sunstein) of *The Cost of Rights: Why Liberty Depends on Taxes* (1999) and (with Moshe Halbertal) of *The Beginning of Politics: Power in the Biblical Book of Samuel* (2017).

Aziz Huq is Frank and Bernice J. Greenberg Professor of Law at the University of Chicago. He previously worked as associate counsel and then director of the Liberty and National Security Project of the Brennan Center for Justice at New York University School of Law, litigating cases in both the US Courts of Appeals and the Supreme Court. He has been a senior consultant analyst for the International Crisis Group, researching constitutional design and implementation in Pakistan, Nepal, Afghanistan, and Sri Lanka. He also clerked for Judge Robert D. Sack of the US Court of Appeals for the Second Circuit and then for Justice Ruth Bader Ginsburg of the Supreme Court of the

United States. His book *How Constitutional Democracy Is Lost (and Saved)*, coauthored with Tom Ginsburg, will be published by the University of Chicago Press in 2018.

Timur Kuran is a professor of economics and political science and Gorter Family Professor of Islamic Studies at Duke University. His research focuses on (1) economic, political, and social change, with emphases on institutions and preferences, and (2) the economic and political history of the Middle East, with a focus on the role of Islam. Among his publications are *Private Truths, Public Lies: The Social Consequences of Preference Falsification* (Harvard University Press), *Islam and Mammon: The Economic Predicaments of Islamism* (Princeton University Press), and *The Long Divergence: How Islamic Law Held Back the Middle East* (Princeton University Press), all translated into multiple languages. He is also the editor of the trilingual, ten-volume compilation *Socio-Economic Life in Seventeenth-century Istanbul: Glimpses from Court Records* (İş Bank Publications).

Martha Minow is Carter Professor of General Jurisprudence at Harvard Law School and Distinguished Service Professor at Harvard University. She served as the dean of the Law School between 2009 and 2017, and on June 30, 2017, she stepped down from her post as Morgan and Helen Chu Dean and Professor of Law at Harvard Law School. She has taught at Harvard Law School since 1981. She would like to thank Melinda Kent, Paloma O'Connor, and Hannah Solomon-Strauss for their research help and advice.

Eric Posner is Kirkland and Ellis Distinguished Service Professor of Law, University of Chicago. His books include *The Twilight of Human Rights Law* (Oxford, 2014); *Economic Foundations of International Law* (with Alan Sykes; Harvard, 2013); *Contract Law and Theory* (Aspen, 2011); *The Executive Unbound: After the Madisonian Republic* (with Adrian Vermeule; Oxford, 2011); *Climate Change Justice* (with David Weisbach; Princeton, 2010); *The Perils of Global Legalism* (University of Chicago, 2009); *Terror in the Balance: Security, Liberty and the Courts* (with Adrian Vermeule; Oxford, 2007); *New Foundations of Cost-Benefit Analysis* (with Matthew Adler; Harvard, 2006); *The Limits of International Law* (with Jack Goldsmith; Oxford, 2005); *Law and Social Norms* (Harvard, 2000); *Chicago Lectures in Law and Economics* (editor; Foundation, 2000); *Cost-Benefit Analysis: Legal, Economic, and Philosophical Perspectives* (editor, with Matthew Adler; University of Chicago, 2001). He is a fellow of the American Academy of Arts and Sciences and a member of the American Law Institute.

Samantha Power is an academic, author, and diplomat who served as the United States Ambassador to the United Nations from 2013 to 2017. Power began her career by covering the Yugoslav Wars as a journalist. From 1998 to 2002, she served as the founding executive director of the Carr Center for Human Rights Policy at the Harvard Kennedy School, where she later became the first Anna Lindh Professor of Practice of Global Leadership and Public Policy. She was a senior adviser to Senator Barack Obama until March 2008. She won a Pulitzer Prize in 2003 for her book *A Problem from Hell: America and the Age of Genocide*, a study of the US foreign policy response to genocide.

Karen Stenner is a political psychologist and behavioral economist and director of Insight-Analytics (Australia). Insight-Analytics provides behavioral insights to political parties and candidates (around the crafting of messages and design of campaigns), as well as to governments, nonprofits, and corporations (in regard to social marketing, sustainability, efficiency, and productivity). Stenner was formerly on the faculty of Princeton University (1998–2005) and Duke University (1996–98) before returning to her native Australia. She teaches political psychology, statistics, and research methodology (especially experimental designs and methods), winning the Stanley Kelly Teaching Award from Princeton's Department of Politics in 2001. Stenner is author of *The Authoritarian Dynamic* (Cambridge, 2005)—which anticipated by a decade the rise of Far Right politics and leaders across the West—along with articles on political psychology and political behavior. She focuses on the use of threatening/reassuring messages to increase/decrease authoritarian behavior in the electorate. Stenner also publishes and consults extensively on energy consumer behavior, including around the design of messages and behavioral interventions to promote energy efficiency and the uptake of renewable energy. She previously served as Senior Research Scientist and Leader of the Behavioural Economics and

Psychological Insights unit at the CSIRO (Commonwealth Scientific and Industrial Research Organisation), Australia's national science agency. Stenner has eclectic interests across the social and behavioral sciences, and favors evidence-based interdisciplinary research that offers actual solutions to real-world problems. She is above all else interested in saving liberal democracy, mostly from itself.

Geoffrey R. Stone is the Edward H. Levi Distinguished Service Professor at the University of Chicago. Mr. Stone joined the faculty in 1973 after serving as a law clerk to Supreme Court Justice William J. Brennan Jr. Stone is the author of many books on constitutional law, including *Sex and the Constitution: Sex, Religion and Law from America's Origins to the Twenty-First Century* (2017); *Speaking Out: Reflections of Law, Liberty and Justice* (2010 and 2016); *Top Secret: When Our Government Keeps Us in the Dark* (2007); *War and Liberty: An American Dilemma* (2007); *Perilous Times: Free Speech in Wartime* (2004); and *Eternally Vigilant: Free Speech in the Modern Era* (2002). He is also an editor of two leading casebooks, *Constitutional Law* (7th ed., 2013) and *The First Amendment* (5th ed., 2016). Stone is an editor of *The Supreme Court Review* and chief editor of a twenty-volume series, *Inalienable Rights*, which is being published by Oxford University Press.

David A. Strauss is Gerald Ratner Distinguished Service Professor of Law and faculty director of the Supreme Court and Appellate Clinic at the University of Chicago

Law School. He is the author of *The Living Constitution* (Oxford University Press, 2010) and has published articles on a variety of subjects, principally in constitutional law and related areas. He is a coeditor of the *Supreme Court Review*. He has been a visiting professor at Harvard and Georgetown, and he has served as an assistant solicitor general of the United States and special counsel to the US Senate Judiciary Committee. He is a fellow of the American Academy of Arts and Sciences.

Cass R. Sunstein is the Robert Walmsley University Professor at Harvard Law School. He clerked for Justice Benjamin Kaplan of Massachusetts Supreme Judicial Court and Justice Thurgood Marshall of the US Supreme Court. He worked as an attorney-advisor in the Office of the Legal Counsel of the US Department of Justice and was a faculty member at the University of Chicago Law School from 1981 to 2008. From 2009 to 2012, he served as Administrator of the White House Office of Information and Regulatory Affairs. From 2013 to 2014, he served on the President's Review Group on Intelligence and Communications Technologies. Sunstein is the author of hundreds of articles and dozens of books, including *Republic.com* (2001), *Nudge: Improving Decisions About Health, Wealth, and Happiness* (with Richard H. Thaler 2008), and *Simpler* (2013). His latest books are *The World According to Star Wars* (2016) and *The Ethics of Influence* (2016). Sunstein received his bachelor of arts from Harvard College in 1975 and his doctorate in law from Harvard Law School in 1978.

Duncan J. Watts is a principal researcher at Microsoft Research and a founding member of the MSR-NYC lab. He is also an AD White Professor at Large at Cornell University. Prior to joining MSR in 2012, he was from 2000 to 2007 a professor of sociology at Columbia University, and then a principal research scientist at Yahoo! Research. His research has appeared in *Nature, Science, Physical Review Letters to the American Journal of Sociology*, and *Harvard Business Review*, and he has been recognized with the 2009 German Physical Society Young Scientist Award for Socio and Econophysics, the 2013 Lagrange-CRT Foundation Prize for Complexity Science, and the 2014 Everett M. Rogers Award. He is also the author of three books: *Six Degrees: The Science of a Connected Age* (W. W. Norton, 2003), *Small Worlds: The Dynamics of Networks Between Order and Randomness* (Princeton University Press, 1999), and, most recently, *Everything Is Obvious: Once You Know the Answer* (Crown Business, 2011).

INDEX